"This book assembles and organizes an imp[...] both old and new. It is admirably clear, coherent, and comprehensive. I hope this book will help to spark a renewed interest in a topic whose neglect has been indefensible."

    —PETER KREEFT, Boston College

"Monsignor Francis Mannion is a serious scholar, but he has shown in his writings an admirable ability to make his insights accessible to the ordinary reader. As we enter into the great Eucharistic Prayer, the priest exhorts God's people: 'Lift up your hearts!' In this profoundly moving set of meditations, Mannion invites us to savor the great joys awaiting us and to live and worship in a way worthy of them."

    —JOHN C. WESTER, Archbishop of Sante Fe

"This book serves up an appreciation of the doctrine of heaven that is engaging to read, theologically rich, and imaginatively traditional. Mannion proves that doctrines are not only to be believed and obeyed; doctrines are also to be enjoyed. We have lost our joy in heaven! This illuminating study refreshes it by moving through eight models, each steeped in Scripture, tradition, art, and prophecy. Most pictures of heaven do not move us; these will."

    —DAVID W. FAGERBERG, University of Notre Dame, emeritus

"Drawing from the treasury of his knowledge of church history and theology, Msgr. Mannion provides a guide to heaven which is as moving as it is instructive: heaven as activity and rest, as the beauty our souls crave, as personal life fulfilled in communion with the blessed Trinity, social life fulfilled in the communion of saints, liturgical life fulfilled in the company of the angels, and earthly life fulfilled in the new creation. A lucid and inspiring portrayal of the contours of Christian hope."

    —CAROL ZALESKI, Smith College

"Monsignor Mannion has been a clear and systematic teacher through his many years as a Catholic priest and scholar, and he continues to be so in Models of Heaven. Here he opens up heaven's mystery in a vivid and compelling way to those of us below and makes it an eternal reward worth working toward."

    —CHRISTOPHER CARSTENS, Diocese of La Crosse, WI

MODELS OF HEAVEN

MODELS *of* HEAVEN

Interpreting Life Everlasting

M. Francis Mannion

WIPF & STOCK · Eugene, Oregon

MODELS OF HEAVEN
Interpreting Life Everlasting

Wipf & Stock
An Imprint of Wipf and Stock Publishers
199 W. 8th Ave., Suite 3
Eugene, OR 97401

www.wipfandstock.com

PAPERBACK ISBN: 978-1-6667-1908-6
HARDCOVER ISBN: 978-1-6667-1909-3
EBOOK ISBN: 978-1-6667-1910-9

DEDICATED TO

OWEN F. CUMMINGS

and

GREGORY A. GLENN

Colleagues and friends of many years.

TABLE OF CONTENTS

ACKNOWLEDGEMENTS

MANY PEOPLE HAVE ASSISTED in the preparation of this book by reading it in whole or in part: David Fagerberg, Christopher Carstens, Patrick Thronson, Michael McCallion, Daria Spezanno, Owen Cummings, Samuel Dinsdale, Mary Strine, Michael O'Brien.

Jeffrey Allen and Ildiko Haycock assisted in preparing the manuscript for submission to the publisher. To them I am most grateful.

My deepest thanks go Susan Burdett, English professor, parishioner, and friend, who used her many skills in typing, editing, and advising. She assisted in every aspect of the book, including helping with the more tedious work of preparing the ancillary material. Without her, this book would never have come to completion.

Many thanks to Matthew Wimer, Caleb Kormann, and Heather Carraher of Wipf and Stock, who were most generous with their time and patient with my one hundred and one questions as the manuscript progressed.

INTRODUCTION

Well, if it comes to that, I suppose I shall enter into eternal bliss,
but I really wish you wouldn't bring up such depressing subjects.
—English vicar on being asked what he expected after death[1]

THE TOPIC OF HEAVEN continues to receive less than favorable reviews. Already, an eighteenth-century Japanese sage predicted much of the modern negativity about the subject: "Judging by pictures, hell looks more interesting than the other place."[2] George Bernard Shaw gave the following verdict on the next life: "Heaven, as conventionally conceived, is a place so inane, so dull, so useless, so miserable, that nobody has ever ventured to describe a whole day in heaven, though plenty of people have described a day at the seaside."[3]

Peter Kreeft, perhaps the premier Catholic writer on heaven today, states: "Our pictures of Heaven simply do not move us; . . . Our pictures of Heaven are dull, platitudinous and syrupy; therefore, so is our faith, our hope, and our love of Heaven."[4] According to Colleen McDannell and Bernhard Lang, "Scientific, philosophical and theological skepticism has nullified the modern heaven and replaced it with teachings that are minimalist, meager, and dry."[5]

Some dismiss the notion of heaven out of hand. For Emily Brontë, the idea of heaven lacks energy and power. She writes:

> O for the time when I shall sleep
> Without identity,

1. Quoted in Alcorn, *Heaven*, 6.
2. Enright, ed., *Oxford Book of Death*, 198.
3. Shaw, *Treatise*, 25.
4. Kreeft, *Everything You Ever Wanted to Know*, 19.
5. McDannell and Lang, *Heaven*, 352.

And never care how rain may steep
Or snow may cover me!
No promised Heaven, these wild Desires
Could all or half fulfil;
No threatened Hell, with quenchless fires,
Subdue this quenchless will![6]

It would appear that some people would rather fade into nothingness after death than enter heaven viewed as a kind of eternal, boring, retirement home where white-robed ghostly figures wander aimlessly between clouds, playing or listening to harp music, vaguely encountering deceased friends and relatives, and occasionally catching a glimpse of a rather remote and dispassionate God.

Though the recovery of eschatology was a central feature of both Catholic and Protestant theology in the twentieth century—so that the twentieth century was regarded as the "century of eschatology"—the topic of heaven remains the poor relation in eschatology. This may be explained in great part by the fact that official teaching authority of the Church over the centuries has had relatively little to say about heaven, due in part, it seems, to aversion to fanciful presentations on the subject, especially those found in private revelations and visions.

I pause here to clarify the meaning of "eschatology." The word *eschaton* refers to the "end," more specifically to what will happen at the end of time when the Kingdom of God is finally and fully established. Eschatology means the theological knowledge of death, the intermediate state, the end of the world, judgment, heaven, hell, and purgatory.[7] (I encourage the reader to keep this description in mind, as it is central to the task of this book.)

A contemporary warning on eschatology is offered in a Letter on Certain Questions Concerning Eschatology promulgated by the Vatican

6. Brontë, "O for the time," 220.

7. I recommend the following for more extensive study: Cummings, *Coming to Christ*; Nichols, *Death and Afterlife*; O'Callaghan, *Christ Our Hope*; Lane, *Keeping Hope Alive*; Grogan, *Where to from Here?*; Schmaus, *Dogma 6*; Hans Schwarz, *Eschatology*; Braaten and Jenson, eds., *The Last Things*; Ratzinger, *Eschatology*; Hayes, *Visions of a Future*; Phan, *Living into Death, Dying to Life*; Daley, *The Hope of the Early Church*; Thiel, *Icons of Hope*; Rausch, *Eschatology, Liturgy, and Christology*; Bloesch, *The Last Things*; Kelly, *Eschatology and Hope*; Habib, *Orthodox Afterlife*. More accessible works include La Due, *The Trinity Guide to Eschatology*, and Phan, *Responses to 101 Questions on Death and Eternal Life*. The standard reference source for the future will be, in my opinion, *The Oxford Handbook of Eschatology*, edited by Walls.

Congregation for the Doctrine of the Faith in 1979, which reads as follows: "When dealing with man's situation after death, one must be especially aware of arbitrary imaginative representations."[8] Indeed, most official—and unofficial—statements on heaven have been simply repetitions of what was stated by the magisterium in the Middle Ages, giving rise to a theology of heaven that had a rather bare-bones character.

In most comprehensive compendia of theology, heaven is found near the back among the "last things" (judgment, heaven, hell, and purgatory)—and is treated with notable brevity. In one of the last manuals of doctrine published before Vatican Council II, *Fundamentals of Catholic Dogma* by Ludwig Ott (English translation, 1955), eschatology is given twenty-three pages out of five hundred and forty-four, and of these roughly nine deal with heaven. A comparable post-Vatican II work, *Catholicism* by Richard McBrien (published in 1981 and revised in 1994), a work of one thousand, two hundred and ninety pages, spends sixty pages on eschatology, with two pages on heaven. Surprisingly, the impressive work, *Eschatology: Death and Eternal Life* by Joseph Ratzinger (Pope Benedict XVI) published in English in 1988, with a revised edition in 2007, has three hundred and seven pages, with only five pages specifically on heaven.

The same critique may be made of official catechisms. *The Catechism of the Council of Trent*, published originally in 1566, is six hundred and three pages long (in the English translation), and accords heaven only nine pages, with seven other mentions. The *Catechism of the Catholic Church* (hereafter *Catechism*), published in a second edition in 2000 (and considered to be the catechism of the Second Vatican Council), is noted for its stronger eschatological orientation, yet deals with heaven explicitly in less than two pages.

While there are a number of books on the history of the idea of heaven and on aspects of heavenly symbolism, there are, except in evangelical/fundamentalist circles, few Catholic or mainstream Protestant books devoted entirely to heavenly existence.

The reticence about describing heaven is expressed pointedly by Ratzinger when he wrote that "the content of eternal life . . . lies completely outside the scope of human experience."[9] He asserts similarly that "the new world cannot be imagined."[10] In this book I will propose that it is precisely

8. Doctrine of the Faith, "Certain Questions Concerning Eschatology," no. 9.

9. Ratzinger, *Eschatology*, 161.

10. Ratzinger, *Eschatology*, 192.

through divinely-inspired imagination that heaven, as well as many other tenets of faith, are expressed.[11]

Although theologians have, for the most part, not provided a vibrant and attractive picture of heaven, this does not mean that modern believers lack complete faith in life after death. Indeed, in a 2014 Pew Research Center poll, 72 percent of Americans professed a belief in heaven—even if often a rather esoteric one—essentially one they make up themselves.[12] Some of this belief comes from wishful thinking, but also from a profound hope that life does not end in death. Human beings are, if anything, fundamentally hopeful.

It seems, for example, that people grasp on to any indicators of heaven, such as accounts of encounters with angels and near-death experiences (NDEs), a subject analyzed first by Raymond A. Moody in his 1975 classic, *Life After Death: The Investigation of a Phenomenon*. This matter is investigated with considerable philosophical and theological sophistication by Carol Zaleski in her 1987 book, *Otherworld Journeys*, and in her 1996 work, *The Life of the World to Come*. Popular imagination has been stirred by movies such as *Heaven is For Real*, and relatively credible books such as neurosurgeon Eben Alexander, *Proof of Heaven*, and that of surgeon Mary C. Neal, *To Heaven and Back*.

If theologians are cautious about describing heaven, so, it seems, are clergy and pastoral ministers. There exists at the pastoral level today what Cardinal Christoph Schönborn calls "eschatological amnesia," a silence about the heavenly dimension of Christian faith.[13] There is nowadays little teaching, preaching, and catechetical formation on eschatological topics; and, in turn, liturgical celebration in the West has, in great part, lost its eschatological orientation. This has probably made believers shy about thinking too much about and setting much store on orthodox Christian views of heaven, and it has led them instead to pin their hopes on New Age and esoteric views on life after death.[14]

---

11. The reluctance to describe heaven may also connect to "negative theology" (the *via negativa*) or apophatic theology. The fundamental conception is that God is beyond all human imagination—therefore so is heavenly existence. A favorite theme of apophatic theology is that comprehension of God is utterly beyond the realm of language and it holds that human conceptions provide very limited insights into the world of the divine, akin to seeing the tip of an iceberg.

12. "Religious Beliefs and Practices," Pew Research Center, 2014.

13. Schönborn, *Death to Life*, 14.

14. Walls, *Heaven*, 30–33.

In this book I propose to show that there is much more to the Christian tradition on heaven, even if implicitly, than we might think, and to indicate that there are many more biblical, theological, liturgical, spiritual, and literary strands that may be drawn together to set forth a more adequate and comprehensive treatment of the subject.

In this book, I will employ a methodology of models, which is useful in the analysis and organization of complex data. This methodology has long been used in the physical and social sciences in the work of scholars such as Max Black, Ian T. Ramsey, and Ian G. Barbour.

The use of models in theology is generally of lesser complexity than it is in scientific theory. Avery (later Cardinal) Dulles, SJ, popularized this methodology by using theological models in his celebrated 1978 *Models of the Church* (subsequently published in an expanded version is 1987). For Dulles, "Models serve to synthesize what we already know or are inclined to believe. A model is acceptable if it accounts for a large number of biblical and theological data and accords with what history and experience tell us about Christian life."[15]

The strength of a methodology of models is that it can bring order and clarity to data that are otherwise scattered and difficult to organize and understand. It can help highlight themes that have received inadequate attention, and put into proper proportion data that are to various degrees either overrated or underrated. Most of all, models are successful when they account for all or most of the relevant data.

The weakness of a methodology of models is that it can oversimplify. Also, models can easily appear to be in competition with each other and to separate data that belong together. Models can seem to place all the data on the same level. Inevitably overlap and duplication in models will occur—something, I would hold, that need not be seen as a weakness, but as a validation of the models scheme, being that all the models are, after all, in their different ways, about the same subject.

I will leave it to the reader to determine if each model is a satisfactory presentation of clusters of ideas about heaven. The reader must ask him or herself whether the number of models is reasonable (too few or too many); if the models are adequate to an organization of the relevant data; and if

---

15. Dulles, *Models of the Church*, 24–25. Numerous authors have used models in their theological writings, among them Kevin W. Irwin (eucharistic theology); Piet Fransen (systematic theology); George S. Worgul and James L. Empereur (sacraments); John F. O'Grady (christology); Stephan B. Bevans (faith and culture); Sallie McFague (God). Dulles himself published *Models of Revelation* in 1992.

there is a sense of proportion and consistency across the scheme of models. The reader must also avoid the danger of assessing the relative value of each model. An adequate methodology of models holds that there is no super-model or "best" model.

The models I am proposing are the following: Resting in Peace; Contemplating Divine Beauty; Participating in the Trinity; Communing with the Saints; Singing with the Angels; Tending the New Creation; Dwelling in the Holy City; Feasting in the Kingdom.

My first task is to *organize* the scriptural, theological, liturgical, social-scientific, and literary data into models; the second is to *interpret* each model by reference to the historical and theological experience of Christians. The second task—that of *interpretation*—will not, I hope, seem overly subjective. Thus, the first model, "Resting in Peace" will make connections between the themes of human restlessness, the "age of anxiety," the eschatological Sabbath, and the theology and practice of the Christian Sunday as the "eighth day."[16]

My approach to the topic of heaven will be undergirded by five theological convictions:

1. Heaven and earth are not totally separate realms, as though the life of one has little to do with the life of the other. Rather, heaven embraces the earth, in its truth and beauty; earth is a kind of sacrament of heaven. Thus, we can say that in the Church's liturgy, heaven "descends" to earth and earth "ascends" to heaven. The British scholar N. T. Wright states that the "place" of heaven will be the earth redeemed. We should not look upwards toward a detached heaven, but to the Second Coming of Christ, which will complete the transformation of the whole universe.[17] This means that all adequate eschatology never distracts from earthly concerns, but inspires action for the cares and obligations of the physical, cultural, and political realms.

2. Heaven is the world's deepest longing—an axiom I have taken from Peter Kreeft's book, *Heaven: The Heart's Deepest Longing*. Kreeft states: "Heaven is earth's model, earth is Heaven's image."[18] What the medieval scholastics called the obediential capacity or

---

16. The reader may wonder why I have not named liturgy as a distinct model. The reason is that the liturgy is the foundation of all the models and is present implicitly or explicitly in all the models examined.

17. Wright, *Surprised by Hope*, 93–108.

18. Kreeft, *Everything You Ever Wanted to Know*, 258.

obediential potency of the human person—an orientation toward
the divine—applies to the whole created order. Karl Rahner speaks
of the supernatural existential, referring to the human orientation
toward God.

3. Heaven is not properly regarded as an extrinsic reward for following the moral code set forth in the scriptures and the commandments of the Church, but as the completion of the transformation
of faithful disciples. Entry into heaven means a deep and intensive
conversion to Christ, himself the model of authentic human being. To be a saint, an inhabitant of heaven, means to have the endless capacity of receiving and reciprocating divine love. Entry into
heaven begins already in Baptism and is carried through in the
Eucharist and the moral life.

4. Imagination is the faculty by which Christians can apprehend and
speak about heaven. All our language about eschatological realities
is, of course, analogical; it is not literal but literate or metaphori-
cal. We know heaven through stories, images, symbols, and metaphors. But, Alistair McGrath points out, "To speak of 'imagining
heaven' does not imply or entail that heaven is a fictional notion,
constructed by deliberately disregarding the harsher realities of
the everyday world. It is to affirm the critical role of the God-given
human capacity to construct and enter into mental *pictures* [my
italics] of divine reality, which are mediated through Scripture and
the subsequent tradition of reflection and development. We are
able to inhabit the mental images we create, and thence anticipate
the delight of finally entering the greater reality to which they
correspond."[19]

5. All Christian doctrine, moral teaching, liturgy, and the many
other elements of tradition are properly viewed in relation to
their heavenly end. Thus the Trinity, Christology, creation, grace,
and redemption should normatively have systematic reference to
the Kingdom to come. Eschatology is, then, not an addendum to
Christian belief and its theological expression, but is the point of
departure and the constant dynamic by which theology moves
forward. This conviction is most notably present in the work of the
Lutheran theologians Jürgen Moltmann and Wolhart Pannenberg,
and in Catholic theologians Johann Baptist Metz and to a lesser
degree Karl Rahner. In Orthodox theology, eschatology is not just
a branch of theological systems, but a theme undergirding all theology; thus the latter in all its aspects is future-oriented.

19. McGrath, *Brief History of Heaven*, 5.

There are many dimensions of eschatology that cannot—and need not—be attended to here: the nature of the resurrection; immortality; the relationship between body and soul; judgment—particular and general; the intermediate state; reincarnation; the various forms of millenarianism; the after-life in Judaism and non-Christian religions; the relationship between the Kingdom of God and the Church; and death itself (including its denial—symbolized by a growing lack of interest in religious "last rites" and funerals).

I am keenly aware of the danger of venturing too far and saying too much in my examination and interpretation of the various aspects of heaven. I keep in mind the truth stated by St. Paul: "But as it is written: 'What eye has not seen, and ear has not heard, and what has not entered the human heart, what God has prepared for those who love him'" (1 Cor 2:9) and the assertion that, "At present we see indistinctly, as in a mirror, but then face to face. At present I know partially; then I shall know fully" (1 Cor 13:12).[20] I take this to mean not that what traditional Christianity believes about heaven is off-base, but that heaven is infinitely more magnificent and inexhaustible than what we now are able to grasp. The models I propose paint cumulatively a picture that is an incomplete reflection of heavenly reality yet can be taken to be reliable.

Finally, this book is not meant primarily for the trained theologian or the specialist—though I hope some may find it useful—but for clergy, seminarians, pastoral theologians, educators, and the inquiring Christian with an interest in deepening his or her knowledge of eternal life. While this book is written by a Roman Catholic from a denominational perspective, I hope that members of the Orthodox, Anglican, and Protestant traditions may find it of some value in their own investigations of heavenly life. These will also note the regular quotation of non-Catholic theologians, making this, in some respects, an ecumenical project.

Conscious of the qualifications and limitations set out in this Introduction, I now take up what John Saward calls "this most beautiful of theological subjects."[21]

20. Unless otherwise noted, biblical quotations are from the *New American Bible, Revised Edition.*

21. Saward, *Sweet and Blessed Country,* 205.

Chapter One

MODEL ONE: RESTING IN PEACE

Anxiety is the most prominent mental characteristic of Occidental civilization.
—R.R. Willoughby[1]

"Rest in Peace" and "Eternal Rest" are probably the most widely-used inscriptions on graves, tombstones, and funeral memorial cards in Western Christianity. However, these expressions are generally used without much definition or understanding.

The concept of resting in peace has been invoked traditionally in Catholic funeral rites, notably in the plainchant and the many choral/orchestral setting of Requiems, as well as in poetry, hymnody, and spiritual writing.

What follows are samples from the 2011 Catholic Funeral liturgy. The Entrance Antiphon of the Funeral Mass is the following:

> Eternal rest grant unto them, O Lord, and let perpetual light shine upon them.[2]

The Communion Antiphon from the Mass has similar wording:

> Let perpetual light shine upon them, with your Saints for ever, for you are merciful. Eternal rest grant unto them, O Lord, and let perpetual light shine upon them, with your Saints for ever, for you are merciful.[3]

---

1. Quoted in Stossel, *My Age of Anxiety*, 8.
2. *Roman Missal*, 1367.
3. *Roman Missal*, 1368.

The Invitation to the Rite of Committal at the place of the interment is the following:

> Our brother/sister N. has gone to his/her rest in the peace of Christ. May the Lord now welcome him/her to the table of God's children in heaven.[4]

The minister concludes the Committal with the more expansive (and well-known) form of the Entrance Antiphon:

> Eternal rest grant unto him/her, O Lord.
> R) And let perpetual light shine upon him/her.
> May he/she rest in peace.
> May his/her soul and the souls of all the faithful departed, through the mercy of God, rest in peace.
> R) Amen.[5]

The *modus operandi* in this chapter will initially be to show how heavenly rest responds to the human experience of restlessness and anxiety. To know what heaven is like requires first a determination of the nature of the human person and the deepest longings of the human heart. I will go on to show how eternal rest is anticipated in the Church's liturgy and in the spiritual as well as creative activities of men and women.

THE RESTLESS HEART

The classical and most widely-quoted statement on the restlessness of the human heart is found at the beginning of the *Confessions* of St. Augustine. Addressing God, Augustine writes: "You have made us for yourself, and our heart is restless until it rests in you."[6] In Christian iconography, Augustine is often portrayed as holding a flaming heart in his hand, symbolizing the fire and energy of the human soul in search of God. Augustine's spiritual restlessness has inspired Christians and religious seekers for fifteen hundred years, and has generated a whole school broadly known as the "Augustinian tradition." In the words of Thomas F. Martin, OSA, "The restless heart of Augustine prompted a searching, a commitment to truth and love, an

---

4. *Order of Christian Funerals*, no. 216.

5. *Order of Christian Funerals*, no. 223.

6. Augustine, *Confessions*, 3.

unrelenting desire to engage the mystery of God that unfolded before him, both overwhelming and beckoning him."[7]

The key to understanding Augustine's spirituality is the *journey*, the endless and restless movement of desire for union with God. Thus, the journey for Augustine is a "heart journey."[8] The heart symbolizes for Augustine the God-inspired journey, a graced and ongoing journey that takes us inward to the center of our being.

Taking up the theme of restlessness, theologian Ronald Rolheiser, OMI, writes: "All of us experience within ourselves a certain restlessness and insatiability. Our hearts and minds are so fashioned that they are never satisfied, always restless; never quiet, always wanting more of everything."[9]

Very often we do not even know what it is that we want; we lack a spiritual compass. A prolonged restlessness leads us into a whirlwind of activities: "But we are still dissatisfied, leaving us no rest and peace, as we search desperately for someone or something to provide us with completion."[10]

Within us, there is a fundamental dis-ease, a deep restlessness that prevents us from finding complete peace. This desire lies at the center of our souls. By nature, we are people who are always restless, always seeking more. We are living lives of quiet desperation, only intermittently experiencing peace.

Whatever form it takes, we are ultimately talking about one thing: a restlessness, a longing, a gnawing nostalgia, a hunger, a deep congenital aching that lies in our souls and is the impetus that drives everything else. This dis-ease is universal, and allows for no exceptions. What we do with it is the stuff of spirituality.

The sense of restless motion with no evident ending is expressed poignantly in *Song of Destiny, op. 54,* by Johannes Brahms in his musical setting of words by Friedrich Hölderlin:

> To us is allotted
> no restful haven to find;
> they falter, they perish,
> poor suffering mortals
> blindly as moment
> follows moment,

7. Martin, *Our Restless Heart*, 13.

8. Martin, *Our Restless Heart*, 41.

9. Rolheiser, *Restless Heart*, 48–49.

10. Rolheiser, *Restless Heart*, 48–57.

like water from mountain
to mountain impelled
destined to disappearance below.[11]

Being spiritually and psychologically lost, without direction, subject to shifting winds, feeling of no significance is the common lot of humanity. D.H. Lawrence captures this mood in his poem "Song of a Man who is Not Loved:"

> The space of the world is immense, before me and around me;
> If I turn quickly, I am terrified, feeling space surround me;
> Like a man in a boat on very clear, deep water, space frightens
> and confounds me.
> I see myself isolated in the universe, and wonder
> What effect I can have. My hands wave under
> The heavens like specks of dust that are floating asunder.
> I hold myself up, and feel a big wind blowing
> Me like a gadfly into the dusk, without my knowing
> Whither or why or even how I am going.
> So much there is outside me, so infinitely
> Small am I, what matter if minutely
> I beat my way, to be lost immediately?
> How shall I flatter myself that I can do
> Anything in such immensity? I am too
> Little to count in the wind that beats me through.[12]

Here, the world is experienced as immense, and our restless experience leaves us helpless and lost. Attempts to achieve significance often bring its opposite: a sense of smallness and lack of direction.

THE AGE OF ANXIETY

The pervasive sense of restlessness has its most severe expression in the experience of anxiety. In 1939, W.H. Auden published a short poem titled, *September 1st, 1939*, about a group of people in a bar in New York seeking to drink away their anxieties. One of the verses states the central theme of the poem:

> Faces along the bar
> Cling to their average day:

11. Hölderlin, *Schicksalslied*.
12. Lawrence, "Song of Man Not Loved," 222–23.

The lights must never go out,
The music must always play . . .
Lest we should see where we are,
Lost in a haunted wood,
Children afraid of the night
Who have never been happy or good.[13]

In 1947, Auden published a longer work, thematically based on his 1939 poem entitled *The Age of Anxiety,* which sought to capture the feelings of fear, doubt, and displacement that followed World War II. While Auden's elaboration of the experience of the four persons in the 1939 poem is set in time of war—the invasion of Poland by Hitler—he makes it clear that the fundamental causes of the anxiety of his characters, as well as of society in general, must be sought on deeper levels than merely a particular occasion such as that of war. The four characters, though different in temperament and background, have in common certain characteristics of the age: the sense of a collapse of faith in Western civilization and of the idea of progress, and the end of the Enlightenment notion that human beings and their society can be made perfect.[14]

The "age of anxiety" made famous by Auden had its modern roots in such diverse figures as Kierkegaard, Freud, and Nietzsche. While each of these differs from the others in emphases, the common thread in all is the reality of existence as a diffuse and often nameless feeling of being adrift in the universe.

The experience of anxiety is certainly not new, and it has beset humankind from the beginning of its reflective journey. Nevertheless, beginning in the nineteenth century, it took on a strong profile in human consciousness and in philosophical and religious reflection, culminating in the "age of anxiety."

13. Auden, *Selected Poems,* 87. Leonard Bernstein was inspired by this poem to compose the Age of Anxiety Symphony No. 2. Choreographer Jerome Robbins composed a ballet on the poem's theme.

14. May, *Meaning of Anxiety,* 51. The psychologist Rollo May has analyzed anxiety from biological, psychological, psychotherapeutic, and cultural perspectives. The contemporary expression of human anxiety is indicated by the extent to which people use anxiety-relieving drugs and alcohol. These seek to assuage the experience of seeking and not finding, searching for meaning amidst the turbulence of life. See also an analysis of the difference between existential and clinical anxiety in Stossel, *My Age of Anxiety,* 3–61.

REDEEMING ANXIETY

The twentieth-century theologian who dealt with anxiety in most detail was the German-born Lutheran Paul Tillich, who spent most of his adult life in the U.S. Tillich described the anxious mood of Europe in the 1930s, and how the ascent of Hitler temporarily assuaged the national mood in Germany of those years: "First of all a feeling of *fear* or, more exactly, of indefinite anxiety was prevailing. Not only the economic and political, but also the cultural and religious security seemed to be lost. There was nothing on which one could build levels; everything was without foundation. A catastrophic breakdown was expected every moment. Consequently, a longing for security was growing in everybody."[15] Hitler seemed to be the answer to the national insecurity—an answer that, we know, proved to be only temporary, and the old anxiety returned with Hitler's demise.

Against feelings of anxiety, especially of meaninglessness and emptiness, Tillich calls the human person to courage as "the universal and essential self-affirmation of one's being" against those elements of human experience that seek to negate it.[16]

Tillich describes the impetus for self-affirmation as the sense of being accepted by something that ultimately is divine grace: "Grace strikes us when we are in great pain and restlessness. It strikes us when we walk through the dark valley of a meaninglessness and empty life. . . . Grace is experienced in moments when our disgust for our own being, our indifference, our weakness, our hostility, and our lack of direction and composure have become intolerable to us. It strikes us when, year after year, the longed-for perfection of life does not appear, when the old compulsions reign within us as they have for decades, when despair destroys all joy and courage."[17]

But, Tillich concludes: "Sometimes at that moment a wave of light breaks into our darkness and it is as though a voice were saying: 'You are accepted. *You are accepted*, accepted by that which is greater than you, and the name of which you do not know. Do not ask for the name now; perhaps you will find it later. . . . *Simply accept the fact that you are accepted!*' If that happens to us, we experience grace."[18]

15. Tillich, *Protestant Era,* 245.

16. Tillich, *Courage to Be,* 3.

17. Tillich, *Shaking the Foundations,* 161.

18. Tillich, *Shaking the Foundations,* 162.

The Swiss theologian Hans Urs von Balthasar published an engaging book titled *The Christian and Anxiety,* in which he analyzes from a different perspective the human experience of anxiety and its redemption in the suffering and Cross of Christ.[19]

Balthasar identifies Sirach 40 as a classic biblical statement of anxiety:

> A great anxiety has God allotted,
> and a heavy yoke, to the children of Adam.
> From the day they leave their mother's womb
> until the day they return to the mother of all the living.
> Troubled thoughts and fear of heart are theirs
> and anxious foreboding until death.
> Whether one sits on a lofty throne
> or grovels in dust and ashes,
> Whether one wears a splendid crown
> or is clothed in the coarsest of garments—
> There is wrath and envy, trouble and dread,
> terror of death, fury and strife.
> Even when one lies on his bed to rest,
> his cares disturb his sleep at night.
> So short is his rest it seems like none,
> till in his daydreams he struggles as he did by day.
> Troubled by the visions of his mind,
> like a fugitive fleeing from the pursuer.
> As he reaches safety, he wakes up,
> astonished that there was nothing to fear. (1–7)

Balthasar sees the solution to anxiety in a sharing in the Cross of Christ, who carries and redeems human anxiety. For Balthasar, the cry of Jesus on the Cross, "My God, my God, why have you forsaken me?" (Matt 27:46; Mark 15:34) is the ultimate expression of anxiety. But on the Cross, Jesus redeems anxiety. Balthasar writes: "Christ has borne the anxiety of the world so as to give to the world instead that which is his: his joy, his peace. . . . And this is absolutely inseparable from his earthly life, from his cross and his descent into hell, and from his resurrection. All grace is the grace of the cross. All joy is joy resulting from the cross, marked with the sign of the cross."[20]

Perhaps nowhere is the consolation of God more poignantly expressed than in the words of comfort offered by Jesus during his public ministry:

19. Balthasar, *Christian and Anxiety,* 88–89.
20. Balthasar, *Christian and Anxiety,* 88–89.

Come to me, all you who labor and are burdened, and I will give you rest. Take my yoke upon you and learn from me, for I am meek and humble of heart; and you will find rest for yourselves. For my yoke is easy, and my burden light." (Matt 11: 28–30)

In his Letter to the Philippians, St. Paul calls the disciples away from earthly anxiety:

Have no anxiety at all, but in everything, by prayer and petition, with thanksgiving, make your requests known to God. Then the peace of God that surpasses all understanding will guard your hearts and minds in Christ Jesus. (Phil 4: 6–7)

The best-known and most-beloved psalm in the Bible, Psalm 23, proclaims God's saving power in the midst of travail:

Even though I walk through the valley of the shadow of death,
will fear no evil, for you are with me;
your rod and your staff comfort me. (Ps 23:4)

While the ministry of Jesus in alleviating anxiety had immediate effects on his hearers, it also had an eschatological reference: Only in the Kingdom of heaven would the end of anxiety be completely realized. Final rest at the end of the world is expressed in the Book of Revelation:

I heard a voice from heaven say, 'Write this: Blessed are the dead who die in the Lord from now on.' 'Yes,' said the Spirit, 'let them find rest from their labors, for their works accompany them.' (Rev 14:13)

An important qualification of the redemption of anxiety is that anxiety will always be a feature of human existence. Only in the Kingdom of heaven will all anxiety be relieved.

REST AND CREATIVITY

If heaven is a place of rest, we may ask: Will there be activity in heaven? Peter Kreeft thinks so: "Creative work is a primary human need, and our conventional pictures of heaven are boring partly because they do not fulfill this need."[21] It is the nature of the human person to be active and creative. We will be released from all laborious work, but not from soulful creativity.

21. Kreeft, *Everything You Wanted to Know,* 51.

Heaven is not a place of idleness, a place of "frozen glory," in the words of Ronda Chervin.[22]

Heavenly rest is not a matter of sleep in the human sense, of unconsciousness and a lack of activity. Rather it is the basis of heavenly work and creativity.

I draw here on Josef Pieper's classic, *Leisure, the Basis of Culture*. For Pieper, leisure is not idleness, but an attitude of mind that fosters silence, contemplation, and receptivity. Leisure, Pieper states, is the basis of culture. Without leisure, culture atrophies and work becomes oppressive and lacking in meaning. Leisure implies "an attitude of non-activity, of inward calm, of silence; it means not being 'busy,' but letting things happen."[23]

The point I wish to make here is that heavenly rest ("Rest in peace," as the Funeral liturgy states) generates activity that is good for the soul and for the common good. It is the kind of work that builds up the holy city. N. T. Wright states: "So far from sitting on clouds playing harps, as people often imagine, the redeemed people of God in the new world will be agents of his love, going out in new ways to accomplish new creative tasks, to celebrate and extend the glory of his love."[24]

In its Pastoral Constitution on the Church in the Modern World (*Guadium et spes*), the Second Vatican Council implied that earthly work will find a place in heaven: "When we have spread on earth the fruits of our nature and our enterprise—human dignity, brotherly communion, and freedom—according to the command of the Lord and in his Spirit, we will find them once again, cleansed this time from the stain of sin, illuminated and transfigured"[25]

Do we have more detail about heavenly work than that? E. J. Fortman, SJ, writes: "Modern man wants a heaven that is dynamic and not static, a heaven that permits an eternal growth in knowing and loving God and people and things, music and art and science, a heaven where each one can make progress in knowing and loving and doing, where each can strive and achieve down to endless 'years of eternity'"[26]

What other kinds of progress might glorified persons make? Fortman answers: "They could use their minds to grow in knowledge—both

22. Chervin, *What the Saints Said*, 111.

23. Pieper, *Leisure, the Basis of Culture*, 46.

24. Wright, *Surprised by Hope*, 105.

25. *Vatican Council II*, p. 938, no. 39.

26. Fortman, *Everlasting Life After Death*, 207.

speculative and practical. They could learn more in any area of knowledge that interested them. In Science. In Art. In Philosophy. In Theology. In Languages. In Music. In Astronomy. In Anthropology. In Sculpture. In History. In Geography. In Literature. In Engineering. In Sociology. And so on and on."[27]

Fortman's description may be overly fanciful, but it makes the point that human work and earthly achievement will not be vague and lacking in dynamism in heaven. The notion of heavenly rest as a semi-comatose, motionless, isolated existence is incorrect. Heaven will not be a sedate and motionless state but a place of dynamic rest, of the expansion of human knowledge and achievement, of intellectual and practical powers and ability, of the dreams expressed in humanity. The popular notion of heaven could not be further from the truth, and the old notion invites ridicule, in the manner of the poet Emily Dickinson, who wrote of eternal rest: "It will take so many beds."[28]

In heaven, work will be adapted to each person's abilities and powers. It will be the work he or she can do best; the work that will give the fullest expression to all that is within him or her. The energy driving human beings, instead of being dissipated at death, will rather be reoriented toward new and transformative activities.

Human beings are active by nature. J. Boudreau writes: "Action is a fundamental dynamic of our existence, which cannot be changed without radically changing our whole nature. In Heaven we shall be far more active than we can possibly be here below."[29]

THE EXPERIENCE OF FLOW

Can we say more about the way people experience rest in heaven? Mihaly Csikszentmihalyi, the social psychologist, has proposed a theory of "flow" which provides some insight into the intensely engaging and "timeless" character of heaven. Csikszentmihaly was fascinated by the way people get lost in their work and in their arts. Artists get so immersed in their work that time seems to stand still. There is no consciousness of past or future, but only a sense of total engagement with the present. Boredom is cancelled out by flow. During flow, people typically experience intense enjoyment,

27. Fortman, *Everlasting Life After Death*, 315.

28. Quoted in McDannell and Lang, *Heaven*, 25.

29. Boudreau, *Happiness of Heaven*, 107.

creativity, and a sense of total involvement. The normal experience of time is suspended.[30] "Most flow activities," Csikszentmihalyi explains, "do not depend on clock time . . . they have their own pace, their own sequences of events marking transitions from one state to another without regard to . . . intervals of duration. . . . Freedom from the tyranny of time does add to the exhilaration we feel during a state of complete involvement."[31]

The most common descriptions of "flow experience" is that time no longer seems to pass in the way it ordinarily does. "The manner in which we measure night and day, or by the orderly progressions of clocks, is rendered irrelevant by the rhythms dictated by the activity."[32] Hours seem to pass by in minutes, and people report that time seems to pass much faster than usual.

Flow experiences, Csikszentmihalyi says, are notably present in games, sports, and recreational activities—for instance, rock-climbing, chess, painting, music-making (and listening). It is also present whenever there is intense and satisfying work, such as that of a surgeon who can perform an operation for hours with little sense of the passage of time.[33]

The opposite of flow is boredom—experienced as disengagement from activities, involvement in uninteresting work, lack of concern for one's surroundings, excessive and depressing self-consciousness, the experience of activities and of personal and social communications that are dull and tiresome. This typically involves oppressive labor and interaction with people with whom one has nothing in common. In activities that generate boredom, the experience of time differs radically from that of flow: minutes become hours and days become weeks.

Boring experiences seem to go on "for eternity." No analysis of eternal rest would be complete without dealing with the basic fear that many people have concerning eternal rest: Is it boring? Isaac Asimov declares: "I don't believe in an afterlife, so I don't have to spend my whole life fearing hell, or fearing heaven even more. For whatever the tortures of hell, I think the boredom of heaven would be even worse."[34] In Randy Alcorn's words:

---

30. It is said that when Michelangelo painted the Sistine Chapel, he worked for days without rest or drink; he would then descend from the scaffolding and eat and sleep briefly, then resume his extraordinary "flow" schedule.

31. Csikszentmihalyi, *Flow*, 66–67.

32. Csikszentmihalyi, *Flow*, 66.

33. Csikszentmihalyi, *Beyond Boredom and Anxiety*, 35–37.

34. Asimov, quoted in Alcorn, *Eternal Perspectives*, 55.

"Satan need not convince us that Heaven doesn't exist. He need convince us only that Heaven is a place of boring, unearthly existence."[35]

Religious and transcendental experiences can also have a flow quality. In the intense experience of worship, for instance, the participant is lifted out of the ordinary experience of time. By the same token, religious activities that are boring seem to last forever.

Using Csikszentmihalyi's theory, we can say that heaven is the ultimate flow experience. We encounter life at its most pleasurable and intense; there is a complete sense of engagement, and nothing is encountered that is boring or anxiety-creating. Time stands still, or, we may say, passes with unimaginable rapidity.

Paul Tillich speaks of "the eternal now," when past and future meet in the present: "The mystery of the future and the mystery of the past are united in the mystery of the present."[36] Humans are the only beings that have a sense of the eternal in the present. They can escape from the bondage of the past and anticipate the future. Past and future, in the experience of the "eternal now," become a present reality.

The Christian liturgical sense of time is also instructive. Liturgy is eternity celebrated in time. *Anamnesis,* the recollection and making real of the past in the present, and *prolepsis,* the calling of the future into the present, is made possible by *epiclesis,* the effective invocation of the Holy Spirit, who is the unifier of time, past and future.

The Church's celebration of the Paschal Mystery, the Lord's suffering, death, resurrection, and ascension, and its consummation in the Kingdom of heaven is always in the *now,* the present moment. Remembrance and hope are unified in liturgical events by the power of the Spirit. In the liturgical celebration, Christ is given to us as food; recalling Christ's death and resurrection, we look forward to the heavenly banquet.

A hint of how time changes when experienced as eternity is found in the words of Psalm 90:4 in which it is said of God: "A thousand years in your eyes are merely a day gone by." Eternal rest is, then, freedom from restlessness and anxiety, and intense engagement in which time seems to stand still, and we experience the eternal now.

35. Alcorn, *Eternal Perspectives,* 59.
36. Tillich, *Eternal Now,* 130.

ANTICIPATING ETERNAL REST

I now turn to the way the liturgy and life of Judaism and Christianity prefigure eternal rest. In biblical history, rest found its most concrete expression in the Jewish observance of the Sabbath, which had its foundation in the story of creation at the beginning of Genesis:

> Thus the heavens and the earth and all their array were completed. On the seventh day God completed the work he had been doing; he rested on the seventh day from all the work he had undertaken. God blessed the seventh day and made it holy, because on it he rested from all the work he had done in creation. (Gen 2:1–3).

This is spelled out further in Deuteronomy, which links the Sabbath with the liberation from Egypt:

> Observe the sabbath day—keep it holy, as the Lord, your God, commanded you. Six days you may labor and do all your work, but the seventh day is a sabbath of the Lord your God. You shall not do any work, either you, your son or your daughter, your male or female slave, your ox or donkey or any work animal, or the resident alien within your gates, so that your male and female slave may rest as you do. Remember that you were once slaves in the land of Egypt, and the Lord, your God, brought you out from there with a strong hand and outstretched arm. That is why the Lord, your God, has commanded you to observe the sabbath day. (Deut 5:12–15)

In the New Testament, many of the disputes between Jesus and the Pharisees had to do with Sabbath observance—the Sabbath being the day on which Jesus chose to work his miracles. Jesus presented himself as the Lord of the Sabbath and his miracles as liberation from evil and sin. His work of healing had a strong eschatological character, and he presented himself as eschatological judge. Already, in his miracles, the new world of health and healing became manifest.

The matter of how the Jewish Sabbath was assumed into the Lord's Day of Christians is a complex one which we need not go into here. Suffice it to say that the memorial of the Lord's resurrection, the first day of the week, became the Sabbath of Christians. In the process, Sunday was given new names: "the day of the Lord," the "dominical day, the *Dies Domini*, "the eighth day," the day beyond all days—the day of eternity.

Willy Rordorf, in his classic work on Sunday, focuses on the Lord's Day as the "eighth day" (language originally used for baptism). "Sunday . . . as the 'eighth day' represented the Kingdom of God, that is to say, the second, new eternal creation at the end of the times."[37] Sunday was the dawn of another world; thus, the concept of the "eighth day." The Lord's Day came to be regarded as standing for eternal rest and it was equated with the eschatological character of the Sabbath. On one day each week Christians enjoyed the fullness of the messianic powers poured out through the ages until the Lord would come again. Sunday was an anticipation of eternal life.

THE *DIES DOMINI* AND ETERNITY

In our own time, Pope John Paul II, in his Apostolic Letter *Dies Domini* (the Day of the Lord), pointed out that Sunday rest has a meaning and importance that goes beyond ordinary Christian conceptions. Rest, the Pope says, is something sacred, because it allows people to withdraw from the often demanding cycle of daily tasks in order to renew an awareness that everything is the work of God.[38] The prodigious power over creation which God has given to humankind can lead it to forget that God is the creator upon whom everything depends.

Through Sunday rest, daily concerns and tasks can find their proper perspective: "The material things about which we worry give way to spiritual values; in a moment of encounter and less pressured exchange, we see the true face of the people with whom we live. Even the beauties of nature—too often marred by the desire to exploit, which turns against us—can be rediscovered and enjoyed to the full."[39] As the day on which people are at peace with God, themselves, and others, Sunday becomes a time when people can appreciate anew the wonders of nature, "allowing themselves to be caught up" in a marvelous and mysterious harmony.[40]

The Church's regulations concerning the Sabbath day should be seen, then, not as restrictive and legalistic, but as motivated by a desire to free people from often oppressive work so that they can give themselves to joyful worship, to communion with others, to the beauties of creation, and to

---

37. Rordorf, *Sunday*, 275–85.
38. John Paul II, *Dies Domini*, 48–49.
39. John Paul II, *Dies Domini*, 50.
40. John Paul II, *Dies Domini*, 50.

the day of eternity. Sunday, then, brings the eschatological future into the present.

The Eucharist, Pope John Paul II writes, has a program of true brotherhood and sisterhood. From Sunday Mass there flows out a program of charity destined to spread into the whole life of the people, inspiring the way in which they live the whole of the Lord's Day. If Sunday is a day of joy, Christians should show by their active behavior that they cannot be happy "by themselves." They look around to find people who may need help. It may be that in their parish, neighborhood, or among those who are sick, elderly, children or immigrants, who feel more keenly on Sundays their isolation, need, and suffering.[41] In these activities the eschatological world beyond time manifests itself.

Pope John Paul names the following activities as appropriate to Sunday: inviting to a meal people who are alone, visiting the sick, providing food for needy families, spending a few hours in voluntary work and acts of solidarity. Lived in this way, "Sunday becomes a great school of charity, justice and peace."[42] The Lord's Day is a "day of solidarity,"[43] which has not only practical means to improve communal life but anticipates the "new heavens" and the "new earth," in which liberation from slavery is finally complete.[44] Sunday involves a "*culture of sharing* to be lived not only among the members of the community itself but also in society as a whole."[45]

The eschatological character of the Sunday Eucharist and the accompanying apostolic works prefigure the future life of the Kingdom in which people eternally worship God and share in a life of giving and receiving within the communion of saints. This is underlined in Pope John Paul's emphasis on the eschatological meaning of Sunday as "the eighth day." Sunday symbolizes the day which will follow the present time, the day without end, in which there will be neither morning nor evening; it will simply be the imperishable age which will never pass away. In celebrating Sunday, which is both the "first" and the "eighth" day, the Christian is led toward the goal of eternal life. The observance of Sunday, the Pope writes, helps "to remind us of *the pilgrim and eschatological character of the People of God.*"[46]

41. John Paul II, *Dies Domini*, 53.
42. John Paul II, *Dies Domini*, 54.
43. John Paul II, *Dies Domini*, 51.
44. John Paul II, *Dies Domini*, 51.
45. John Paul II, *Dies Domini*, 52.
46. John Paul II, *Dies Domini*, 28–29.

Looking beyond Sunday, John Paul II says, we may expand the list of simple activities that have an implicit eschatological orientation: family get-togethers, anniversaries, recreations of various kinds including sports, vacations, artistic activities, reading, music, time spent with friends, and sports. All good and edifying activities have an intrinsic eschatological character—whether this is explicitly adverted to or not; they point beyond themselves to the life of the Kingdom of heaven, and anticipate the coming of the Kingdom into the present.

In his classic work on the Sabbath, Abraham Joshua Heschel writes, from a modern Jewish perspective, about the Sabbath as an "eschatological day." (The Christian reader will adapt this to the Sunday observance.) "Six days a week we wrestle with the world, wringing profit from the earth; on the Sabbath we especially care for the seed of eternity planted in the soul. The world has our hands, but our soul belongs to Someone Else. Six days a week we try to dominate the world, on the seventh day we try to dominate the self."[47]

The Sabbath is, then, a reminder of two worlds—the present world and the world to come, the eternal day of joy, holiness, and rest. The Sabbath is no time for anxiety or care, for the Sabbath prefigures eternity. We are thus called already to be "in love with eternity."[48] Created things "are our tools; eternity, the Sabbath, is our mate. Israel is engaged to eternity."[49]

For Heschel, the Sabbath is not isolated from the rest of the week, but overflows into it. The Sabbath "cannot survive in exile, a lonely stranger among days of profanity. It needs the companionship of all other days. All days of the week must be spiritually consistent with the Day of Days."[50] Thus, our whole life should be a pilgrimage to the seventh day. Accordingly, "the Sabbath is the counterpoint of living; the melody sustained throughout all agitations and vicissitudes which menace our conscience; our awareness of God's presence in the world."[51] Unless one learns to relish the Sabbath while still in this world, unless one is initiated into the appreciation of eternal life, one will be unable to enjoy the reality of eternity in the world to

47. Heschel, *Sabbath*, 13.
48. Heschel, *Sabbath*, 48.
49. Heschel, *Sabbath*, 48.
50. Heschel, *Sabbath*, 89.
51. Heschel, *Sabbath*, 89; also Brueggemann, *Sabbath As Resistance*.

come. "Sad is the lot of him who arrives inexperienced and when led to heaven has no power to perceive the beauty of the Sabbath."[52]

For Jews, then, the Sabbath has an eschatological foundation. For Christians, Sunday is the eschatological day. Sunday worship overflows into the prayer, work, and contemplative activities of the "ordinary" day.

CONCLUSION

While Christians, especially writers and commentators, must exercise appropriate caution in imagining what goes on in heaven, it may be said with certainty that heavenly rest will be one of intense and joyful activity—as the models to be treated in the coming chapters will indicate. But until the Kingdom comes, restlessness and anxiety will remain features of human existence. In this life, flow and tension, anxiety and peace will remain contrasting and oppositional companions. Heavenly rest allows the human person to be active in a manner fitted to his or her nature and in a way that meets the heart's desires. In eternal rest there is no toil or difficulty; all is accomplished in joy and peace. Heaven is at once the most intense activity and the highest form of rest. In heaven, we will experience the ultimate glory of resting, not in isolation, but in the embrace of the holy Trinity, the saints, and glorified humanity. It is such rest that we properly have in mind when we pray for "eternal rest" and invoke the words "rest in peace" as we commend our deceased brothers and sisters to the Lord. Thus, in the meantime we are required to learn how to live creatively with restlessness and anxiety, recognizing St. Augustine's dictum that our hearts are restless until they rest in God.

To return to the beginning of this chapter, we frequently find in the liturgy the word "rest." We pray that the dead will "rest in peace." The ultimate resting in God is not a passive resting from an often laborious life, but a participation in the eternal activity of God

---

52. Heschel, *Sabbath*, 74.

Chapter Two

MODEL TWO:
CONTEMPLATING DIVINE BEAUTY

It is beauty that will save the world.
—Fyodor Dostoevsky[1]

ROBERT (NOW BISHOP) BARRON, founder of the evangelical Word on Fire Catholic Ministries, begins his engaging book *And Now I See . . . A Theology of Transformation* by writing: "Christianity is, above all, a way of *seeing*. Everything else in Christian life flows from and circles around the transformation of vision. Christians *see* differently, and that is why their prayer, their worship, their action, their whole way of being in the world have a distinctive accent and flavor."[2] Barron points both to the conviction of Pierre Teilhard de Chardin, whose fundamental vocation as a Christian was to help people *see*, and to Thomas Aquinas' basic assertion that the ultimate goal of Christian life is the *beatific vision*, an act of *seeing*.[3]

This chapter will deal with the beatific vision, the eternal vision of God, as one of the principal features of heavenly existence—traditionally regarded as the most important one. It will take up the notion of the contemplation of divine beauty, and the way in which the inhabitants of heaven are beautified, becoming themselves makers of beauty. It will finally show the power of liturgy as a foretaste of the beauty of heaven.

Accordingly, I assume a theological connection between the enjoyment of the beatific vision and the contemplation of divine beauty.

1. Quoted in Dostoevsky, *Idiot*, 432.
2. Barron, *Now I See*, 1.
3. Barron, *Now I See*, 1.

Theologian John Navone puts the relationship between the two as follows: "Eternal happiness is the beatific vision of Beauty Itself."[4] The words "beatific," possessing eternal happiness, and "beauty," have separate and distinct meanings; yet their common, albeit distant, origins in the Latin word *bonus*, good, connect them directly. Both name the divine object of enjoyment and contemplation. Accordingly, the "beatific vision" and the "contemplation of divine beauty" will be seen to be two sides of the same reality.

THE BEATIFIC VISION

The *Catechism* provides a number of paragraphs that together constitute the main elements of a theology of the beatific vision. Here is one:

> Because of his transcendence, God cannot be seen as he is, unless he himself opens up his mystery to man's immediate contemplation and gives him the capacity for it. The Church calls this contemplation of God in his heavenly glory "the beatific vision."[5]

Later, the *Catechism* says:

> Desire for true happiness frees man from his immoderate attachment to the goods of this world so that he can find his fulfillment in the vision and beatitude of God. "The promise [of seeing God] surpasses all beatitude. . . . In Scripture, to see is to possess. . . . Whoever sees God has obtained all the goods of which he can conceive."[6]

Purity of heart, the *Catechism* says, is a precondition for the vision of God's beauty:

> The "pure in heart" are promised that they will see God face to face and be like him [1 Cor 13: 12; 1 Jn 3:2]. Purity of heart is the precondition of the vision of God. Even now it enables us to see *according to* God, to accept others as "neighbors"; it lets us perceive the human body—ours and our neighbor's—as a temple of the Holy Spirit, a manifestation of divine beauty.[7]

The beatific vision, then, is not merely something one experiences without a proper disposition. It requires conversion of heart and a clear,

4. Navone, *Theology of Beauty*, vi.
5. *Catechism*, no. 1028.
6. *Catechism*, no. 2548.
7. *Catechism*, no. 2519.

faith-filled attitude. Thus, there is both continuity and discontinuity in the relationship between the beginning of the beatific vision in present life and the fulfillment of the beatific vision in eternal life.

The human experience of the vision of God in the Old Testament is ambiguous: God is sometimes seen, sometimes not. In Exodus 33:20, God says to Moses: "You cannot see my face, for no one can see me and live." However, in Exodus 33:11 we read, "The Lord used to speak to Moses face to face, as a person speaks to a friend," thus, transforming the face of Moses. In the Book of Numbers there is the blessing, "The Lord let his face shine upon you, and be gracious to you!" (Num 6:25–26).

In the Christian dispensation, Jesus is the revelation of God's "face." Thus, the glory of God appears at the birth of Jesus, at the transfiguration, in the post-resurrection appearances, and at the ascension. Matt 18: 10 states that the angels in heaven "always look upon the face of my heavenly Father." 1 John 3:2 speaks of the future state in which humankind shall see divinity: "We do know that when it is revealed we shall be like him, for we shall see him as he is." Paul draws a contrast between our knowledge of God now and our knowledge in the Kingdom to come: "At present we see indistinctly, as in a mirror, but then face to face" (1 Cor 13:11–12). The implication is that the beatific vision begins in earthly existence.[8] We can experience it in all that is beautiful in human reality. In Paul's Letter to the Colossians, Jesus is viewed as "the image of the invisible God" (Col 1:15). In the Eastern tradition, and to a lesser extent in the West, Jesus is viewed as the icon of God.[9]

In examining the reality of the beatific vision, we find that heaven is no cold and abstract reality, but a vital and dynamic one. Nor is the beatific vision a matter of "staring" at the face of God. We will, in fact, encounter the totality of Christ, and all that he beatifies. In the words of theologian Peter Phan, "Heaven is not only vision of the divine essence, but also sharing in the life of the Triune God, communion with other human beings, and harmony with the cosmos."[10] The beatific vision, then, will be an ecstatic rather than a static reality; it will be comprehensive in scope, and embrace all created reality.

---

8. *Catechism*, no. 633. Hell is viewed as a radical self-imposed deprivation of the vision of God.

9. See Nichols, *Art of God Incarnate*; Schönborn, *God's Human Face*.

10. Phan, *Responses to 101 Questions*, 78.

THE PROCESS OF DIVINIZATION

The experience of God in the present makes us holy; it divinizes us. Divin-ization, also called "deification" and *theosis*, refers to the process by which Christians are radically and profoundly transformed by grace, primarily by the sacraments of Baptism, Confirmation, and the Eucharist, and by encounter with Christ across the whole range of Christian spirituality and action. Here we link divinization with the contemplative seeing of Christ, with the beatific vision. This process is never complete in this life, but only in the Kingdom of heaven. It is a process that is beyond all earthly com-prehension, a transformation that Greek Catholic theologian Jean Corbon calls "astonishing."[11]

The biblical warrant for divinization is found in Second Peter, which states that as believers, the baptized "may come to share in the divine na-ture" (2 Pet 1:3–4). In 2 Corinthians, the baptized are transformed into Christ's very likeness (2 Cor 3:18). Divinization is expressed in 1 John in these words: "See what love the Father has bestowed on us that we may be called the children of God. Yet so we are. . . . We do know that when it is revealed we shall be like him, for we shall see him as he is (1 John 3:1–2).

The *Catechism* elaborates on this in terms of the notion of the human/divine exchange that is fundamental to the Christian faith:

> The Word became flesh to make us *"partakers of the divine na-ture"* [2 Pet. 1–4]: "For this is why the Word became man, and the Son of God became the Son of man: so that man, by entering into communion with the Word and thus receiving divine sonship, might become a son of God" [St. Irenaeus, *Adv. haeres.* 3, 19, 1]. "For the Son of God became man so that we might become God" [St. Athanasius, *De inc.*, 54, 3]. "The only-begotten Son of God, wanting to make us sharers in his divinity, assumed our nature, so that he, made man, might make men gods" [St. Thomas Aquinas, *Opusc.* 57: 1–4].[12]

What begins in Baptism continues in spiritual contemplation, as the *Catechism* states:

> Contemplation is a *gaze* of faith, fixed on Jesus. "I look at him and he looks at me": this is what a certain peasant of Ars used to say while praying before the tabernacle. This focus on Jesus is a

11. Corbon, *Wellspring,* 217.
12. *Catechism,* no. 460.

renunciation of self. His gaze purifies our heart; the light of the countenance of Jesus illumines the eyes of our heart and teaches us to see everything in the light of his truth and his compassion for all men. Contemplation also turns its gaze on the mysteries of the life of Christ.[13]

The word "contemplation" and the phrase "gaze of faith" could easily give the impression that the beatific vision is both in its present form and in its eternal fulfillment passive or static. The beatific vision is not static, but dynamic and transformative. Christians are being drawn in an ongoing way into the trinitarian life of God. What is contemplated reaches out and embraces us; we become one with what we contemplate. Australian theologian Anthony Kelly writes:

> The beatific vision must be understood—as with everything that can be said about heaven—in Trinitarian terms. The vision of God is not simply beholding the Trinity "from the outside." God is not one object, however sublime, among many that the blessed now see. They do not so much see what God is like as to become transformed into the divine likeness. To see God is to be "deified" or, if you will, "trinified." The essential meaning of the beatific vision lies in our future participation in God's own self-knowledge and joy.[14]

Kelly continues: "The beatific vision is what can be described as participatory knowledge. It is not a matter of looking at God 'from the outside,' but a knowledge born of an immersion in the boundless ocean of Trinitarian life. It is to live from, with, and in God."[15]

The beatific vision changes and transforms human vision. We see from within the triune God. We are given divine vision, so that we look *in God* at our fellow men and women, at creation, and at history in divine light. We do not so much see God as see *in* God. We look outward and see everything bathed in glory. Gazing into God's face reveals to us who we really are. In this light our fellow men and women become beautiful.

Kelly develops the notion that the beatific vision even in heaven is always incomplete and always unfolding:

> Even though God is "seen" and "possessed" in the glory of heaven, God does not cease to be absolute and inexhaustible mystery. God

13. *Catechism*, no. 2715.

14. Kelly, *Eschatology and Hope*, 172.

15. Kelly, *Eschatology and Hope*, 172.

is not an object bounded by the limits of finite vision. God is not possessed as something held and grasped. The immediacy of face-to-face vision does not mean that the mind now masters what was once too difficult or too obscure. No doubt many mysteries will be resolved in the light of God, but the abiding mystery of God is not one of them. For God can never be placed in some larger context. There are no other points or frames of reference or comparison. The infinite mystery essentially—and forever—surpasses all contexts, all reference points, and the universe itself.[16]

Poet Gustav Davidson provides a summary of the experience of the beatific vision in this life in a short poem that deftly captures the change of vision that comes with heavenly perspective:

All things are holy,
even the profane.
And whether we move in
illusion or reality,
if anything concerns us,
this already is its sanctification.
For there is nothing without its aura,
only it is for us to perceive it
and walk in the midst of it,
enchanted and haloed.[17]

THE DIVINIZING LITURGY

Since liturgy is the source and summit of the Christian life, it is also the source and summit of the process of divinization. The liturgy is the central dynamic of divinization, the beginning of the process by which humankind is transformed in Christ.

Andrew Hofer writes on this:

Divinization begins in the grace of Baptism for the individual made in the image of God and born into this world, and divinization ends in the final transformation of glory for the one destined to look upon him forever in heaven.[18]

16. Kelly, *Eschatology and Hope*, 173. For useful histories of divinization in Eastern and Western Christianity, see Collins, *Partaking in Divine Nature*; Christensen and Witting, eds., *Partakers of the Divine Nature*; Meconi and Olson, *Called to be the Children of God*; in the latter, see David W. Fagerberg, "Liturgy and Divinization," 274–83.

17. Davidson, *All Things are Holy*, 56.

18. Hofer, *Divinization*, 7.

Baptism means the reception of Christ through the Spirit; Confirmation is the deepening of initiation into the Spirit of Christ.[19] The various moments of the initiation process celebrate the different dimensions of incorporation into Christ by the power of the Spirit. One of the most impressive elements of the process of the Order of the Christian Initiation of Adults (OCIA) is the Acceptance into the Order of Catechumens. Those who are be initiated are marked by the sponsors or catechists on various parts of the body with the following words by the celebrant:

> Receive the cross on your forehead.
> It is Christ himself who now strengthens you
> with this sign of his love.
> Learn to know him and follow him.
> Receive the sign of the cross on your ears,
> that you may hear the voice of the Lord.
> Receive the sign of the cross on your eyes,
> that you may see the glory of God.
> Receive the sign of the cross on your lips,
> that you may respond to the word of God.
> Receive the sign of the cross over your heart,
> that Christ may dwell there by faith.
> Receive the sign of the cross on your shoulders,
> that you may bear the gentle yoke of Christ.
> Receive the sign of the cross on your hands,
> that Christ may be known in the work which you do.
> Receive the sign of the cross on your feet,
> that you may walk in the way of Christ.

Then the celebrant says:

> I sign you with the sign of eternal life
> in the name of the Father, and of the Son,
> and of the Holy Spirit.

He concludes with these words:

> Lord, we have signed these catechumens
> with the sign of Christ's cross.
> Protect them by its power,
> so that, faithful to the grace which has begun in them,

---

19. That is why Baptism and Confirmation properly belong together, as they do now in all Catholic initiation rites, except in the Confirmation of people, mostly teenagers, baptized in infancy, an anomaly to be corrected. Baptism and Confirmation are properly seen and practiced as two sacraments in a single rite.

they may keep your commandments
and come to the glory of rebirth in baptism.
We ask this through Christ our Lord.
R.) Amen[20]

These rites express the truth that incorporation into Christ is a trans-formation of the whole person. Divinization is not a cerebral matter, but a transformation of the body as well as the soul. In the invitation to the sacrament of Confirmation following Baptism, the following address is made to the candidates by the celebrant:

> My dear newly baptized, born again in Christ by baptism, you have become members of Christ and of his priestly people. Now you are to share in the outpouring of the Holy Spirit among us, the Spirit sent by the Lord upon his apostles at Pentecost and given by them and their successors to be baptized.

Then he says:

> The promised strength of the Holy Spirit, which you are to receive, will make you more like Christ and help you to be witnesses to his suffering, death, and resurrection. It will strengthen you to be active members of the Church and to build up the Body of Christ in faith and love.[21]

The celebrant then addresses the people:

> My dear friends, let us pray to God our Father, that he will pour out the Holy Spirit on these newly baptized to strengthen them with his gifts and anoint them to be more like Christ, the Son of God.[22]

This is followed by the laying on of hands and the words:

> N., be sealed with the Gift of the Holy Spirit.[23]

Jean Corbon sums up the divinizing character of the ritual process I have just described by attending to its life-changing effects:

> Through baptism and the seal of the gift of the Holy Spirit we have become "sharers of the divine nature" (2 Pet 1:4). In the liturgy

20. *Christian Initiation*, nos. 56, 57, 27–28
21. *Christian Initiation*, no. 233, 162.
22. *Christian Initiation*, no. 233, 162.
23. *Christian Initiation*, no. 235, 163.

of the heart, the wellspring of this divinization streams out as the Holy Spirit, and our individual persons converge in a single origin. But how is this mysterious synergy to infuse our entire nature from its smallest recesses to its most obvious behaviors? This process is the drama of divinization in which the mystery of the lived liturgy is brought to completion in each Christian.[24]

The Eucharist is similarly a sacrament of divinization, a sacrament which gives a share in Christ's divinity. The consecration of the bread and wine into the sacramental body and blood of Christ by the power of the Holy Spirit enables us to speak of the Eucharist as a sacrament of divinization. Indeed, in this sense, every sacrament, including the sacraments of vocation (Holy Orders and Matrimony) and the sacraments of healing (Penance and the Anointing of the sick) are sacraments of divinization. They all have their end in the Christian's conformity to Christ.[25]

Andrew Hofer points out about the divinizing features of the Eucharist:

> All the elements of the Eucharist divinize . . . from the opening sign of the cross, with the greeting that the Lord be with the people and the priest celebrant, to the dismissal with the blessing and sending forth into the world.[26]

He states further that the divinizing power of the Eucharist

> must not be seen as terminating with the closing of the Mass. Rather, since the Mass is the source and summit of Christian life, we see divinization extending not only toward the Mass in its intensification but also from the Mass in its diffusion through evangelization.[27]

A typical example of the theme of divinization in the Eucharist is found in one of the collects for Christmas Mass:

> O God, who wonderfully created the dignity of human nature and still more wonderfully restored it, grant we pray, that we may share in the divinity of Christ who humbled himself to share in our humanity.[28]

---

24. Corbon, *Wellspring of Worship*, 217.

25. Hofer, *Divinization*, 7–11.

26. Hofer, *Divinization*, 9.

27. Hofer, *Divinization*, 10.

28. *Roman Missal*, 164.

The same theme is found in the first antiphon of Evening Prayer of the Solemnity of Mary, Mother of God:

> O Marvelous exchange! Man's creator has become man, born of a virgin. We have been made sharers in the divinity of Christ who humbled himself to share in our humanity.[29]

Pope Benedict XVI wrote on this matter:

> Stressing the mysterious nature of this food, Augustine imagines the Lord saying to him: "I am the food of grown men; grow, and you shall feed upon me; nor shall you change me, like the food of your flesh, into yourself, but you shall be changed into me" (*Confessions* VII 10, 16). It is not the Eucharistic food that is changed into us, but rather we who are mysteriously transformed by it."[30]

At every Mass, the holy exchange of the human and the divine is expressed in the silent prayer the priest says at the washing of hands:

> By the mystery of this water and wine may we come to share in the divinity of him who humbled himself to share in our humanity.[31]

Heaven, then, gives us a clear, transformative vision in which all the glorious things we have ever seen will become fully manifest. We will see "in Christ," from *within* the Trinity. We will be endowed with insight into the vast panorama of all that God has created. We will become trinified.

GOD THE BEAUTIFUL

In the second half of this chapter, I will connect the notions of the beatific vision, the process of divinization, and the divinizing liturgy with a theology of divine beauty, the process of beautification, and the beauteous liturgy by which God's glory is manifest and believers are transformed. This second part of the chapter is intended to deepen the notion of the beatific vision by reference to a theology of beauty. This brings us into the area of philosophical and theological aesthetics.[32]

29. Antiphon, Evening Prayer I for the Solemnity of Mary, Mother of God, in *Liturgy of Hours*, 477.

30. Benedict XVI, "Sacrament of Charity" (*Sacramentum Caritatis*), 70.

31. *Roman Missal*, Nos. 24, 512; See Hofer, *Divinization*.

32. Aesthetics is by character a complex subject. Accessible works include Scruton, *Beauty*; O'Donohue, *Beauty*.

Cutting through the many complex philosophies of beauty, we may say that, in the widest sense, beauty embraces any person, place, thing, taste, sound, and the like, that are spiritually pleasing to the senses. The beautiful has something to do with pleasing order and form. For instance, there is something about a great work of art, a newborn baby, an attractive natural scene that has perfect order and form. We can, by the same token, identify things that are not beautiful because they lack pleasing order; they are *disordered* and without form. Following the concise medieval description, we can say that beauty is that which give pleasure when seen. St. Thomas has a rather detailed treatment of beauty, where he names the qualities of integrity or perfection, proportion or harmony, and brightness or clarity.

For Thomas Aquinas, beauty not only has its origins in God, but God himself is beauty:

> The beautiful—that is, God—is the ultimate source and goal of all things. For everything was made in order to reflect, in some way or other, the divine Beauty. . . . From this divine Beauty flows the being of all that exists—and thus, it is clear that all existence is derived from divine Beauty. . . . There is nothing which does not share in goodness and beauty, for according to its form each thing is both good and beautiful.[33]

Numerous examples may be provided of the truth that God is beauty and that created things have their foundation in the beauteous God. St. Augustine wrote:

> Question the beauty of the earth, of the truth that God is beauty.
> The beauty of the sea,
> the beauty of the wide air around you,
> the beauty of the sky;
> question the order of the stars,
> the sun whose brightness lights the day,
> the moon whose splendor softens the gloom of night;
> question the living creatures that move in the waters,
> that roam upon the earth,
> that fly through the air;
> the spirit that lies hidden,
> the matter that is manifest;
> the visible things that are ruled,
> the invisible that rule them;

---

33. *On the Divine Nature*, 90. For a comprehensive treatment of Aquinas' aesthetics, see Christopher Scott Sevier, *Aquinas on Beauty*.

question all these.
They will answer you:
"Behold and see, we are beautiful."
Their beauty is their confession of God.
Who made these beautiful changing things,
if not one who is beautiful and changeth not.[34]

Augustine held that God is not only the maker of the beautiful, but is himself unchanging beauty. He wrote:

Late have I loved you, beauty so old and so new; late have I loved you. And see, you were within and I was in the external world and sought you there, and in my unlovely state I plunged into those lovely created things which you made. You were with me, and I was not with you. The lovely things kept me far from you, though if they did not have their existence in you, they had no existence at all. You called and cried out loud and shattered my deafness. You were radiant and resplendent, you put to flight my blindness. You were fragrant, and I drew in my breath and now pant after you. I tasted you, and I feel but hunger and thirst for you. You have touched me, and I am set on fire to attain the peace which is yours.[35]

This brings me to the matter of aesthetics. A sub-set of the wide-ranging field of aesthetics is theological aesthetics or aesthetic theology, a topic that has been greatly neglected in Western Christianity, though not in the East. First a word about theological aesthetics: Beauty remains the Cinderella of Western theology. The *Catechism* allows it only five paragraphs explicitly (nos. 2500–2503, 2513). However, this dearth has begun to be made up for in recent decades by the appearance of works on theological aesthetics or aesthetical theology. In Catholicism the great leader here may well turn out to be the preeminent theologian of the second half of the twentieth century: Hans Urs von Balthasar.[36] The contributions in Catholicism to the theology of beauty represent a new and welcome turn in

34. St. Augustine, "Beauty of Creation," 1669.

35. St. Augustine, *Confessions*, 10, 38. For a more extensive treatment, see Carol Harrison, *Beauty and Revelation in the Thought of St. Augustine*.

36. Hans Urs von Balthasar's great work on the theology of beauty is *The Glory of the Lord*, vol. 1. Accessible introductions to Balthasar's aesthetics are found in Nichols, *Key to Balthasar*; and Riches, ed., *Analogy of Beauty*.

Western theology generally.[37] The influence of Eastern Orthodoxy is clearly evident in these developments.

Ancient and medieval philosophers and theologians clarified the nature of beauty by setting forth a scheme called the transcendentals: truth, goodness, and beauty. Theologian Brian Zahnd writes succinctly as follows:

> The ancient Greek philosophers, and later the early church fathers, spoke of three prime virtues: truth, goodness, and beauty. As prime virtues, truth, goodness, and beauty need no further justification—they are their own justification, which is a way of saying that truth, goodness, and beauty don't need to be made practical—they don't have to *do* anything to be of value. The value of a virtue is inherent; we simply choose truth, goodness, and beauty because they are true, good, and beautiful.[38]

Zahnd continues:

> Early Christian theologians located the source of these prime virtues as proceeding from God himself—truth, goodness, and beauty are virtues because God is true, good, and beautiful. Thus this trinity of virtues becomes a guide to Christian living as we seek to *believe* what is true, *be* what is good, and *behold* was is beautiful.[39]

It is this third virtue, beauty, which has been most marginalized and least valued in Western Christianity historically. Zahnd writes on this:

> Christianity has suffered a loss of beauty—a loss that needs to be recovered. With an emphasis on truth, we have tried to make Christianity persuasive (as we should). But we also need a corresponding emphasis on beauty to make Christianity attractive. Christianity should not only persuade with truth, but it should also attract with beauty. Along with Christian apologetics, we need Christian aesthetics. Christianity needs not only to be defended as true—it also needs to be presented as beautiful.[40]

Theological aesthetics holds that God is not only beautiful, but beauty itself. To say that God is beautiful and beauty itself is to say that all beauty

---

37. On theologies of beauty, see Harries, *Art and the Beauty of God*; Sherry, *Spirit and Beauty*; Thiessen, ed., *Theological Aesthetics*; Forte, *The Portal of Beauty*; Nichols, *Redeeming Beauty*.

38. Zahnd, *Beauty Will Save*, 59.

39. Zahnd, *Beauty Will Save*, 59–60.

40. Zahnd, *Beauty will Save*, 60.

may be traced to and has its foundations in God. God is the origin and summit of beauty. All beauty begins in God and finds its apex in him. The beatific vision is a vision of the beautiful God.

Jacques Maritain, the preeminent modern philosopher of art and the aesthetic, in reflecting on the relationship between beauty and God, wrote: "God is beautiful. He is the most beautiful of all beings. . . . His Beauty is without change or vicissitude, without increase or diminution. He is beautiful by Himself and in Himself, beautiful absolutely."[41]

The relationship between God and beauty has been further set forth by Orthodox theologians Merisor Dominte and Stelian Onica. The reader will note the Eastern Christian ethos in this quotation:

> The Holy Fathers [of the early Church] reiterated the biblical concept of the greatness and beauty of God revealed in the beauty of the created world to which they added the belief that God, the source of this beauty, is Himself pure, perfect beauty, Beauty itself, where we can arrive through faith, contemplation and continuous spiritual exercise. Since God is equivalent with beauty, He contains in Himself the beauty of the world, of everything that exists, including man and His other creations. Therefore, the Holy Fathers name Him all-beautiful. All the beauty in the world has its origin in God the Beautiful, to which it aspires through spiritual exercise. God the Beautiful is the creator of all things beautiful in the world, whatever they may be.[42]

John Navone states: "The life story of Jesus Christ is the beautiful icon disclosing God, Beauty Itself, to the world (John 12:45; 14:9). The risen Christ is the paradigmatic image for Christian faith of divine and human beauty."[43]

Navone continues: "As the Son and Word of Beauty Itself incarnate, Jesus Christ makes God beautifully visible. He manifests the splendor of Supreme Beauty, the glory of the Father, which transfigures humankind into beautiful, living icons through the gift of the Spirit."[44] This beauty is fully manifest, however, after the resurrection. (In contrast to theologians like Balthasar, I hold that the Cross is beautiful only in retrospect, after the resurrection. Here I have in mind the first reading of the Good Friday

---

41. Maritain, *Art and Scholasticism*, 44–45.

42. Dominte and Onica, *Concept of Beauty*, 11.

43. Navone, *Theology of Beauty*, 17. See also Navone, *Enjoying God's Beauty*.

44. Navone, *Theology of Beauty*, 17.

liturgy from Isaiah 53:2: "He had no majestic bearing to catch our eye, no beauty to draw us to him.")

As the authors cited above attest, God is the beginning and end of beauty. He is beauty itself, the heart of the process by which men and women are made beautiful and ennobled by the beatific vision.

THE PROCESS OF BEAUTIFICATION

The beauty we experience on earth is a prefigurement of the beauty we will experience in heaven. By the same token, the process of beautification, of making beautiful, as experienced in our earthly life will only be complete in heavenly existence. We look at earthly beautification with an eye always to what it will be like in heaven. As divinization is the process of being conformed to Christ, so beautification corresponds to the process of entering into the life of the beautiful God.

How we enter into the life of God is dealt with in Barron's book *And Now I See*, which is to a considerable extent about Christian aesthetics in that it devises a theology of transformation based on a number of important authors, including Dante, William Faulkner, and Flannery O'Connor. These authors show how narrowness of vision and of soul gives rise to a restricted perspective on the world. The tragedy of being unable to *see* leads to exclusiveness, self-righteousness, and egotism. Barron distils a theology of transformation that may be used to articulate an understanding of the beautification process in Christian life. What Barron says about our participation in the incarnation applies to our engagement with the beautiful. The beautiful God, he says, is not someone to be "admired from the outside, but rather an energy in which to participate."[45] In his earthly ministry, "Jesus urges his listeners to change their way of knowing, their way of perceiving and grasping reality, their perspective, their mode of *seeing*."[46]

Barron writes further, "When we meditate on an icon of the Virgin [Mary] . . . we allow ourselves to be drawn into the 'field of force' of that picture, allowing the icon to 'work on us' through a type of spiritual osmosis."[47] The iconic allows "the elevation of human beings toward their final end, the contemplation of God."[48] The whole range of Christian ideas, symbols, and

45. Barron, *Now I See*, 3.
46. Barron, *Now I See*, 4.
47. Barron, *Now I See*, 9.
48. Barron, *Now I See*, 12.

narratives bring about a soulful contemplation. To see Jesus, Barron says, is "to glimpse, in hope, what is beautiful in us and to taste, in ecstasy, the God who summons us to union."[49] Reflecting Balthasar, Barron writes that beauty is "a force that prompts a sort of alchemy in the soul, lifting it up, coalescing its powers, and finally focusing on the divine source of beauty."[50]

The beautiful is not a self-contained, introverted reality, but it invites a response; it is provocative and disturbing, "it must be *seen* and taken in, dealt with."[51] When confronted by the beautiful, "one realizes that the hidden ground of all is a challenging, provocative, and inviting Beauty."[52]

Barron continues:

> An encounter with the deeply beautiful—what is not merely entertaining or diverting—is a meeting that concerns and shakes and changes the subject. People sometimes speak of the aesthetic experience as "enrapturing" or "transporting," signaling that one is taken away (rapt), stolen, translated into a different realm of existence. The beautiful cannot leave us indifferent, unaffected, but rather it works its way into our bones, into the sinews of our life, indelibly making us and setting us off.[53]

The human being is given a "new identity" and a new "practical purpose" through encounter with the beautiful.[54] Thus the beautiful "seizes a person, orients her radically toward the transcendent source of beauty and then sends her outward as a missionary. There is an expansive, propulsive, centrifugal energy to the beautiful, causing an enlargement, a broadening of the powers of the soul."[55]

This process of human transformation by *seeing* is set forth by English writer John Berger: "It is seeing which establishes our place in the surrounding world; we explain that world with words, but words can never undo the fact that we are surrounded by [the world]."[56]

Berger explains: "We are always looking at the relation between things and ourselves. Our vision is constantly active, continually moving,

---

49. Barron, *Now I See*, 15.

50. Barron, *Now I See*, 70.

51. Barron, *Now I See*, 71.

52. Barron, *Now I See*, 71.

53. Barron, *Now I See*, 72.

54. Barron, *Now I See*, 73.

55. Barron, *Now I See*, 74.

56. Berger, *Ways of Seeing*, 7.

continually holding things in a circle around itself, constituting what is present to us as we are."[57]

According to Mihalyi Csiksentmihalyi, the beautiful artwork brings about "transcendence" or "loss of ego." "Attention is so completely focused, so completely enmeshed in the interaction with the artwork, that the viewer gives up, at least momentarily, his most human attribute: self-consciousness."[58]

Just as the beatific vision brings about a profound beautification of the believer, so the God who is beauty transforms the very being of the Christian. The beautification of the human person allows him or herself to encounter, if never completely, God the most beautiful. By the same token, every earthly beauty prefigures the beauties of heaven. Together, the beatific vision and the contemplation of divine beauty set before us, around us, and in us infinite and eternal beauty. In heaven we shall have an eternal vision of a beautiful God, a vision which transforms all things.

There is a memorable passage in C. S. Lewis that is relevant here. For Lewis, the human person desires not only to encounter beauty but to enter into it:

> We do not want merely to *see* beauty. . . . We want something else which can hardly be put into words—to be *united* with the beauty we see, to pass into it, to receive it into ourselves, to bathe in it, to become part of it.[59]

Lewis continues:

> At present we are on the outside of the world, the wrong side of the door. We discern the freshness and purity of morning, but they do not make us fresh and pure. We cannot mingle with the splendours we see. But all the leaves of the New Testament are rustling with the rumour that it will not always be so. Someday, God willing, we shall get *in*.[60]

Beauty grasps us at the most profound level of our being. In turn we seek to grasp *it*. In this is the beautification of the seeker, and, by extension, the beatification of the one who encounters the beatific vision.

---

57. Berger, *Ways of Seeing*, 9.
58. Csikszentmihalyi and Robinson, *Art of Seeing*, 122.
59. Lewis, *Weight of Glory*, 42.
60. Lewis, *Weight of Glory*, 43.

A BEAUTEOUS LITURGY

I turn now to beauty in the liturgy which transforms by encounter with the beatific vision. In looking at the matter of the beauty of the liturgy, we immediately come up against the fact that there is virtually little writing on the topic. Certainly, there is more and more writing on beauty as a theological topic, especially from the second part of the twentieth century. However, I notice something quite extraordinary in all the new writing on beauty: how little the liturgy of the church is referred to and how feebly liturgical considerations enter into the fabric of new theologies of the aesthetic. An issue of *Liturgy Digest* in 1996, edited by liturgical theologian Nathan Mitchell, devoted to theological aesthetics, points out that the use of aesthetic language about Christian worship "is rarely the object of critical reflection."[61] Indeed, "treatments of the aesthetic dimensions of the liturgy are still too few to warrant the naming of a sub-discipline as 'Liturgical Aesthetics.'"[62]

That the Churches have not always been theoretically and practically successful in the correlation of liturgy and beauty is signified by the oft-quoted report given to Vladimir, Prince of Kiev (958–1015), by emissaries he sent in search of the most beautiful and impressive liturgy in the known world. They found the liturgy in Constantinople, not that of the West, the most satisfactory. He reported:

> We knew not whether we were in heaven or on earth, for surely there is no such splendor or beauty anywhere on earth. We cannot describe it to you: only this we know, that God dwells there among men, and that their services surpass the worship of all other places. For we cannot forget that beauty.[63]

Thus it is not surprising that those concerned about liturgy and beauty today look to the East, where eschatological beauty always has had high profile. This is symbolized by the new interest in the West in Eastern iconography, which serves to unite the human and divine, earth and heaven, in a quasi-sacramental fashion.[64]

I am not proposing to outline a full liturgical aesthetics here, but rather to suggest the importance of the ethos of beauty that should suffuse the liturgy. Going back to the earlier part of this chapter, I suggested that

61. Mitchell, "Toward a Liturgical Aesthetic," 4.

62. Mitchell, "Toward a Liturgical Aesthetic," 72.

63. Quoted in Ware, *Orthodox Church*, 269.

64. Visal, *Icons*.

the beauty of the liturgy is founded in the beauty of the triune God revealed in Christ.

St. Augustine states: "For in that Trinity is the supreme source of all things, and the most perfect beauty and the most blessed delight."[65] For theologian Douglas F. Kelly, the perfect relations between the trinitarian persons are the source of beauty: "This beauty of loving and giving, receiving and sharing the gift within the three persons of Holy Trinity lies behind God's original giving of himself to reveal himself to his image-bearers" (Gn 1:27, 28).[66]

Jesus "coming down to us in the flesh is an aspect of the internal beauty of God."[67] Kelly writes: "The God whose own inner-trinitarian relations are beautiful has created beauty outside himself, and such creative beauty says something significant about who God is in his own Being."[68] The ultimate revelation of the triune beauty has taken place in Christ, the image of the beautiful Trinity. In Christ is the perfection, beauty, and splendor of God.[69]

How is divine beauty made present in the world? Through the beautiful Jesus Christ. But how is Christ mediated in the world? Primarily in the Church, the sacraments, and in the quasi-sacramental blessings of persons, places, and things (the sacramentals). He is present also in creation, in "natural" sacraments.

Two books published in 1963, in the middle of the Second Vatican Council, help us understand how beauty is mediated. The books are Karl Rahner, *The Church and the Sacraments*, and Edward Schillebeeckx, *Christ the Sacrament of the Encounter with God*.[70] While there are differences in the approach of each theologian, there is a remarkable similarity.

For Rahner, the Church is the "fundamental sacrament." Thus, we do not begin sacramental theology by examining the rituals of the Church, but by starting with the Church, which is the "continuance, the perpetual presence of the task and function of Christ in the economy of redemption, his contemporaneous presence in history, his life, the Church in the full and proper sense."[71] The seven sacraments are, in turn, the self-actualization of

65. Augustine, *On the Trinity*, 16.

66. Kelly, *Systematic Theology*. 16.

67. Kelly, *Systematic Theology*, 17.

68. Kelly, *Systematic Theology*, 21.

69. Kelly, *Systematic Theology*, 18.

70. Rahner, *Church and Sacraments*; Schillebeeckx, *Christ the Sacrament*.

71. Rahner, *Church and Sacraments*, 13.

the Church. The sacraments are, therefore, the saving acts of Christ. They are primarily personal, not quasi-physical, means of grace, as neo-scholastic theology held. Applying this to beauty (which Rahner does not do), the beautiful Christ is made present in the beautiful (if imperfect) Church; the Church is made present in the beautiful (if imperfect) sacraments; the sacraments are made present in the rites called sacramentals.

Schillebeeckx follows generally the same line of thought, except that he does not begin with the Church, but with Christ, the "primordial sacrament," the means by which we encounter God, the ongoing sanctifying presence of Christ in the world.[72] He is the divine one who is himself "sacramental," that is, the primordial presence of God in the human world.[73]

Schillebeeckx sees the Church as the means by which Christ is present and active in the world. Schillebeeckx writes, "The earthly Church is the visible realization of . . . the saving reality in history. The Church is the visible communion of grace."[74]

Like Rahner, Schillebeeckx views the seven sacraments as follows:

> Through the sacraments we are placed in living contact with the mystery of Christ the High Priest's saving worship. In them we encounter Christ in his mystery of Passover and Pentecost. The sacraments *are* this saving mystery in earthy guise.[75]

Applying this again to beauty, it may be said that through the Church and the sacraments, we encounter Christ the beautiful and the beautiful Trinity. This encounter is eschatological in that it draws us up into the heavenly realm. The sacraments bring heavenly beauty to earth and the beautiful sacraments raise us up to heaven and give us a foretaste of it. The Christian is called to enter into the beautiful sacraments by active participation, by an interiorization of divine beauty, thus a foretaste of heaven.

On a more concrete level, we may say that authentic liturgy is solemn and glorious, profound and ecstatic, serene and exuberant, weighty and festive, artful, graceful, elegant, contemplative, majestic, delightful, awesome, glorious. The liturgy properly abandons the strictures of functionalism and practicality, features of much modern liturgical theology and practice. The

---

72. Schillebeeckx, *Christ the Sacrament*, 7.
73. Schillebeeckx, *Christ the Sacrament*, 15.
74. Schillebeeckx, *Christ the Sacrament*, 47.
75. Schillebeeckx, *Christ the Sacrament*, 45.

liturgy of heaven needs its earthly counterpart, and the earthly must take on the superabundance of the worship of the heavenly City.

CONCLUSION

At the beginning of this chapter, I attended to Robert Barron's thesis that *seeing* is the fundamental and most comprehensive feature of the beatific vision and of human contemplation of divine beauty. These are two aspects of the same activity, two languages about a single aspect of Christian faith.

Seeing is the most basic feature of human existence. Without seeing, we are fundamentally hampered. To see heaven even partially in this life is to see as through a glass darkly. The beatific vision begins in earthly existence. To grow in sanctity is to grow in encounter with the beatific vision.

Anything that is authentically beautiful is a kind of sacrament of the world to come. In heaven all partial earthly beauty flowers and flourishes. We shall see everything in its fullness. In heaven we shall not only see God, but grow eternally together in knowledge of the inexhaustible mystery of God. We shall see God not as an object, but we shall see *in* God, with God-sight. Therefore, we shall see everything as God sees it. Everything will be revealed in the fullness of beauty, and the beautified in heaven will become makers of beauty. Eternity will be an endless celebration of all that is wondrous and beautiful; it will be an unending "feast for the eyes."

Chapter Three

MODEL THREE:
PARTICIPATING IN THE TRINITY

I would believe only in a God that knows how to dance.
—Friedrich Nietzsche[1]

FOR MANY CHRISTIANS, THE doctrine of the Trinity is the most obscure and least interesting feature of Christian faith. The renowned theologian Karl Rahner wrote in his book *The Trinity* that if the trinitarian doctrine were abolished, it would make little difference to the majority of Christians, and the life of faith would continue as usual. It would seem, he wrote, that most Christians are in effect monotheists or unitarians; that is, they hold a belief in the oneness of God, but much less in divine triunity.[2]

Already in the late eighteenth century, the German philosopher Immanuel Kant could state:

> The doctrine of the Trinity, taken literally, has no practical relevance at all, even if we think we understand it; it is even more clearly irrelevant, if we realize that it transcends all our concepts. Whether we are to worship three or ten persons in the Deity makes no difference.[3]

The purpose of the first section of this chapter is to explore the manner in which the life of believers in heaven will be a joyful participation in the

---

1. Nietzsche, *Zarathustra*, 69.

2. Rahner, *Trinity*, ix.

3. Kant, *Religion*, 264.

life of the Trinity.[4] While there are many theologies of the Trinity, notably the Western paradigm that begins with the divine substance and the oneness of God, and the Eastern paradigm that begins with the person of the Father. In this chapter, I choose the paradigm which begins with the trinitarian God, the perichoretic paradigm.[5]

In what follows, I will explore the character of the triune God along perichoretic lines. I will examine the nature of dance as a metaphor for trinitarian relations. Next I will look at the way in which believers come to participate in the triune God in heaven, and even now in present life. The way in which there are vestiges of the Trinity (*vestigiae trinitatis*) in the various aspects of human experience will engage my attention. Finally, I will look at what it means to give glory to the trinitarian God.

THE PERICHORETIC TRINITY

A perichoretic trinitarian paradigm begins with the triunity of God, the three person of the Trinity rather than the oneness of God (though, of course to be theologically correct we must also affirm the oneness of God). This paradigm envisions the Trinity as dynamic, mobile, and inclusive. In the eighth century, John Damascene used the term *perichōrēsis* to underscore the dynamic and vital character of the trinitarian community of the three divine persons. The perichoretic Trinity is relational, vital, dynamic: the three persons exist interdependently.[6]

In a historical review I have gleaned the following terms characterizing *perichōrēsis:* inhabiting, enveloping, self-giving, intertwining, permeating, interacting, co-inhering, cooperating, inter-weaving, indwelling. No

---

4. For those who wish to explore trinitarian history and theology more extensively, I recommend the following: Fortman, *The Triune God*; Kasper, *The God of Jesus Christ*; O' Collins, *The Tripersonal God*; Hill, *The Three-Personed God*. Invaluable resources include *The Oxford Handbook of the Trinity*, eds. Emery and Levering; *The Cambridge Companion to the Trinity*, ed., Peter Phan. More accessible works include: La Due, *The Trinity Guide to the Trinity*; Downey, *Altogether Gift*; Lorensen, *The College Students' Introduction to the Trinity*.

5. By "paradigm" I mean simply a way of seeing, viewing, or understanding. I would use the term "model" but that is already taken in the structure of this book, and I want to avoid a muddle in terminology.

6. LaCugna, *God for Us*, 270–78. For a general review of the patristic notions of *perichōrēsis*, see Twombley, *Perichōrēsis and Personhood*; Gifford, Jr., *Perichōrētic Salvation*, esp. 33–77. In chapters three and four of his book, Gifford provides a good summary of the early history of *perichōrēsis*.

person of the Trinity exists alone; rather each person exists in relation to the others. Each person is drawn irresistibly to the other and pours himself into the others. Yet, there is no blurring of the individuality of each trinitarian person.[7]

Catherine Mowry LaCugna stresses the truth that immobile, physical objects do not do justice to the threeness-in-community of God, so she looks to the analogy of the dance as a metaphor, a metaphor that is ancient and venerable. The term *perichōrēsis* was first used by Gregory of Nazianzen in christological context to underscore the mutual interdependence of the two natures of Christ, the divine and the human. The term was also closely related to the word *circumincessio*, which means "to move around."

Various analogies have been used to depict *perichōrēsis*. According to LaCugna, these include the analogy of household lamps; in one household and wholly permeating each other, the lamps are "unified in one undifferentiated light."[8] There is also the example of perfumes, which are sprayed into the air; one cannot say where one scent begins and the other ends. There is the analogy of the three dimensions of a physical object: length, width, and depth or height.[9]

LaCugna summarizes the dynamics of *perichōrēsis* when she writes that the metaphor of the dance is highly effective.

> Choreography suggests the partnership of movement, symmetrical but not redundant, as each dancer expresses and at the same time fulfills him/herself towards the other. In interaction and inter-course the dancers (and the observers) experience one fluid motion of encircling, encompassing, permeating, enveloping, outstretching. There are neither leaders nor followers in the divine dance, only an eternal movement of reciprocal giving and receiving, giving again and receiving again. To shift metaphors for a moment, God is eternally begetting and being begotten, spirating and being spirated. The divine dance is fully personal and interpersonal, expressing the essence and unity of God. The image of the dance forbids us to think of God as solitary. The idea of trinitarian *perichōrēsis* provides a marvelous point of entry into contemplating what it means to say that God is alive from all eternity as love.[10]

7. LaCugna, *God for Us*, 270–71.
8. LaCugna, *God for Us*, 271.
9. LaCugna, *God for Us*, 273.
10. LaCugna, *God for Us*, 272.

According to Roderick Heupp, "If today's devotees of trinitarian theology learn only one technical term, *perichōrēsis* should be it."[11]

A DANCING GOD

The notion of a dancing trinitarian God may seem somewhat frivolous and
superficial, but I will explore in greater detail how the concept serves to
revitalize trinitarian theology from excessive abstraction and affective dry-
ness, thus correcting the perceptions of Kant and Rahner set forth at the
beginning of this chapter.[12] Here I will explore the treatment of the trinitarian dance by C. Baxter Kruger, Richard Rohr (with Michael Morrell), and
Hugo Rahner, SJ.

Kruger, an American Reformed theologian, has written a most engaging book entitled *The Great Dance: The Christian Vision Revisited,* in
which he deals with Trinity, creation, salvation, and eschatology using the
metaphor of dance. He describes the great dance of the Trinity as follows:

> The great dance is all about the abounding life—the fellowship and
> togetherness, the love and passion and joy—shared by the Father,
> Son and Spirit. The incarnation is the staggering act of this God
> reaching out to share the great dance with us. Our humanity is
> the theatre in and through which the great dance is played out in
> our lives, and human history is the harrowing experience through
> which we are educated as to the truth of our identity.[13]

Kruger wishes to get away from a view of God as abstract, distant,
austere, and cold. The Trinity, he says, is a "circle of shared life, and the life
shared is full, abounding, and rich and beautiful, not lonely and sad and
boring."[14] The great dance is about the magnificent life shared by the Father,
Son, and Spirit—and into whose community we are called—a call that will
be completed by our full trinitarian participation in heaven.

This reality is described by Kruger in the following way: First, there
is the triune God and the great dance shared by Father, Son, and Spirit;
second, there is the interconnection as the Trinity reaches down to us, thus

11. Heupp, *Trinitarian Theology,* 71–72. The term *perichōrēsis* is notably used today
in the writings of Volf, Torrance, Gunton, Boff, and Möltmann.

12. The unfolding of Christ's life, death, and resurrection as dance is exemplified in
Sydney Carter's hymn, *Lord of the Dance.* Available in many hymnals.

13. Kruger, *Great Dance,* 21.

14. Kruger, *Great Dance,* 22.

extending the circle, their great dance to humankind by the dance of the Spirit.[15]

The Trinity is inadequately understood if it is described apart from humanity. While the Trinity does not *need* humankind, the dance of the triune God elaborates trinitarian life and fulfills humanity. We can say that the beauty and glory of the great triune dance are played out in us, even now, and will be fully played out in the Kingdom of heaven.

Kruger rejects any notion that God may be known in any way except as Trinity. God never became triune; he was triune before time began. Furthermore, God was oriented to creation and redemption from the beginning. Kruger sets out the relationship of creation and redemption as a joyful sequence of events in history:

> First, there is the Trinity and the Triune life, the fellowship and joy and glory of the Father, Son and Spirit, the great dance. Second, this God speaks the universe, the earth and humanity, and all things into existence. And the gracious and astonishing purpose of this creative activity is to extend the dance to us. The Father, Son and Spirit created us so that we could participate in their life together, so that we could share in their knowledge and laughter and fellowship, in their insights and creativity and music, in their joy and intimacy and goodness, so that all of it could be played out in us and in our ordinary lives.[16]

Incarnation and redemption may be described in terms of the joyful divine *perichōrēsis*. In the incarnation, the beloved Son stepped out of eternity into history, uniting humanity and divinity. In his incarnate life, death, and resurrection he forged a union between the triune God and the human race: "He opened the great dance and drew us into it."[17]

Kruger spends much of his book on the incarnation, by which, through Christ's life, death and resurrection, we are made links in the great dance of life.[18] In his incarnation, death, and resurrection, Christ forges a connection between the Trinity and the human race. He opens the great dance and draws us within it. In summary, Kruger writes:

15. Kruger, *Great Dance*, 23.

16. Kruger, *Great Dance*, 26.

17. Kruger, *Great Dance*, 27.

18. Here Kruger is influenced by St. Athanasius and by his teacher and mentor, the distinguished Scottish theologian James B. Torrance.

The truth is, this world belongs to the Holy Trinity and is permeated by the great dance of life shared by the Father, Son and Spirit. You and your life have been overtaken by the abounding philanthropy of the Triune God. You have been included in the great dance. That is your identity, who you are and what your life is all about. That is what your motherhood and fatherhood are all about. That is what your gardening and your cookouts and your carpentry and work and love and friendships are all about. They are the ways the great dance of the Trinity is being played out in you.[19]

As I have shown, Kruger provides an attractive and moving account of human participation in the triune God, even now, but ultimately in the Kingdom to come. The divine dance in the meantime meets on earth all kinds of obstacles and is rendered incomplete. However, in the Kingdom of God all will be resolved: all joy, beauty, communion, and creativity will be achieved in a perfect dance, and the fullness of the triune God will be encountered.

The second author I want to look at on the matter of how we participate in the Trinity now and in eternity is Richard Rohr, who, with Mike Morrell, wrote *The Divine Dance: The Trinity and Your Transformation*.[20] As the title of the book suggests, there is much in common with Kruger's view. Both view the Trinity in dynamic, vital, circling terms and the ethos of Rohr's view of the Trinity is joyful, beautiful, uplifting.

Rohr uses the image of "circling around" as a primary metaphor for the Trinity: "Whatever is going on in God is a *flow*, a *radical relatedness*, a *perfect communion between the three*—a circle dance of love."[21] He quotes from Br. Elias Marechal, who sets forth a conception of the "circling around" of the Trinity. Br. Elias writes:

The ancient Greek Fathers depict the Trinity as a Round Dance: an event that has continued for six thousand years, and six times six thousand, and beyond the time when humans *first* knew time. An infinite current of love streams without ceasing, *to and fro, to and fro, to and fro*: gliding from the Father to the Son, and back to the Father, in one timeless happening. This circular current of Trinitarian love continues night and day. . . . The orderly and rhythmic

19. Kruger, *Great Dance*, 33.

20. Rohr and Morrell, *Divine Dance*.

21. Rohr and Morrell, *Divine Dance*, 27.

process of subatomic particles spinning round and round at immense speed echoes its dynamism.[22]

Rohr emphasizes the truth that knowledge of the Trinity is "participatory knowledge"—if we know God, we know him from within.[23] We do not merely *watch* the Trinity, we *dance* the Trinity.[24]

Rohr uses the famous icon of Andrei Rublev written in the fifteenth century called "The Trinity" as an image of the way we are called into the communion of the Trinity. Father (signified by gold), Son (signified by blue), and Spirit (signified by green), surround the table/altar on three sides. But on the front there is the mysterious little rectangular opening. Rohr and others think there was a mirror there once, so that the viewer saw him or herself in the mirror, and thus one's own face became the fourth face in the icon. Whatever the case, the opening seems to invite the viewer into communion with the Trinity, so that the fourth face in the icon is ours. Rohr comments: "It's stunning when you think about it—there was room at this table for a fourth."[25] Rohr states that this three-fullness does not like to eat alone. This invitation to share at the divine table is probably the first biblical hint of what we would eventually call "salvation."[26]

In all this we are required to provide some biblical protocol for the metaphor of dance. Does the "dance" appear in the scriptures? Even a cursory reading shows it does. In the Old Testament, on many occasions, the people dance for joy. The most-often quoted is the dance of David before the Ark. In fact, before creation, dance was the expression of God's self-interaction.[27] A reading of the New Testament yields up numerous passages in which the trinitarian persons relate to each other perichoretically. They may be systematized as follows:

---

22. Marechal, *Innocent God*, 7.

23. Rohr and Morrell, *Divine Dance*, 49.

24. Rohr and Morrell, *Divine Dance*, 64.

25. Rohr and Morrell, *Divine Dance*, 31.

26. Rohr and Morrell, *Divine Dance*, 31. Other books on the Trinity in the perichoretic tone and style are Reeves, *Delighting in the Trinity*; and Foster, *Trinity: Song and Dance*.

27. Hugo Rahner, *Man at Play*, 15–21. Hugo Rahner was the older, lesser-known brother of Karl Rahner, and was himself a distinguished patristic scholar. He was once asked what he planned to do in retirement. He responded that he would try to translate Karl's works into German! (Karl wrote in German.)

The Father is in the Son:

- If I do not perform my Father's works, do not believe me; but if I perform them, even if you do not believe me, believe the works, so that you may realize [and understand] that the Father is in me, and I am in the Father. (John 10: 37–38)

- Do you not believe that I am in the Father and the Father is in me? The words that I speak to you I do not speak on my own. The Father who dwells in me is doing his works. Believe me that I am in the Father and the Father is in me, or else, believe because of the works themselves. (John 14: 10–11)

The Son is in the Father:

On that day you will realize that I am in my Father and you are in me and I in you. (John 14: 20)

The Spirit is in the Son:

- Filled with the Holy Spirit, Jesus returned from the Jordan and was led by the Spirit into the desert. (Luke 4: 1)

- You know the word [that] he sent to the Israelites as he proclaimed peace through Jesus Christ, who is Lord of all, what has happened all over Judea, beginning in Galilee after the baptism that John preached, how God anointed Jesus of Nazareth with the holy Spirit and power. (Act 10:36–38)

The Spirit is in the Father:

- This God has revealed himself to us through the Spirit. For the Spirit scrutinizes everything, even the depths of God. Among human beings, who knows what pertains to a person except the spirit of the person that is within? Similarly, no one knows what pertains to God except the Spirit of God. (1 Cor 2:10–11)

The Father is in the Spirit:

- Through him the whole structure is held together and grows into a temple sacred in the Lord; in him you also are being built together into a dwelling place of God in the Spirit. (Eph 2:21–22)
- One body and one Spirit, as you were also called to the one hope of your call; one Lord, one faith, one baptism; one God and Father of all, who is over all and through all and in all. (Eph 4:4–6)

The Son is in the Spirit:

- And I will ask the Father, and he will give you another Advocate to be with you always, the Spirit of truth, which the world cannot accept, because it neither sees nor knows it. But you know it, because it remains with you, and will be in you. I will not leave you orphans; I will come to you. (John 14:16–18)
- For this reason I kneel before the Father, from whom every family in heaven and on earth is named, that he may grant you in accord to the riches of his glory to be strengthened with power through his Spirit in the inner self, that Christ may dwell in your hearts through faith. (Eph 3:14–17)

TRINITY AND COMMUNITY

I turn now to another theme in trinitarian theology, which has to do with the way the Trinity is reflected variously in the human person, in society, and even in creation—prefigurements of what will come to fulfillment in heaven.

Again I observe that the Trinity is a Trinity-in-communion. The three persons of the Trinity exist as a communion of persons—a model of human communion. God is not self-enclosed, but is intrinsically open so that the human community may be drawn into the life of the triune God. The Croatian Protestant theologian Miroslav Volf put this point as follows:

> Because the Christian God is not a lonely God, but rather a communion of three persons, faith leads human beings into the divine communion. One cannot, however, have a self-enclosed communion with the triune God—a "foursome," as it were—for the Christian God is not a private deity. Communion with this God

is at once also communion with those others who have entrusted themselves in faith to the same God. Hence one and the same act of faith places a person into a new relationship both with God and with all others who stand in communion with God.[28]

That the persons of the triune God exist in relationship also tells us something about the nature of the human person. We are used to the idea that humans are made in the image of God (*imago dei*). We are less familiar with the notion that we are made in the image of the Trinity (*imago trinitatis*). The human person is not independent, self-enclosed, complete in him or herself—which is the modern view of the human person.

Catherine LaCugna elaborates this matter as follows:

> By definition a person is ecstatic, toward-another; we are persons by virtue of relationships to another. Persons know and are known, love and are loved, and express themselves in freedom. To think of a person without thinking of that person in relationship to another person defeats what it means to be a person.[29]

LaCugna's view of the human person has its foundation in the doctrine of the Trinity. Her trinitarian conception of personhood contradicts the modern Enlightenment view of persons as autonomous, all-sufficient, self-enclosed. She proposes a view of personhood that reflects the Holy Trinity. The human person exists in openness to Christ—and, therefore, to the Trinity. Just as God is intrinsically communitarian, so human beings are trinitarian.[30]

PARTICIPATING IN THE TRINITY

One of the positive developments in trinitarian theology in recent decades is the proposition that human society is an image of the Trinity. I have already explored the notion of the human person as an image of the Trinity. Building on that, I look now at how the trinitarian God illuminates the

---

28. Volf, *Likeness*, 173.

29. LaCugna, "Practical Trinity," 173. Significantly, LaCugna avoids the terms "individual" in favor of the word "person" to underscore the fact that "person" suggests openness, relationality while "individual" does not. This is also a feature of the writings of Pope John Paul II.

30. LaCugna draws on the philosophical concept of person in John Macmurray, *The Self as Agent*, and Macmurray, *Persons in Relation*.

proper shape of society. Theologian Timothy Ware summarizes the essential point here:

> Each social grouping—family, parish, diocese, Church council, school, office, factory, nation—has as its vocation to be transformed by grace into a living icon of [the holy Trinity], . . . to effect a reconciling harmony between diversity and unity, human freedom and mutual solidarity, after the pattern of the Trinity. Our belief in a trinitarian God, in a God of social inter-relationship and shared love, commits us to opposing all forms of exploitation, injustice and discrimination.[31]

Some theologians, then, see traces of the Trinity (*imago trinitatis*) located in human community, and in social institutions generally.[32]

The trinitarian society of heaven is a paradigm for human society; correlatively, human society when organized along trinitarian lines is a prefigurement of heavenly society. Leonardo Boff writes:

> The communion that is to be fashioned between human beings is one that embraces their whole being, right down to the roots of their love. It must also manifest itself in every aspect of life, including economic, social, and political life. Produced by the Father, the Son, and the Holy Spirit, it is the communication of their own Trinitarian communion.[33]

Theologian Frederick Christian Bauerschmidt deals with the way in which trinitarian faith is a resource for thinking about political life. Bauerschmidt shows—contra Kant—that the Trinity is a "practical" resource for human political life. The Trinity as the communion of persons shows how unity in diversity can be achieved; how political life is about communion; and how the economic, educational, and social orders can be coordinated for the common good. As there is a just balance among the persons of the

---

31. Ware, "Human Person," 17–18.

32. Institutions that are oppressive and dehumanizing do not, of course, serve adequately as images of the Trinity. Feminist and liberation theologians point out that a radically hierarchical view of the Trinity can reflect societies that offend against human flourishing. They emphasize for that reason the equality of the three persons of the Trinity, avoiding seeing the Father as the foundation of the Trinity, a position that a hierarchical trinitarian paradigm would regard as inadequate.

33. Boff, *Holy Trinity*, 42.

Trinity, so society can be balanced in just social structures.[34] Boff himself speaks of the world as a sacrament of the Trinity:

> All creation is the work of the blessed Trinity. The Persons act on the basis of their own proper qualities so that signs of the triune God can be seen everywhere. God in God's own mystery can never be adequately represented. That is why the Fourth Lateran Council (1215) taught that the unlikeness between Creator and creature is greater than the likeness. But that does not mean that we do not have the traces of the divine stamped on all creation.[35]

Peter J. Leithart describes how traces of the Trinity appear in myriad ways in everyday life, from our relations with others, to sexuality, language, music, ethics, and logic. The Trinity may be regarded as a kind of "theory of everything." Marriage, for instance, is a reflection of the Trinity in that man and woman, according to Pauline theology, symbolize the love of Father and Son. The fruit of marital love is children, so that children may be seen to symbolize the Holy Spirit. Thus, father, mother and children may be regarded as an image of the triune God. Indeed, we might say that every authentic human relationship, including friendship, images the Trinity. The participants in the relationship signify the Father-Son/Son-Father, and the fruit of that love is the good works inspired by the Holy Spirit. The nature of all human relationships is to have a self-giving, a gift-giving character.

Leonardo Boff points out that the renowned psychologist Carl Jung studied the symbolism of the number three. The number is an archetype found in all cultures. "The number three symbolized the human demand for integration, association, and totality."[36] In preaching, "analogies and figures have been borrowed from material life to express the Trinity of persons, and their unity and communion."[37] Some speak of the sun, its rays, and its heat. Others speak of fire that radiates light and produces heat. Still others point to three lit candles that meet in a simple flame. Catechists have often explained the Trinity by showing children the shamrock of St. Patrick, which is a leaf made up of three small leaflets.[38] For Boff, "creation exists in order to welcome the Trinity into itself. . . . The Trinity in creation seeks

---

34. Bauerschmidt, "Trinity, Politics," 531–43.
35. Boff, *Holy Trinity*, 44.
36. Boff, *Holy Trinity*, 45
37. Boff, *Holy Trinity*, 45.
38. Boff, *Holy Trinity*, 45.

to bring creation into the Trinity."[39] He continues: "The universe, after the millions and millions of years of its rise, after the unfolding of its latent potentialities, at last, overt, after the cosmic crisis by which it has been purified of all evil, will finally attain the reign of the Trinity."[40]

Boff says again:

> Nature is not mute; the stones speak, the sea expresses itself, and the firmament sings God's glory. Nothing is juxtaposed or thrown in randomly. Everything is related and enters into communion: the wind with the rock, the rock with the earth, the earth with the sun, and the sun with the universe. Everything is drenched in the communion of the Blessed Trinity.[41]

Last but not least, as Miroslav Volf puts it, the Church itself is a sacrament of the Trinity, a sign of the Church's present life and its fulfillment in the Kingdom.[42] While Volf is critical of the vagueness of the correlation of the Church and the Trinity, he does affirm that "the correspondence is grounded in Christian Baptism. Through Baptism 'in the name of the Father, of the Son, and of the Holy Spirit,' the Spirit of God leads believers simultaneously into both trinitarian and ecclesial communion."[43] Referring to John Zizioulas, Volf says that if the Church is genuinely "to be a church transcended eschatologically, it must be identical with Christ and for that reason also be understood as a strictly eschatological reality."[44]

Boff points to Tertullian, the third-century theologian, who emphasizes that, "Where the Father, the Son, and the Holy Spirit are, there also is the church, which is the body of the Three."[45] Being a liberation theologian, Boff is critical of what he sees as operationally oppressive structures in the Church, and he would be the last person to divinize the Church; still he does not hesitate to see the Church and the Trinity in perichoretic relationship.[46]

---

39. Boff, *Holy Trinity*, 109.

40. Boff, *Holy Trinity*, 109.

41. Boff, *Holy Trinity*, 46.

42. Volf, *After Our Likeness*, 173.

43. Volf, *After Our Likeness*, 195.

44. Volf, *After Our Likeness*, 102.

45. Boff, *Holy Trinity*, 43.

46. Boff, *Holy Trinity*, 43.

TRINITARIAN DOXOLOGY

We live in a perichoretic world through the appropriation of the various categories set forth in the earlier part of this chapter: the Trinity as salvific dance, the persons in communion, and the Church as a body in communion.

It is in the liturgy, however, that we find the fullest expression of the doxological, the worship of the Trinity. A doxology is typically an expression of praise to the Trinity, Father, Son, and Spirit. The best-known doxological hymn is the "Old Hundredth" found in many Christian hymnals:

> Praise God, from whom all blessings flow,
> Praise Him, all creatures here below;
> Praise Him above, ye heavenly host;
> Praise Father, Son, and Holy Ghost.

Doxologies are found in the primary sacraments of Baptism and the Eucharist—two sacraments that stand in the present but with their consummation in the glory of heaven. In fact, all the liturgies and blessings of the Church are doxological.

Theologian Susan K. Wood shows how the fullest knowledge of the trinitarian God in the liturgy is through active participation. She says: "Our participation in the liturgy gives us access to a certain kind of knowledge of God, which I am identifying as participatory knowledge."[47] This participatory knowledge is mediated through the symbol system of the liturgy, including the scriptures, liturgical actions, sacraments, and prayers.[48] Wood writes: "It is primarily a knowledge of who God is for us within a Trinitarian economy wherein God sends the Son to give the Spirit that we may be constituted into the body of the Son and return to the Father in his gift of himself and our gift of ourselves."[49] The liturgy of the Church is permeated by the power of the Trinity. The triune God is above and beyond the liturgy, but it is also made present and active sacramentally and is internalized by the power of the Spirit into the many dimensions of Christian discipleship.

---

47. Wood, "Participatory Knowledge," 95.

48. Wood, "Participatory Knowledge," 95.

49. Wood, "Participatory Knowledge," 95. See also Pivarnik, *Toward a Trinitarian Theology of Liturgical Participation*. Pivarnik offers a concise analysis of the fundamental liturgical aim of the modern liturgical movement and of Vatican II and after: to bring worshippers into "active participation" by a profound interiorization of the mystery of the Lord's ministry, death, resurrection, and ascension.

One of the most expressive statements of the believers' dwelling in God is found in St. Patrick's breastplate. I have replaced the word "Christ" in the acclamations with "Triune God" in order to underscore the comprehensive power of our human dwelling in the triune God:

Today I put on
a terrible strength
invoking the Trinity,
confessing the Three
with faith in the One
as I face my Maker.
Triune God beside me,
Triune God before me,
Triune God behind me,
Triune God within me,
Triune God beneath me,
Triune God above me,
Triune God on my right hand,
Triune God on my left,
Triune God where I lie,
Triune God where I sit,
Triune God where I rise,
Triune God in the hearts of all who think of me,
Triune God in the mouths of all who speak to me,
Triune God in every eye that sees me,
Triune God in every ear that hears me.
Today I put on
a terrible strength,
invoking the Trinity,
confessing the Three,
with faith in the One
as I face my Maker.[50]

THE DANCE AGAIN

I turn again to the theme of the dance of the Trinity. While theorists are not agreed on the extent—if at all—that dance was part of the early Christian liturgy, there is a widely recognized perspective that extra-liturgical dance was used as an image of trinitarian life. In Hugo Rahner's work *Man at Play* mentioned earlier, the author explores the language of play and dance

50. Based on a traditional Irish prayer.

as metaphors for Christian existence. But he argues that dance was rarely used within the liturgy itself.[51] Yet he says, as does Marilyn Daniels and others, that religious or sacred dance, as distinct from liturgical dance, was common from the beginning of Christianity until the middle of the second millennium.[52] Religious or sacred dance served to unite body, soul, and spirit, to symbolize ecclesial structure, to introduce joy, festivity, and merriment into communities, and to promote social order. It served not least to prefigure the dance of heaven.

Rahner writes:

> All that pious men have sought to express in the dance by means of gesture and music is but a secret preparatory exercise for the object of their longing, the dance of everlasting life. What was lost by man at the beginning of the world is once more to be regained by him, and he is to know once again the blessed harmony of body and soul. There is no other image under which he can more eloquently describe the bliss of this everlasting life than under that of a heavenly dance.[53]

Gregory of Nyssa uses the rubric of the dance for describing salvation history:

> Once there was a time when the whole of rational creation formed a single dancing chorus looking upwards to the one leader of this dance. . . . And the harmony of that motion which was imparted to them by reason of his law found its way into their dancing. [54]

Gregory states that original sin destroyed this dance-like harmony of the spirit, and it will be only at the end of all things that all will again be as it once was. He continues: "Our first parents still danced in among the angelic powers. But the beginning of sin made an end of the sweet sounds of this chorus."[55]

> Since then, man has been deprived of this communion with the angels, and, since the fall, must sweat and most arduously toil

51. H. Rahner, *Man at Play*, 75–76.

52. Daniels, *Dance in Christianity*. An extensive treatment of religious dance is found in Gerardus van der Leeuw, *Sacred and Profane Beauty*, esp. 11–112.

53. H. Rahner, *Man at Play*, 87.

54. Gregory of Nyssa, *Homilies on the Psalms*, 6; translation in H. Rahner, *Man at Play*, 111.

55. Gregory of Nyssa, *Homilies on the Psalms*, 6; translation in Rahner, *Man at Play*, 111.

to do battle with and conquer the spirit that, thanks to sin, now weighs upon him; but the spoils of victory will be these: that which was lost in his original defeat will once more be his to enjoy, and once again he will take part in the dancing of the divine chorus. . . . And this victory will come, and thou shalt be found in the dancing ranks of the angelic spirits.[56]

The great Easter hymn of praise of Hippolytus of Rome sees the return of humankind to glory in dance terms:

O thou leader of the mystic round-dance! O divine Pasch and new feast of all things! O cosmic festal gathering! O joy of the universe, honour, ecstasy, exquisite delight by which dark death is destroyed,. . . and the people that were in the depths arise from the dead and announce to all the hosts of heaven: "The thronging choir from earth is coming home."[57]

Much later, Mechtild of Magdeburg wrote:

Here too the Spirit shafts
Such heavenly floods of light
On all the Blest that they,
Filled and enchanted, sing
For joy, and laugh and leap
In ordered dance. They flow
And swim and fly and climb
From tierèd choir to choir
Still upward through the heights. [58]

CONCLUSION

Participation in the triune God has the character of the dance, of *perichōrēsis*. The process of salvation is worked out by a dancing God drawing humankind into himself in a never-ending choreography. We are not drawn in as "individuals" but as "persons" in communion, a relational communion that marks all human institutions, and, perfectly, the communion of heaven—a communion of dynamism, movement, and eternal joy. The dance is an image of the Trinity and the paradigm for all human institutions and

---

56. H. Rahner, *Man at Play*, 89-90.

57. Hippolytus, *Homilies on the Pasch/Easter*, 6: translation in *Man at Play*, 108.

58. Mechtild of Magdeburg VII.1; translation in *Man at Play*, 79.

communities. Heaven will be an everlasting dance in which all persons, communities, and creation will move in ordered glory, ecstasy, and joy.

Chapter Four

MODEL FOUR:
COMMUNING WITH THE SAINTS

There is but one regret: not to have become a saint.
—Léon Bloy[1]

SALT LAKE CITY, WHERE I live, is the world headquarters of the Church of Jesus Christ of Latter-day Saints (Mormon). As the title of the Church suggests, Mormons are called "saints"—not only those who have died, but all living adherents. There is no canonization process in Mormonism; one becomes a saint simply by being baptized.

Non-Mormons often find the use of "saint" in this way to be presumptuous and ill-founded. The truth, of course, is that Mormonism is on firm biblical ground in using the term "saint" for its adherents. St. Paul regularly speaks of Christian disciples as "saints." Before Paul's conversion, we read how Ananias, during his vision of the Lord, complained about Paul:

> Lord, I have heard from many about this man, how much evil he has done to your saints in Jerusalem." (Acts 9:13)

In the same chapter, we read:

> Now as Peter went here and there among all the believers, he came down also to the saints living in Lydda. (Acts 9:32)

Again, Paul writes in 1 Corinthians 1:2–3:

> To the church of God that is in Corinth, to those who are sanctified in Christ Jesus, called to be saints, together with all those who

1. Bloy, *La Femme pauvre*, 206.

in every place call on the name of our Lord Jesus Christ, both their Lord and ours: Grace to you and peace from God our Father and the Lord Jesus Christ.[2]

Similar use of the word "saint" may be found in the openings of Paul's letters to the Romans, Ephesians, Philippians, and Colossians. Thus, it is clear that the designation of the faithful Christian as a "saint" is well founded in the scriptures.

In this chapter, I will elaborate on the character of the saint; then explore the communion of saints—a communion that unites earthly life with the life of heaven. I will examine the notion of the communion of saints and explain the manner by which the living and the dead are united now and in eternity. I will go on to look at the heavenly reunion of family and friends.

WHAT IS A SAINT?

Notre Dame University theologian Lawrence Cunningham offers a broad and comprehensive definition of the saint:

> A saint is a person so grasped by a religious vision that it becomes central to his or her life in a way that radically changes the person and leads others to glimpse the value of that vision.[3]

Cunningham develops his understanding of the saint in the broadest possible way by reference to psychologist William James' description of saintly life, which Cunningham abbreviates as follows:

- A feeling of being in a wider life than that of this world's selfish little interests; and a corresponding conviction, not merely intellectual, but, as it were, sensible, of the existence of an Ideal Power.

- A sense of the friendly continuity of the Ideal Power with our own life, and a willing surrender to its control.

- An immense elation and freedom, as the outlines of the confining selfhood melt down.

---

2. These excerpts are from the *American Standard Version*. Some Bibles use the words *holy ones*, not *saints*. I use *saints* to bring out the essential point I want to make.

3. Cunningham, *Meaning of Saints*, 65; italics in original. See also by Cunningham, *Brief History of Saints*. These two books are among the best introductions to the history and theology of sainthood.

- A shifting of the emotional centre towards loving and harmonious affections, towards "yes," "yes" and away from "no" where the claims of the non-ego are concerned.[4]

For Cunningham, sainthood can evolve in the soul quite dramatically, or in a quiet, almost imperceptible manner over time. He writes:

> What is crucial is not the suddenness or the slowness of the transformation; what is crucial is the change that it causes in the person. Whether the conversion is dramatic or not is somewhat irrelevant to its essential nature. What is important is the new affirmation that derives from the transformation, an affirmation, either implied or fully articulated, that radically changes a person's perspective about the self and about others.[5]

The *Christian* saint, with whom Cunningham is primarily concerned, is grasped by the Christian vision with Christ as the center. The vision is not merely aesthetic or moral, but truly religious (to use Sören Kierkegaard's term). Sainthood involves a radical conversion—not necessarily instantaneous (like that of St. Paul on the road to Damascus), but one that takes place over time (like that of St. Augustine).

The saint, whether living or dead, is an eschatological figure. He or she embodies a Christ-like way of life. Saints are models of life fully lived, models of radical Christian existence. The living saint is the man or woman fully flourishing, fully living according to the example of Christ and providing inspiration to others. One may say that saints are sacraments of God and his Kingdom.

Yet the saints on earth (a vocation to which every Christian is called) may not be perfect; they may struggle and fail, encounter imperfections and set-backs. The key element of earthly saints is that, despite their imperfections, they seek Christ and follow him in a radical manner.

The process of canonization, the Church's formal recognition of the extraordinary holiness of particular Christians, has varied over history from a less formal popular acclamation to the more formal procedure, signified today by a process that involves the Vatican Congregation for the Cause of Saints, and ending in a papal edict.[6]

---

4. Cunningham, *Meaning of Saints*, 66. William James sets forth the meaning of sainthood in his book, *The Varieties of Religious Experience*.

5. Cunningham, *Meaning of Saints*, 66.

6. On the process of canonization, see Cunningham, *Meaning of Saints*, 34–61; also by Cunningham, *Brief History of Saints*, esp. 28–53. See also Woodward, *Making Saints*.

Many commentators hold that the number of canonized saints should be broadened to include more lay people, especially women. Currently the official list of saints is mostly made up of clergy. The achievements of saints could also be expanded to include men and women dedicated to such causes as social justice and cultural transformation.[7]

While Cunningham has Christian saints particularly in mind, he suggests that the word "saint" may be broadened to include figures who are not Christian (well-known figures like Mahatma Gandhi, the Dalai Lama, Simone Weil, and Dag Hammarskjold).

It is notable that the *Lutheran Book of Worship* contains such figures as Martin Luther King; Dietrich Bonhoeffer; John XXIII, Bishop of Rome; Florence Nightingale; and Seattle, chief of the Duwamish Confederacy.[8] *The Book of Common Prayer* of the Episcopal Church in the United States has a similar, though less extensive, list of saintly figures not found in the Roman calendar.[9]

A SAINTLY COMMUNION

To examine sainthood in individual terms would be inadequate. Saints are members of a community united to Christ. It is not as though one first becomes a saint and then joins the communion of saints. The saintliness of the baptized person has its beginning and finality in the saintly communion of heaven and earth.[10]

In his book *Being and Communion*, Orthodox theologian John Zizioulas explores the relationship between person and communion, arguing that persons are adequately understood only in communal terms. We exist not as individuals who become part of a communion; rather, communion is the very ground of our existence. For Zizioulas, there is no true being without

7. See, for instance, Vogt, *Saints and Social Justice*.

8. See *Lutheran Book of Worship*, 9–12.

9. See *The Book of Common Prayer*, 19–33.

10. For those who wish to deepen their knowledge of the communion of saints, I recommend Garijo-Guembe, *Communion of the Saints*; Benko, *The Meaning of Sanctorum Communio*; Emery, *The Communion of Saints*; McGinnis, *The Communion of Saints*; Kirsch, *The Doctrine of the Communion of Saints*; Molinari, *Saints*; Bonhoeffer, *The Communion of Saints*; Philip Graham Ryken, ed., *The Communion of Saints*; McCarthy, *Sharing God's Company*; Perham, *The Communion of Saints*; DeLorenzo, *Work of Love*; Walford, *Communion of Saints*; Maloney, *Communion of Saints*; Madrid, *Any Friend of God Is a Friend of Mine*.

communion. By the same token any kind of communion that overrides the person is inauthentic.[11]

The Apostles' Creed professes faith in "the communion of saints" after having first professed faith in "the holy catholic Church." The *Catechism* states that the Church is constituted by the assembly of the saints; by the same token, the communion of saints makes up the Church.[12]

Quoting Thomas Aquinas, the *Catechism* states:

> "Since all the faithful form one body, the good of each is communicated to the others . . . We must therefore believe that there exists a communion of goods in the Church. But the most important member is Christ, since he is the head . . . Therefore, the riches of Christ are communicated to all the members, through the sacraments" (St. Thomas Aquinas. *Symb.*, 10). "As this Church is governed by one and the same Spirit, all the goods she has received necessarily become a common fund."[13]

The treasury of the saints is a rich reality. A central aspect is the truth that the saints assist us even now according to their particular vocations. Paul Claudel writes:

> We have at our disposal for loving, understanding, and serving God not only our own powers but everything from the Blessed Virgin in the summit of heaven down to the poor African leper who, bell in hand, whispers the responses of the Mass through a mouth half eaten away. The whole of creation, visible and invisible, all history, all the past, the present, and the future, all the treasures of the saints, multiplied by grace—all that is at our disposal as an extension of ourselves, a mighty instrument. All the saints and the angels belong to us. We can use the intelligence of St. Thomas, the right arm of St. Michael, the hearts of Joan of Arc and Catherine of Siena, and all the hidden resources that have only to be touched to be set in action. Everything of the good, the great, and the beautiful from one end of the earth to the other—everything that *begets* sanctity (as a doctor says of a patient that he has *got* a fever)—it is as if all that were our work. The heroism of the missionary, the inspiration of the Doctors of the Church, the generosity of the martyrs, the genius of the artists, the burning prayers of the Poor Clares and Carmelites—it is as if all that were ourselves;

---

11. Zizioulas, *Being as Communion*. See also Zizioulas, *Communion and Otherness*.

12. *Catechism*, no. 974.

13. *Catechism*, no. 974.

it is ourselves. All that is one with us, from the North to the South, from the Alpha to the Omega, from the Orient to the Occident; we clothe ourselves in it, we set it in motion.[14]

HOLY THINGS, HOLY PEOPLE

The *Catechism* goes on to say that the term "communion of saints" has two, closely-linked meanings: communion "in holy things *(sancta)*" and "among holy persons *(sancti)*." It elaborates as follows:

> *Sancta sanctis!* ("God's holy gifts for God's holy people!") is proclaimed by the celebrant in most Eastern liturgies during the elevation of the holy Gifts before the distribution of communion. The faithful *(sancti)* are fed by Christ's holy body and blood *(sancta)* to grow in the communion of the Holy Spirit *(koinonia)* and to communicate it to the world.[15]

The communion of saints has its foundation in the Body of Christ as expressed in the Eucharist, which binds all together in a radical manner. The *Catechism* makes this point about the *sanctorum communio*, the communion of saints:

> "None of us lives to himself, and none of us dies to himself." (Rom 14:7) "If one member suffers, all suffer together; if one member is honored, all rejoice together. Now you are the body of Christ and individually members of it." (1 Cor 12:26–27) "Charity does not insist on its own way." (1 Cor 13:5; cf. 10.24). In this solidarity with all men, living or dead, which is founded on the communion of saints, the least of our acts done in charity redounds to the profit of all. Every sin harms this communion.[16]

Those who hear and act on God's word become members of the Body of Christ. The passion, death, resurrection, and ascension of Christ are communicated to them. This is especially true of Baptism and the Eucharist. The Eucharist is the completion of baptismal initiation into the Body of Christ by which we are made one in communion with Christ and one another.

---

14. Jullien, *Paul Claudel interroge Le Cantique,* 156–57. Translation in Henri de Lubac, *Splendor of the Church,* 238–39.

15. *Catechism,* no. 948.

16. *Catechism,* no. 953.

What goes on in heaven relative to the communion of saints? The answer is, of course, all the activities examined in the chapters of this book. But beyond these, the most characteristic element of heavenly life is love, *agape, caritas,* which, when placed in a trinitarian framework, has profound significance.

I stated in chapter three (Participation in the Trinity), that the basis of all love is the Trinity, the relationship between Father, Son, and Holy Spirit. The essential trinitarian dynamic is of God as giver, given, and gifting—or simply gift! One can put it, as St. Augustine did, as lover, loved, and love. *Agape* is the distinctively Christian love, involving self-giving and self-sacrifice.[17]

In chapter three, I said that the Christian community not only apprehends the Trinity intellectually, but is drawn into the dynamic life of the trinitarian God. The Trinity draws us into the never-ending dance of God; it imprints itself on our souls. Since God's intra-trinitarian love is self-emptying and kinetic, human love at its most authentic is self-giving, *agapic.*

Theologian Michael Downey writes:

> What is most mysterious is God's superabundant life pouring itself forth, the love of God who gives and gives again but is never emptied in the giving. This self-giving is at the very heart of who God is. The incomprehensibility of God lies in the utter gratuity of life and love, in God's constant coming as gift. God is inexhaustible Gift, Given and Gift/ing in and through love. This is who God is and how God is.[18]

Our participation in God's self-giving love for humankind begins in Baptism and is fulfilled in the Eucharist. But our at-one-ment with the communion of saints is still partial, and will be only fulfilled in the eucharistic life of heaven. This is why it is so important to say that the Church's liturgy always has an orientation toward the eschatological future.

This means, as pointed out already, that the human person is called to be a self-giver, a going-out-of-oneself in love. Divine self-giving love passes through us, so to speak, and passes into the other. Downey writes:

17. See Outka, *Agape*; Nygren, *Agape and Eros*. A review of the different kinds of love is found in Jeanrond, *A Theology of Love*; C. S. Lewis, *The Four Loves*, 116–41, provides the most readable and lucid presentations of the theme of love. What others call *agape*, Lewis calls "charity."

18. Downey, *Altogether Gift*, 43. For a similar portrait of the Trinity, see Navone, SJ, *Self-Giving and Sharing*.

From the very first moment of existence, the infant is toward the other, ordinarily the mother or father, who is in turn toward and for the infant. From our origin we are related to others. We are from others, by others, toward others, for others, just as it is in God to exist in the relations of interpersonal love. God is Love, three in the one Love: Father, Son, Spirit.[19]

The *agapic* union between heaven and earth is not merely to be grasped intellectually and to be divorced from experience, but is expressed and experienced in various ways, principally in the Eucharist. This communion is also expressed in good works and common prayer in union with the company of saints.[20]

THREE STATES OF THE CHURCH

I now turn to the three states of the Church, the three states of the communion of saints. This has been enumerated traditionally as follows: the Church on earth (the Church militant), the Church in heaven (the Church triumphant), and the Church in purgatory (the Church suffering). These are not fundamentally separated, but are three dimensions of the Church which will be unified at the end of time. The Vatican II Dogmatic Constitution of the Church (*Lumen gentium*) explicates this truth:

> When the Lord will come in glory, and all his angels with him (cf. Matt 25:31), death will be no more and all things will be subject to him (cf. 1 Cor 15:26–27). But at the present time, some of his disciples are pilgrims on earth. Others have died and are being purified, while still others are in glory, contemplating "in full light, God himself triune and one, exactly as he is" [Council of Florence, *Decretum pro Graecis,* Denz. 693.]. All of us, however, in varying degrees and in different ways share in the same charity towards God and our neighbors, and we all sing the one hymn of glory to our God. All, indeed, who are of Christ and who have his Spirit form one Church and in Christ cleave together (Eph 4:16). So it is that the union of the wayfarers with the brethren who sleep in the peace of Christ is in no way interrupted, but on the contrary, according to the constant faith of the Church, this union is

19. Downey, *Altogether Love,* 63.

20. A comprehensive treatment of the communion of saints in the Body of Christ is found in Murphy-O'Connor, *Becoming Human Together.*

reinforced by an exchange of spiritual goods. Being more closely united to Christ, those who dwell in heaven fix the whole Church more firmly in holiness, add to the nobility of the worship that the Church offers to God here on earth.[21]

THE CHURCH IN PURGATORY

I will now look briefly at purgatory, the third state of the Church (the Church suffering). Heaven, the final condition of salvation, is united to purgatory, the state in which those who have died without perfection are conformed to Christ.

Purgatory is the most controversial feature of ecumenical dialogue; it is rejected by Protestants and Anglicans (with rare exceptions) and is held with ambiguity by the Orthodox Churches. The doctrine of Purgatory stands at the core of inter-church debates about justification and sanctification.

Essentially, purgatory is the "place" or process by which those who have died in imperfection are brought by God's grace to the full stature of the saints. The *Catechism* states: "All who die in God's grace and friendship, but still imperfectly purified, are indeed assured of their eternal salvation; but after death they undergo purification, so as to achieve the holiness necessary to enter the joy of heaven."[22] The *Catechism* states, furthermore, "The tradition of the Church, by reference to certain texts of Scripture, speaks of a cleansing fire."[23]

The *Catechism* continues:

> As for certain lesser faults, we must believe that, before the Final Judgment, there is a purifying fire. He who is truth says that whoever utters blasphemy against the Holy Spirit will be pardoned neither in this age nor in the age to come. From this sentence we understand that certain offenses can be forgiven in this age, but certain others in the age to come.[24]

---

21. *Vatican Council II*, no. 49, p 409.
22. *Catechism*, no. 1030.
23. *Catechism*, no. 1031.
24. *Catechism*, no. 1031.

However, purgatory is not, as Joseph Ratzinger pointed out, "Some kind of supra-worldly concentration camp where man is forced to undergo punishment in a more or less arbitrary fashion. Rather, it is the inwardly necessary process of transformation, in which a person becomes capable of Christ, capable of God, and thus capable of unity with the whole communion of saints."[25] The transformation of purgatory is "the fire that burns away our dross and re-forms us to be vessels of eternal joy."[26]

This same view was expressed by St. Catherine of Genoa. For Catherine, the fire of purgatory is not a fire of destruction, but the "burning love by which the divine majesty draws the deceased into the perfect vision of God."[27] This is not a fire of desolation, but a fire which burns away all that is imperfect. Catherine writes: "Unceasingly God draws the soul to Himself and breathes fire into it, never letting it go until He has led it to the state from which it came forth—that is, the state of pure cleanliness in which it was created."[28] The fire of purgatory, then, is a loving fire, the fire of the Holy Spirit: "When with its inner sight the soul sees itself drawn by God with such loving fire, then it is melted by the heat of the glowing love for God, dear Lord, which it feels overwhelming it."[29]

THE SAINTS AND LITURGY

The union between heaven and earth is found most expressively in the celebration of the Eucharist, especially in Eucharistic Prayer I (*The Roman Canon*), where we read:

> In communion with those whose memory we venerate,
> Especially the glorious ever-Virgin Mary,
> Mother of our God and Lord, Jesus Christ,
> And blessed Joseph, her Spouse,

25. Ratzinger, *Eschatology,* 230–33. Theologically reliable treatments of purgatory are found in Taylor, *Purgatory*; Hahnenberg, *Purgatory*; Ombres, *The Theology of Purgatory*; Solkeld, *Can Catholics and Evangelicals Agree about Purgatory and the Last Judgment?* An excellent and extensive treatment of purgatory is provided—ironically—by the Baptist theologian Jerry L. Walls, in his book *Purgatory*. A brief treatment of purgatory from an Anglican perspective is offered by Macquarrie, *Principles of Christian Theology*, 367–68.

26. Ratzinger, *Eschatology,* 231.

27. Catherine of Genoa, *Fire of Love!* 53.

28. Catherine of Genoa, *Fire of Love!* 54.

29. Catherine of Genoa, *Fire of Love!* 53–54.

Your blessed Apostles and Martyrs,
Peter and Paul, Andrew,
(James, John,
Thomas, James, Philip,
Bartholomew, Matthew,
Simon and Jude;
Linus, Cletus, Clement, Sixtus,
Cornelius, Cyprian,
Lawrence, Chrysogonus,
John and Paul,
Cosmas and Damian)
And all your Saints;
We ask that through their merits and prayers,
In all things we may be defended
By your protecting help.
(Through Christ our Lord. Amen.)

Later, in the same Eucharistic Prayer, the list of saints is expanded:

To us, also, your servants,
who, though sinners,
hope in your abundant mercies,
graciously grant some share
and fellowship with your holy Apostles and Martyrs:
with John the Baptist, Stephen,
Matthias, Barnabas,
(Ignatius, Alexander,
Marcellinus, Peter,
Felicity, Perpetua,
Agatha, Lucy,
Agnes, Cecilia, Anastasia)
and all your Saints;
admit us, we beseech you,
into their company,
not weighing our merits,
but granting us your pardon,
through Christ our Lord.[30]

The invocation of the saints takes place most solemnly at the Easter Vigil:

30. *Roman Missal*, no. 86, p. 620.

Holy	Mary, Mother of God,
Saint	Michael
Holy	Angels of God,
Saint	John the Baptist,
Saint	Joseph
Saint	Peter and Saint Paul
Saint	Andrew
Saint	John
Saint	Mary Magdalene
Saint	Stephen
Saint	Ignatius of Antioch
Saint	Perpetua and Saint Felicity
Saint	Agnes
Saint	Gregory
Saint	Augustine
Saint	Athanasius
Saint	Basil
Saint	Martin
Saint	Benedict
Saint	Francis and Saint Dominic
Saint	Francis Xavier
Saint	John Vianney
Saint	Catherine of Siena
Saint	Teresa of Jesus
All holy men and women,	
Saints of God.[31]	

These invocations serve not merely a catechetical function, but represent a calling upon the saints to encircle the celebrating community, uniting the saints in heaven and on earth.[32]

31. See, for instance, *Order of Christian Initiation of Adults*, no. 221, 144–45.

32. A meditative treatment of the invocation of the saints in Eucharistic Prayer I of the Mass is found in Walsh, *In Memory of Me*, 67–77, 161–97. Popular presentations of

FAMILY AND FRIENDS IN HEAVEN

One of the questions that most engages Christians (and many others) on the matter of death and the afterlife is whether or not they will know their family and friends in heaven. I answer yes on the grounds that this is an outcome of the communion of saints. Since we live in relationship on earth, we cannot but know in heaven spouses, family, friends—indeed eventually all men and women. Since we do not exist as isolated individuals but as persons whose existence is intrinsically relational, our very being is constituted by relationship. We are who we are because of those who brought us into existence. Our families and friends have given us our identity; the whole social and material environment in which we are born, live, and die shapes us deeply.

What will be the relationships between people (spouses, children, friends, and others) in heaven? Here we have to be careful to avoid saying too much (and too little). The scriptures do not give us any kind of detailed or comprehensive picture. Yet we are not prevented from teasing out a broader picture from scripture, the nature of the human person, community, Christian spirituality, and human experience generally.

Bede the Venerable, the early English ecclesiastical historian, provides a comprehensive account of this matter: "A great multitude of dear ones is there expecting us; a vast and mighty crowd of parents, brothers, and children, secure now in their safety, anxious yet for our salvation, long that we may come and embrace them to that joy which will be common to us and to them."[33]

Evangelical writer Larry Dick writes of how in heaven all earthly alienations will have passed away and all human pain and difficulty will be overcome:

> All the misunderstandings, hasty judgments, disappointments, resentments and hurts of the past that can happen in even the best relationship, will be forgiven and forgotten. There will only be unconditional love and ecstatic joy at seeing each other again. More than this, you will have the opportunity to meet and spend time with your ancestors that made it into heaven. What a fascinating

---

human relationship to the saints are found in Ellsberg, *Saints' Guide to Happiness*; and Martin, *My Life with the Saints*.

33. Bede, "Sermon on All Saints' Day," 6–7.

experience to hear and see first-hand how God has worked down through the generations to you!"[34]

Taking up this theme, philosopher Peter Kreeft writes that we shall meet all our ancestors and descendants in heaven; every life will enter into every other life. Paraphrasing philosopher Richard Purtill, Kreeft states that there will be three tasks in heaven:

> First, we review our past life with divine understanding and appre-
> ciation of every single experience, good and evil: we milk all our
> meaning dry. Then we do the same to others' lives from within. We
> know them more intimately and completely than we could ever
> know our most intimate friend on earth because we share God's
> knowledge of each one. When these two preliminary lessons are
> complete—when we know, love, understand, and appreciate com-
> pletely by inner experience everything we and everyone else have
> ever experienced—only then are we spiritually mature enough
> to begin the endless and endlessly fascinating task of exploring,
> learning and loving the facets of infinity, the inexhaustible nature
> of God.[35]

The eighteenth-century New England Puritan Jonathan Edwards spells out the blessed reunion of the living with those who have entered heaven: "There the Christian father, and mother, and wife, and child, and friend, with whom we shall renew the holy fellowship of the saints, which was interrupted by death, but shall be commenced again in the upper sanctuary, and then shall never end. There we shall have communion with the patriarchs, the fathers and mothers, and the saints of the Old and New Testaments."[36]

As mentioned, the holy Trinity will be the foundation of all heavenly relations. We cannot know anyone in heaven except through the Holy Trinity. Edwards continues:

> And there, above all, we shall enjoy and dwell with God the Father,
> whom we have loved with all our hearts on earth; and with Jesus
> Christ, our beloved Savior, who has always been to us the chief
> among ten thousands, and altogether lovely; and with the Holy

---

34. Dick, *Taste of Heaven*, 47.

35. Kreeft, *Everything You Wanted to Know*, 52; see Purtill, *Thinking about Religion*, 143.

36. Edwards, *Heaven*, 18.

Spirit, our Sanctifier, and Guide, and Comforter; and shall be filled with all the fullness of the Godhead forever![37]

Accordingly, the early twentieth-century Church of Ireland (Anglican) theologian J. Paterson-Smyth writes that the notion of heaven as a place in which people dwell in isolation is profoundly wrong: "We know that Heaven would scarce be Heaven at all if we were to be but solitary isolated spirits amongst a crowd of others whom we did not know or love. We know that the next world and this world come from the same God who is the same always."[38] He continues: "We have seen what a prophecy of recognition lies deep in the very fibers of that nature which God has implanted in us. If we shall not know one another, why is there this undying memory of departed ones, the aching void that is never filled on earth?"[39]

Paterson-Smyth uses the example of a mother who has lost her child:

> The lower animals lose their young and in a few days forget them. But the poor, human mother never forgets. When her head is bowed with age, when she has forgotten nearly all else on earth, you can bring the tears into her eyes by mentioning the child that died in her arms forty years ago. Did God implant that divine love in her only to disappoint it? God forbid! A thousand times, no. In that world the mother shall meet her child, and the lonely widow shall meet her husband, and they shall learn fully the love of God in that rapturous meeting with Christ's benediction resting on them.[40]

Writing in 1871, Fr. J. Boudreau, SJ, writes of the blessedness of the heavenly home and the absence of all discord:

> There we shall love everyone with the most perfect charity, and everyone will return our love. There we shall have no enemies; no one to think uncharitably of us; no one to criticize our sayings and conduct; no one to spread reports injurious to our character; no one to put an unfavorable construction upon our most innocent actions. "God is charity," and as "we shall be like him because we shall see him as he is," it follows that we, too, shall possess that divine charity, in a far high degree than is attainable here below.

37. Edwards, *Heaven*, 18.
38. Paterson-Smyth, *Gospel of the Hereafter*, 225.
39. Paterson-Smyth, *Gospel of the Hereafter*, 226.
40. Paterson-Smyth, *Gospel of the Hereafter*, 226.

Our social intercourse with the blessed will, therefore, ever be the source of the purest and sweetest joy.[41]

FUNERALS AND HEAVEN

A privileged source of Christian belief about the union of the living and the dead in the communion of saints is the liturgy of the Church. The Catholic *Order of Christian Funerals* is replete with references to reunification with the deceased in heaven.

Referring to the deceased, the first Invitation to Prayer in the Final Commendation at the Funeral Mass states: "One day we shall joyfully greet him/her again when the love of Christ, which conquers all things, destroys even death itself."[42] The second Invitation to the Commendation uses similar language: "There is sadness in parting, but we take comfort in the hope that one day we shall see N. again and enjoy his/her friendship."[43] The Prayer of Commendation itself asks God to "help us who remain to comfort one another with assurances of faith, until we all meet with Christ and are with you and with our brother/sister."[44] The Invitation to the Rite of Committal ends with the words: "May we who mourn be reunited one day with our brother/sister; together may we meet Christ Jesus when he who is our life appears in glory."[45]

This is why all earthly relationships are of ultimate importance. And this is why we can expect to meet our fathers and mothers, spouses, brothers, sisters, children, and friends in heaven. (How God deals with relationships that were dysfunctional and destructive in life, only he knows. That, I assume, is partly what purgatory is about.) Accordingly, our relationships with the dead do not end at the grave. There is profound communion between the living and the dead, expressed especially in the Eucharist; when we say "farewell" at a funeral, we are beginning a new phase of relationship with the departed.

41. Boudreau, *Happiness of Heaven*, 146–47. In their engaging book on heaven, McDannell and Lang show how in Christian history the notion of heaven has shifted back and forth between an individualist, God-focused conception (theocentric) and a communal view (anthropocentric) in which friends and relatives live together and interact constantly. See also Lang, *Meeting in Heaven*.

42. *Christian Funerals*, no. 171 (A), 89.

43. *Christian Funerals*, no. 171 (B), 89.

44. *Christian Funerals*, no. 175 (A), 90.

45. *Christian Funerals*, no. 216 ((B), 113.

St. Simeon of Thessalonica speaks of the funeral farewell as follows: "We sing for his departure from this life and separation from us, but also because there is a communion and a reunion. For even dead, we are not at all separated from one another, because we all run the same course and we will find one another again in the same place. We shall never be separated, for we live for Christ, and now we are united in Christ as we go toward him ... we shall all be together in Christ."[46]

CONCLUSION

The communion of saints—a theme unfortunately having today less profile in Christian consciousness than in the past—stands as a central model of life in heaven. The saints are the glory of God and the inspiration of all men and women of good will. The whole of humankind is called to sainthood. It is in the liturgy of the Church that we find the fullest expression of the communion of saints as a "great cloud of witnesses" (Heb 12:1) living now and forever.

---

46. Simeon of Thessalonica, *Concerning the Order of Burial*, 336. Quoted in *Catechism*, no. 1690.

Chapter Five

MODEL FIVE:
SINGING WITH THE ANGELS

Music is well said to be the speech of Angels.
—Thomas Carlyle[1]

IN A BOOK TITLED *Angels: An Endangered Species,* published in 1990, religion commentator Malcolm Godwin argued that belief in angels had fallen on hard times.[2] Godwin stated that at that time less than half of Americans believed in angels; most thought of angels as sentimental, romantic, and harmless—essentially decorative creatures.

In the years since Godwin's book appeared, there seems to have been a greater increase in belief in angels—as the religion/spirituality section of bookstores demonstrates. But, the understanding of angels has become more notably flavored by New Age and esoteric religious movements. While some orthodox and theologically solid works on angels have been produced in recent decades, there are many more that do not meet the criteria of orthodox Christianity.[3]

1. Carlyle, "Opera," 123.

2. Godwin, *Angels,* 6–15.

3. While there are dozens of books on angels of questionable merit published in recent times, I recommend the following more substantive works for those who wish to broaden and deepen their knowledge of angelic beings: Kreeft, *Angels (and Demons)*; Parente, *The Angels in Catholic Teaching*; Aquilina, *Angels of God*; Mother Alexandra, *The Holy Angels*; Patella, *Angels and Demons*; Shapiro, *The Angelic Way*; Bulgakov, *Jacob's Ladder*; Miller, *Lifted by Angels*; Vonier, *The Angels*; Jones, *Angels.* A positive assessment of angels by a non-believer is found in Adler, *The Angels and Us.* Particularly valuable are Guiley, *Encyclopedia of Angels*; Davidson, *A Dictionary of Angels Including Fallen Angels.* The most extensive bibliography on angelology is found in Marshall, *Angels.* A summary

As the title suggests, the fundamental concern in this chapter will be with music as the angelic language, and the participation of all humanity redeemed in the music of heaven. It will argue that music raises the human being to heaven, where humanity and angels sing together. As music descends from heaven, humanity is transformed and made holy. In this process humanity is enabled to participate in cosmic worship. Words from two familiar hymns, "O Worship the King" and "Holy God We Praise Thy Name" provide a general orientation for this chapter. The first is as follows:

> O measureless might, ineffable love,
> While angels delight to hymn thee above,
> Thy humbler creation, though feeble their lays,
> With true adoration shall sing to thy praise.[4]

A hymn version of the *Te Deum* provides the basis for the second:

> Hark! The loud celestial hymn
> Angel choirs above are raising,
> Cherubim and seraphim,
> In unceasing chorus praising;
> Fill the heavens with sweet accord:
> Holy, holy, holy, Lord.[5]

THE NATURE OF ANGELS

Is the traditional notion of angels out of date in modernity? I don't think so. For instance, given our modern knowledge of outer space, we should be more open than ever to life forms beyond what we now know. The Anglican theologian John Macquarrie has written perceptively on this: "More than ever nowadays, as we learn more and more of the inconceivable vastness of space and time and of the infinite proliferation of worlds, it becomes a probability of the highest order that there are or have been or will be beings that surpass man in the hierarchy of beings."[6]

Belief in angels, Macquarrie says, opens our eyes to the vast, unimaginable, divine creation. The panorama of the created order "must be far

---

of angelology is provided in K. Rahner. "Angels," in *Encyclopedia of Theology, Concise Sacramentum Mundi*, 4–12.

4. Grant, "O Worship the King," 1833. Found in various hymnals.

5. Franz, "Holy God We Praise Thy Name." Found in various hymnals.

6. Macquarrie, *Principles*, 234.

more breathtaking than we can guess in our corner of the cosmos, for there must be many higher orders of beings whose service is joined with ours under God."[7]

Angels play an important role in the Old and New Testaments. The sixth-century Christian writer Pseudo-Dionysius developed a system of angelic beings in terms of choirs: seraphim, cherubim, thrones, dominations, virtues, powers, principalities, archangels, and angels. These have different roles in relation to God and to humanity. Rather than being regarded as a confusion of angelic beings, they should be seen as a profusion of God's orderly creation.[8] Many theologians took up this theme, notably Hildegard of Bingen in the thirteenth century, for whom music echoed through creation and united the great cosmic realities in symphonic terms.[9]

Philosopher Peter Kreeft answers in one page the question, "What can you tell me about angels?" My (slight) adaptation of Kreeft is as follows. (1) Angels really do exist, not just in our minds or in humanly fabricated religious myths or symbols. (2) Angels are present to human beings in the here-and-now. (3) Angels are not cute, cuddly, comfortable, chummy, or "cool;" they can be fearsome and formidable, and often act as warriors in the face of injustice and human cruelty. (4) Angels are the real "extra-terrestrials"; they are the real "Supermen." (5) Angels have minds more brilliant than Albert Einstein. (6) Angels can literally move the heavens and earth if God permits them. (7) There also exist evil angels, fallen angels, demons or devils, demon possessions and exorcisms. (8) Angels are aware of human beings, though we cannot hear or see them. (9) Every person has his or her own guardian angel. (10) Angels often appear in disguise. (11) Human beings are on a protected part of a great battlefield between angels and devils. (12) Angels are sentinels, standing at the crossroads where life meets death.[10]

SINGING ANGELS

Angels have forever been associated with music, specifically with singing—although some Fathers of the Church were cautious about the use of music

---

7. Macquarrie, *Principles*, 237.

8. Pseudo-Dionysius, "Celestial Hierarchy," 143–91.

9. Hildegard of Bingen, *Symphonia*.

10. Kreeft, *Angels (And Demons)*, 17.

in the liturgy.[11] While this cautious position is held by some today, it is difficult to imagine that angels do not sing, while earthly worshipers do. (My friend Anthony Ruff, OSB, says that it is unlikely that the angels in heaven *recite* the *Sanctus* (Holy, Holy). By the same token it is difficult to envisage eighty thousand people at the Super Bowl *reciting* the national anthem.) Some reticence about music in the liturgy continued in the West well into patristic times. However, in the patristic East there was less concern about the relationship between music and paganism, so that in the East music was seen to have an intrinsic role in the liturgy.[12]

While there are many expressions of singing in the scriptures, particularly in the Psalms and the Book of Revelation, I will focus here on the *Sanctus*.[13] The *Sanctus* finds two chief expressions in the scriptures, in Isaiah and in the Book of Revelation. The first is in Isaiah 6. The power of the seraphim in the court of heaven is described as follows:

> In the year King Uzziah died, I saw the Lord seated on a high and lofty throne, with the train of his garment filling the temple. Seraphim were stationed above; each of them had six wings: with two they covered their faces, with two they covered their feet, and with two they hovered. One cried out to the other: "Holy, holy, holy is the Lord of hosts! All the earth is filled with his glory."
>
> At the sound of that cry, the frame of the door shook and the house filled with smoke. (Isa 6:1–4)

In the Book of Revelation (Rev 4:6–11) the *Sanctus* appears a second time:

> In the center and around the throne, there were four living creatures covered with eyes in front and back. The first creature resembled a lion, the second was like a calf, the third had the face like that of a human being, and the fourth looked like an eagle in flight. The four living creatures, each of them with six wings, were covered with eyes inside and out. Day and night they do not stop exclaiming:

11. On this see Quasten, *Music and Worship in Pagan and Christian Antiquity*; also Stapert, *A New Song for an Old World*.

12. Sánchez-Escobar points out that "Orthodox liturgical music, as well as other church arts such as architecture or iconography, is part of the dogmatic tradition of the Orthodox Church and thus of its Holy Tradition. . . . Singing and praying are two elements intrinsically joined in Orthodox worship." Sánchez-Escobar, *Orthodox Church Music*, 7.

13. Spinks, *Sanctus*.

"Holy, holy, holy is the Lord God almighty,
who was, and who is, and who is to come."

Whenever the living creatures give glory and honor and thanks to the one who sits on the throne, who lives for ever and ever, the twenty-four elders fall before the one on the throne and worship him, who lives forever and ever. They throw down their crowns before the throne, exclaiming:

Worthy are you, Lord our God,
to receive glory and honor and power,
for you created all things;
because of your will they came to be and
were created. (Rev 4: 6–11)

The use of the *Sanctus* in the eucharistic liturgy in many Christian traditions is well known:

Holy, Holy, Holy Lord God of hosts.
Heaven and earth are full of your glory.
Hosanna in the highest.
Blessed is he who comes in the name of the Lord.
Hosanna in the highest.[14]

In the angelic world, music is associated with the Seraphim, the first choir of the hierarchy of angels. Pascale Parente writes: "The primary duty of the seraphim is to sing without ceasing to God, celebrating above all the other attributes of the Holiness of God."[15] Angels have a language all of their own; they are able to talk to each other, to sing to and with each other—and most of all they sing and talk to humanity.[16]

SINGING HEAVEN

At first hearing, singing the *Sanctus* repeatedly can seem like a monotonous activity. But it is actually the vital, self-renewing song of creation, a song of celebration. It is a primary expression of love: "It is a creative, resonating field of life. The Seraphim are in direct communion with God and as such are beings of pure light and thought who resonate with the Fire of Love."[17]

14. *Roman Missal*, in the various eucharistic prayers.
15. Parente, *Angels*, 28–33.
16. Parente, *Angels*, 79.
17. Godwin, *Angels*, 25.

An anonymous litany of the angels sets forth the role of the angels in salvation history:

> O God, who by the Archangel Michael didst overthrow the rebel angels,
> Have Mercy upon us.
> Who by the Archangels Gabriel didst foretell the birth of St. John the Baptist,
> Have Mercy upon us.
> Who by the Archangel Gabriel didst announce to Mary the incarnation of God,
> Have Mercy upon us.
> Who by angels and archangels art ever worshipped in heaven,
> Have Mercy upon us.
> O ye Angels of God, Guardians of his people Israel,
> Pray for us.
> Announcing the birth of Jesus,
> Pray for us.
> Ministering to Jesus in the wilderness,
> Pray for us.
> Strengthening Jesus in his agony,
> Pray for us.
> Appearing at his Resurrection,
> Pray for us.
> Comforting the disciples at the Ascension,
> Pray for us.
> Ministering to the heirs of salvation,
> Pray for us.
> Rejoicing over the sinner that repents,
> Pray for us.
> O ye Angels of God, protecting us with ceaseless care.
> Pray for us.[18]

In the liturgy of the Catholic Church, it is not only the seraphim who sing around God's throne, but the whole hierarchy of angels. The Eucharistic Preface I of the Nativity of the Lord has the following:

> And so, with Angels and Archangels,
> with Thrones and Dominions,
> and with all the hosts and Powers of heaven,
> we sing the hymn of your glory,
> as without end we acclaim:

18. Unpublished litany. Origin unknown.

Holy, Holy, Holy Lord God of hosts . . .[19]

The Preface I of Easter is as follows:

Therefore, overcome with paschal joy,
every land, every people exults in your praise
and even the heavenly Powers, with the angelic hosts,
sing together the unending hymn of your glory,
as they acclaim:
Holy, Holy, Holy Lord God of hosts ...[20]

The Preface I of the Blessed Virgin Mary proclaims:

Through him the Angels praise your majesty,
Dominions adore and Powers tremble before you.
Heaven and the Virtues of heaven and the blessed Seraphim
worship together with exultation.
May our voices, we pray, join with theirs
in humble praise, as we acclaim:
Holy, Holy, Holy Lord God of hosts ...[21]

The highest expression of angelic music in heaven is found in the Book of Revelation:

I looked again and heard the voices of many angels who surrounded the throne and the living creatures and the elders. They were
countless in number, and they cried out in a loud voice:

"Worthy is the Lamb that was slain,
to receive power and riches, wisdom and strength,
honor and glory and blessing."

---

19. *Roman Missal*, 520, no. 35.

20. *Roman Missal*, 540, no. 45.

21. *Roman Missal*, 574, no. 62. Here I take up again the question of heavenly boredom. Do the angels and the inhabitants of heaven sing unceasingly and without repetition? Do the angels and the inhabitants do anything else? I observed in chapter one (Resting in Peace) that heavenly "time" is eternal and that all human time, past, present, and future, are collapsed into timelessness. When we say that the company of angels sings unceasingly, we mean that in heaven everything has the unending beauty and harmony of many songs and that every heavenly activity is transfigured with music. The angels praise God, singing unceasingly. That does not mean flattering God endlessly, but being what God intended angels to be: expressions of his being. Heavenly music has an endless variety because of the unfathomable activity of God and of the inhabitants of heaven. To say that heaven could be boring is to say that God is boring—hardly an arguable position.

Then I heard every creature in heaven and on earth
and under the earth and in the sea, everything in the universe, cry out:

"To the one who sits on the throne
and to the Lamb
be blessing and honor and glory and might,
forever and ever."

The four living creatures answered, "Amen," and the elders fell
down and worshiped. (Rev 5:11–14)

MUSIC'S LADDER

The image of the musical ladder is useful in articulating the relationship
between the music of heaven and the music of earth. We read the following
in Genesis:

Jacob departed from Beer-sheba and proceeded Haran. When he
came upon a certain place, he stopped there for the night, since the
sun had already set. Taking one of the stones at the place, he put it
under his head and lay down in that place. Then he had a dream: a
stairway rested on the earth, with its top reaching to the heavens;
and God's angels were going up and down it. (Gen 28:10–12)

The angels descending and ascending the ladder represent the descending and ascending of worshipful music. Russian Orthodox theologian
Sergius Bulgakov writes: "One can say that only a certain participation in
song and music, which fill the angelic life as doxology, is accessible to humankind and the human world."[22]

Angels ascending and descending Jacob's ladder symbolize the angelic
beings bringing heavenly music to earth and earthly music to heaven. Bulgakov writes: "The foundation for the art of sound is found in the angelic
world, in its harmonies."[23] The musical art is founded in the music of the
heavenly spheres. "Between heaven and earth the holy angels ascend and
descend unceasingly."[24]

Bulgakov goes on to say: "In *song* humankind and all creation truly unite with the song of angels as such, despite all the difference in its

---

22. Bulgakov, *Jacob's Ladder*, 126.

23. Bulgakov, *Jacob's Ladder*, 126.

24. Bulgakov, *Jacob's Ladder*, 164.

perfection and quality."[25] Angelic sound is the prototype of earthly music; the foundation for the art of sound is heavenly art. Bulgakov continues:

> The *singing* of angels is the prototype of any singing, and in particular of our own; the doxology of the angels is the foundation of our human doxology, in which, as the Church puts it, the holy angels also participate. We have direct testimony about the doxology of the angels in Isaiah 6:3 concerning the seraphim: "And they called out one to another and said, 'Holy, holy, holy, the Lord Sabbaoth! All the earth is full of His glory.'"
>
> This *Trisagion* [Holy, Holy] of the angels is praise of the Holy Trinity, which the seraphim, while flying, *call out one to another.* This is an important indication that the doxology contains not only each angel's personal address to God but also forms the beginning of their mutual communion, common life, and collectivity: it is not only prayer, but also common, mutual, creative inspiration, which in human language we call *art.*[26]

Bulgakov says of hymnody, "a human song is united with an angelic one and is in a certain sense homogenous. For that reason the possibility of a joint service of humans and angels becomes comprehensible."[27]

GOD THE MUSICIAN

I turn now to an ancient theme: that music has an intrinsic relationship to God and to the whole cosmic order. Traditionally this has been spoken of in terms of the "music of the spheres."

Pythagoras is credited with having discovered the idea of music of the spheres. It is also present in Boethius and—and while it fell into disrepute for centuries—it has been recovered somewhat in new and creative ways.[28] The essential notion of music of the spheres is that there is order and harmony in the universe. All things cohere: the earth, sun, moon, stars. This order has a music-like quality; indeed, music is regarded as the key to the universe. To seek to understand the universe is to understand music; and

---

25. Bulgakov, *Jacob's Ladder,* 125.

26. Bulgakov, *Jacob's Ladder,* 119.

27. Bulgakov, *Jacob's Ladder,* 124.

28. On this theme, see Godwin, ed., *Harmony of the Spheres*; Godwin, ed., *Harmonies of Heaven and Earth*; Godwin, ed., *Music, Mysticism and Magic*; Godwin, ed., *Cosmic Music.*

to understand music is to understand the universe. Music has a cosmic character.

Not many scientists today accept the view that the universe has an underlying musical order but is rather the result of a random set of accidents. The universe, it is held, is governed by the processes of evolution. Yet, as musicologist Jamie Jones writes:

> Despite the odds, the ancient tradition of the musical cosmos, embracing and unifying noble rationalism and ecstatic mysticism, has survived. What we may call the great theme—the belief that the cosmos is a sublimely harmonious system guided by a Supreme Intelligence, and that man has a place preordained and eternal in that system—runs throughout Western civilization, even if during the declining era of Romanticism it is a muted leitmotif. As the orthodox culture focused its attention earthward and selfward, the impulse to connect with the universal became more and more esoteric.[29]

Theologian Eric Peterson states that it is no accident that medieval musical treatises begin with reference to the music of the spheres. Since the church's praise turns into the praises of the cosmos "any consideration of the place of music in Church worship must take account of the sort of praise offered by sun, moon and stars."[30] In the great symphony, Peterson says, "the harmony of the spheres rings out, and angel song resounds, the liturgy of the Church has found its voice. The sun makes music because it circles round, the angel sings because he stands firm, and man takes part in the praise of the cosmos and of the angels."[31] There is an inner connection "between the movement of the spheres and their music, as there is between the poise of the angels and their singing. The universe makes music out of its own being and declares by its order that it does not transgress the law of God."[32]

Peter Kreeft speaks of the music in heaven, affirming that heaven is a musical reality. He holds that "great earthly music is particularly Heavenly."[33] What is dimly suggested in all earthly music . . . is precisely Heavenly

---

29. Jones, *Music of the Spheres*, 19.

30. Peterson, *Angels and Liturgy*, 29.

31. Peterson, *Angels and Liturgy*, 29.

32. Peterson, *Angels and Liturgy*, 29–30.

33. Kreeft, *Everything You Wanted to Know*, 46.

music.[34] Indeed, "it may well be *in* music that the world was created."[35] It is not that music is in heaven; rather "Heaven is in music."[36]

MUSIC AND THE *ESCHATON*

Going further, it may be said that God is the original musician, the one from whom music emanates throughout the whole cosmos. God is song and humankind is the singer; indeed, it may be said that Christ is the Song incarnate. In "The Singer and the Song," Peter Davison offers the following verses:

> When long before time and the worlds were begun,
> when there was no earth and no sky and no sun,
> and all was deep silence and night reigned supreme,
> and even our Maker had only a dream . . .
> . . . the silence was broken when God sang the Song,
> and light pierced the darkness and rhythm began,
> and with its first birth-cries creation was born,
> and creaturely voices sang praise to the morn.
> To you, God the Singer, our voices we raise,
> to you, Song Incarnate, we give all our praise,
> to you, Holy Spirit, our life and our breath,
> be glory for ever, through life and through death.[37]

Similarly, David A. Robb probes the divine celestial sphere in this hymn text:

> Praise the living God who sings,
> pulsing through created things,
> harmonizing nature's arts,
> voicing hope in human hearts!
> Alleluia! Alleluia!
> God's eternal anthem rings!
> Alleluia! Alleluia!
> Tell the nations God still sings!
> Celebrate creation's God!
> Magnify redemption's Lord!

34. Kreeft, *Everything You Wanted to Know*, 46.

35. Kreeft, *Everything You Wanted to Know*, 46.

36. Kreeft, *Everything You Wanted to Know*, 46.

37. Davison, "Singer and Song," 145. Of special note here is that God is not only composer and singer, but that the Son of God is "Song Incarnate."

Praise the Spirit's power to bring
understanding as we sing!
Alleluia! Alleluia!
Wake the woodwinds, pipes, and strings!
Alleluia! Alleluia!
Join the anthem, God still sings![38]

The themes of God as composer and Christ as singer—indeed of Christ as the Incarnate Song—are found in many of the early Christian writers. There is nothing esoteric in this, only a salvific interpretation of music: God as music as the ultimate foundation of all heavenly and earthly music. A modern rendering of this theme is found in scripture scholar Eugene LaVerdiere:

> In the beginning was the Song, and the Song was with God, and the Song was God. That Song was life, and everything that came to be came alive with the life of that Song. The Song came into the world and was made flesh. The noise of the world tried to destroy the Song but the noise could not drown it out. The Song of God would always be there.[39]

It is surprising how many great theologians have awakened to the divine feature of even "secular" music: notably Karl Barth, Hans Urs von Balthasar, and Hans Küng. Barth, reflecting on the eschatological character of Mozart's music, "writes" to the composer as follows:

> What I thank you for is simply this: Whenever I listen to you, I am transported to the threshold of a world which in sunlight and storm, by day and by night, is a good and ordered world. Then, as a human being of the twentieth century, I always find myself blessed with courage (not arrogance), with tempo (not an exaggerated tempo), with purity (not a wearisome purity), and with peace (not slothful peace). With an ear open to your musical dialectic, one can be young and become old, can work and rest, be content and sad: in short, one can live.[40]

Balthasar's musical theology is explored by Edward T. Oakes in his book *Patterns of Redemption*. Oakes points to Balthasar's enthusiasm for music, especially that of Mozart. Balthasar's theology, Oakes says, has a strong musical ethos, and it uses musical analogies in the elaboration of his

---

38. Robb, "Praise God Who Sings," 146.

39. LaVerdiere, "Musician," 31–42.

40. Barth, *Mozart*, 22.

thought. Oakes writes: "It would be difficult to exaggerate the importance of music in the construction of Balthasar's theology."[41] The transcendent character of music is similarly found in Hans Küng.[42]

An increasing number of composers are influenced by the notion that music has some connection to the heavenly and the cosmic. Contemporaries for whom music is eschatological and brings us to heaven are Arvo Pärt, Henryk Górecki, and John Tavener. Their music, even when not explicitly religious, is shot through with a transcendent character.[43]

ANGELS AND THE LITURGY

In the liturgy, the songs of the angels and of humankind find their most complete expression. Of course, this worshipful music will reach its fullest form only in the Kingdom of heaven. Cyprian Vagaggini, OSB, in his book *Theological Dimensions of the Liturgy* details the liturgical presence of the angels in the worship of both the Eastern and Western churches. I have already given much attention in this chapter to the *Sanctus*. Vagaggini develops this liturgical feature further when he writes:

> The inclusion of the Sanctus, therefore, is intended to emphasize that the supreme thanksgiving, that supreme praise and blessing which we render to God in the Mass is the best way by which we can associate ourselves here below with the eternal heavenly liturgy of the angelic world, and the moment in which the unity of the angelic world and of the human world finds its highest expression.[44]

Vagaggini goes through the prayers in the ancient traditions, observing that the unity of the angelic world with the human world attained a

41. Oakes, *Patterns of Redemption,* 133.

42. Küng, *Mozart.*

43. For a general analysis of Pärt, Górecki, and Tavener, see Mellers. *Celestial Music?* This work is an excellent analysis of the intersection of music and theology in Western musical history. See also the chapter entitled "Music of the Spheres" in Olsen, *The Turn to Transcendence,* 156–207. On Tavener in particular, see his book, *The Music of Silence.* This book provides insight into Tavener's musical genius (as well as his exceedingly eccentric world view!). The essence of Tavener's musical theology is set forth as follows: "All music already exists. When God created the world, he created everything. It's up to us as artists to find that music." Tavener, *The Music of Silence,* 73. See also, Haydon, *John Tavener.*

44. Vagaggini, *Theological Dimensions,* 353.

most vivid expression.[45] He traces the place of the angels in Baptism, Penance, Matrimony, Holy Orders, the Anointing of the Sick, Funerals, the Liturgy of the Hours, the official blessings, and the liturgical year.[46]

In the pre-Vatican II baptismal rite, Vagaggini notes that there is clear allusion to the angel of Baptism: "We pray to You, O Lord, see fit to send Your holy angel from heaven to protect likewise this Your servant N. and lead him to the grace of Baptism. Through Christ our Lord."[47] Regarding Penance, he quotes the words of Jesus: "There is joy among the angels of God over one sinner who does penance" (Luke 15:20). From this text is derived the patristic concept of "the angel of penance."[48] For the presence of the angels in Matrimony, Vagaggini cites the text of Tertullian which speaks of "the happiness of that marriage . . . which the angels proclaim, and which has the Father's approval."[49] In the rite of the Ordination of bishops in the presence of the Holy Spirit, the approval of the people must be expressed as if they were in the tribunal of God and Christ (Heb 1:14).

Notable in the pre-Vatican II tradition is the extent of the mention of angels in the liturgies for the ill, the dying, and Funerals. References to the angels are found, for example, in the Funeral service. The *Proficiscere,* which finds its way into the post-Vatican liturgy—with some curtailed reference to angels—said at the time of death, is particularly strong and moving:

> Go forth, Christian soul, from this world, in the name of God the
> almighty Father who created you; in the name of Jesus Christ, the
> Son of the living God, who suffered for you; in the name of the
> Holy Spirit, who has been poured forth upon you; in the name
> of the glorious and holy Mother of God, the Virgin Mary; in the
> name of the blessed Joseph, illustrious spouse of that same Virgin;
> in the name of the angels and of the archangels; in the name of the
> thrones and dominations; in the name of the principalities and

45. What is notable is the extent to which the post-Vatican II prayers of the Eucharist and the sacraments have been in great part shorn of references to the angels and archangels. This has architectural and iconic parallels in the way images of angels are often completely missing in modern churches. The familiar principle "out of sight, out of mind" finds ample expression here!

46. Vagaggini, *Theological Dimensions,* 354–60. While Vagaggini focuses mostly on the recent pre-Vatican II liturgy, Daniélou, and Peterson conduct similar commentaries on the ancient liturgy. See Daniélou, *The Angels and their Mission,* 55–67; also Peterson, *Angels and the Liturgy.*

47. Vagaggini, *Theological Dimensions,* 354–61.

48. Vagaggini, *Theological Dimensions,* 356.

49. Vagaggini, *Theological Dimensions,* 356.

power; in the name of the virtues, of the cherubim, and of the seraphim; in the name of the patriarchs and prophets . . . May peace be your dwelling today, and may holy Sion be your habitation.

The sense of the union of the human world with the world of the angels is no less evident in the following Funeral prayers in the pre-Vatican II rite:

> I commend you, dear brother [sister], to almighty God. . . . Then, when your soul goes forth from your body, may the radiant company of angels come to meet you. May the assembly of the apostles, our judges, welcome you.
>
> Come to his [her] aid, O saints of God; come forth to meet him [her], angels of the Lord, receive his [her] soul, and present it to the Most High. May Christ, who has called you now receive you, and may the angels lead you forth to the bosom of Abraham.
>
> May the angels lead you forth to paradise. At your coming may the martyrs welcome you and lead you on into the holy city of Jerusalem. May the choir of angels welcome you, and with Lazarus, who once was poor, may you have eternal rest.[50]

The burial rite speaks of an angel charged with guarding the place of burial:

> O God, by whose mercy the souls of the faithful find rest, see fit to bless this tomb and assign Your holy angel to guard it.[51]

The French theologian Jean (later Cardinal) Daniélou carries on a similar review of the role of the angels in the liturgy. The participation of the angels, he says, extends to the whole liturgical life and especially to the celebration of the Christian feasts.[52] The angels preside at every Christian assembly. When the saints are assembled together, there is "a twofold Church present, that of men and that of angels."[53] Daniélou quotes John Chrysostom, who, he says, develops this idea most expressively:

> The angels are present here. The angels and the martyrs meet today. If you wish to see the angels and the martyrs, open the eyes

---

50. Vagaggini, *Theological Dimensions*, 357. The work, *The Dream of Gerontius* by John Henry Newman, and set to music by Edward Elgar, is an unsurpassed statement of the role of the angels in bringing the souls of the dead to the throne of God and then gently carrying them to purgatory.

51. Vagaggini, *Theological Dimensions*, 335–61.

52. Daniélou, *Angels*, 66.

53. Daniélou, *Angels*, 66.

of faith and look upon this sight. For if the very air is filled with angels, how much more so the Church! And if the Church is filled with angels, how much more is that true today when their Lord has risen into heaven! The whole air about us is filled with angels.[54]

In regard to the resurrection, Daniélou again quotes Chrysostom:

It is not only earth, but heaven as well which has part in today's feast. The Angels exult, the Archangels rejoice, the Cherubim and the Seraphim join us in the celebration of today's feast . . . What room is there for sadness?[55]

I conclude this chapter on the role of the angels in life and in the liturgy by suggesting briefly what liturgical music looks like when viewed as an expression of the heavenly character of sacred music.

IMPLICATIONS FOR SACRED MUSIC

I propose that there are eight characteristics of sacred music, particularly liturgical music.

- Sacred music is sacramental when it manifests the beauty of God. Sacramentality is the presence of the divine among us, something we receive from God, a divine art which grasps the musician and the congregation. Worship music is not primarily self-expressive, a human initiative, or a human work, but the musician's service of God's self-expression. God is in the music.

- Sacred music is eschatological in that it pulls us toward heaven. It lifts us out of everyday life and raises our hearts, souls, and spirits—ourselves—to union with the world of angels and saints.

- Sacred music is cosmic. Angels are the guardians of the vast space of the universe. According to cosmic vision, in the Kingdom of heaven the world of humankind, materiality, corporality, history, and inspired human achievement are drawn up into praise of God. Salvation embraces not only the individual person, or a particular community, but all that God has made.

---

54. John Chrysostom, "Sermon on the Ascension," translation from Daniélou, *Angels*, 66–67.

55. John Chrysostom, "Sermon on the Resurrection," translation from Daniélou, *Angels*, 67.

- Sacred music is evocative of the great space of the universe, not the small space of the inner self. Sacred music is "music for a great space" (to borrow a phrase from the composer Richard Proulx); it must not be music of the impoverished acoustical ambience of a typical modern church but the "acoustics" of the whole cosmos. This is possible even in a small church with good musical acoustic.

- Sacred music is doxological. It is often said that since Vatican II Catholic liturgy lacks beauty, majesty, and splendor. Liturgy easily becomes trivial, commonplace, without exuberance, pale, lifeless, and uninspiring. An absence of depth and significance often appears to characterize liturgy and its music today. Music that is doxological must reverse these characteristics and once again become beautiful and magnificent.

- A renewal of the glorious in music as well as in the word (including homilies), art, architecture, ministerial artistry, is required to renew the sense of the glorious. For this reason, liturgy must be solemn and profound, serene and weighty, and festive. The earthly liturgy must take on the superabundance of the festival of the heavenly city.

- Sacred music must be able to comprehend, articulate, and celebrate the breadth, length, height, and depth of human reality. It expresses the whole range of the thought, experience, and feelings of Christian believers. It moves away from the narrow expressive range that characterizes much Catholic liturgical music today.

- It is important that in the Church's liturgical repertoire there is music for funerals that differs markedly from music for weddings or for Holy Week. Our modern worship and its music is not deep or wide enough to equip people to face human tragedy and shoulder the Cross.

CONCLUSION

Music is a fundamental feature of human life, something that has its foundation in God. In great music, God and humanity are caught up in an eternal love-song. Angels are the original ministers of music in the whole process of bringing heavenly music to earth and earthly music to heaven. This is a dialogue that has gone on since creation, and it will only be complete in the Kingdom of heaven.

Music that comes from heaven edifies, transforms, and beautifies the human world—and then returns to heaven to give glory to God. All good music raises the soul to heaven and glorifies God. This is true not only of liturgical music but also of all music that has a sacred and transcendent character.

In heaven we shall sing eternally with the angels, as all together redeemed humanity and creation give praise to God. Even now in the liturgy of the Church, we are surrounded by the choirs of angels.

Chapter Six

MODEL SIX:
TENDING THE NEW CREATION

The world is charged with the grandeur of God.
—Gerard Manley Hopkins[1]

HEAVEN IS A GARDEN-CITY, meaning a city which is consciously designed
to integrate city and country, culture and nature. The notion of the garden-
city was first proposed at the end of the nineteenth century by Sir Ebenezer
Howard in Great Britain.[2] Howard called for urban renewal in which
people lived in harmony with nature. He believed that the overwhelming
deterioration of cities was one of the most troublesome issues of the time,
and that the creation of garden-cities could begin to provide a solution.

Heaven may be regarded as the perfect garden-city, in which human
culture and physical nature, city and country, are perfectly integrated.
However, for the purposes of this chapter, garden and city will be separately
examined. This strategy has been followed by Oxford University theologian
Alister E. McGrath in his book *A Brief History of Heaven*.[3] Like McGrath,
I recognize that garden (New Creation) and city (Holy City) belong inti-
mately together and each finally blends into the other. Thus, chapter six
is named "Tending the New Creation," and chapter seven will be titled
"Dwelling in the Holy City."

What follows in this chapter is a brief review of the creation narratives
in Genesis which set forth creation history, and the hope of Israel for a

1. Hopkins, "God's Grandeur," 27.

2. Howard, *To-morrow*, 1898.

3. McGrath, *Brief History*, 1–69.

renewed creation. This matter is expressed also in the writings of Isaiah, St. Paul, and the Book of Revelation. I will look at the ecological question which has to be considered in any discussion of creation; and finally I propose a meaning to the expression "tending" the new creation.

CREATION, EDEN, FALL

Genesis 1:1–31 narrates the beginning of creation. First came light, then day and darkness; next came water, followed by a dome, and the separation of the waters above the dome from the waters below; from this came the sky; and after that the dry land and the sea; then came forth vegetation and every kind of fruit-bearing plant. God then called forth day and night, the seasons and the years. Then God created living creatures in the waters and birds in the air, great sea monsters, and living creatures with which the waters teem, and all kinds of birds. Next came every sort of living creature, animals both tame and wild. Finally, God made human beings in his own image, giving them dominion over all the animals he had created, and ordering Adam and Eve to be fertile and multiply, to fill the earth and subdue it. They were to have dominion over the fish, the birds, and all created things, over green plants grown for food. God gave them every seed-bearing plant and every tree that has seed-bearing fruit. God looked at all he had created and found it "very good" (Gen 1:31). On the seventh day, God had completed his work and rested.

The process of God's creation is narrated differently in Genesis 2:4–3:24. We read that when the Lord God made the earth there were neither fish nor grass—and no rain. Then God formed Adam out of the dust of the earth and placed him in the Garden of Eden. Out of the ground the Lord made trees that were delightful to look at and good for food, with the "tree of life" in the middle of the garden and the "tree of knowledge of good and evil" there, too. The Lord took the man and settled him in the Garden of Eden to cultivate and care for it, telling him that he could eat from any of the trees, except from the tree of knowledge of good and evil, warning him that if he should eat from that tree he would die. The Lord then said it is not good for man to be alone; thus came forth Eve.

These narratives provide the elements of a creation theology: God created all that is, he did so in an orderly fashion, and he found it to his satisfaction. He created man and woman to have dominion over the earth, and of all the animals he had created. Thus, the earth, the first man and woman, and animals were created from the dust of the earth, which the human person was to "cultivate," "dominate," and "subdue."[4]

We are familiar with the story of the Fall in Genesis. The serpent, symbol of evil and cunning, convinced the woman to eat of the tree of knowledge, and so she did, and gave the fruit to her husband. God then said to the serpent:

> Because you have done this,
> cursed are you
> among all the animals, tame or wild;
> On your belly you shall crawl,
> and dust you shall eat
> all the days of your life.
> I will put enmity between you and the woman
> and between your offspring and hers;
> They will strike at your head,
> while you strike at their heel.
> To the woman God said:
> I will intensify your toil in childbearing;
> in pain you shall bring forth children.
> Yet your urge shall be for your husband,
> and he shall rule over you. (Gen 3:16)
> To the man [God] said:
> Because you listened to your wife and ate from the tree about
> which I commanded you, You shall not eat from it,
> Cursed is the ground because of you!
> In toil you shall eat its yield
> all the days of your life.
> Thorns and thistles it shall bear for you,
> and you shall eat the grass of the field.
> By the sweat of your brow
> you shall eat bread,
> Until you return to the ground,
> from which you were taken;
> For you are dust, and to dust you shall return. (Gen 3:14–19)

Then we read:

> The Lord God therefore banished him from the garden of Eden,
> to till the ground from which he had been taken. He expelled the

---

4. The word "dominate" is generally taken to mean despoiling or abusing. But the word comes from the Latin verb *dominare*, which relates to the noun *dominus*, Lord. The kind of domination God exercises is a domination that protects, advances, and flourishes. This is the kind of domination humankind is called to exercise.

man, stationing the cherubim and the fiery revolving sword east
of the garden of Eden, to guard the way to the tree of life. (Gen
3:22–24)

God, who created the world with all its animals and growing things,
now cursed the earth due to the sin of Adam and Eve. Some interpretations
offer a more subtle view of the curse: it is not that God cursed the earth,
but that he cursed the relationship between humankind and the earth. Or
perhaps Adam and Eve themselves cursed their relationship to the earth?

The fall from grace of the first couple was accompanied by a fall of
the whole created order. Nature, ordered in beauty and harmony, began to
unravel—a process that will continue until the renewal of the natural order
in the New Creation.

The fundamental point of interest here is that nature was not merely
the background to the history of creation, but an integral part of it. When
humankind sinned, human enterprise became toil, and every child born
became a burden. The serpent (and all animals) became cursed; humankind and the snake became enemies; the wife became subject to her husband; and work became slavery. Finally, the first couple was expelled from
Eden into a hostile world.

VISIONS OF RENEWAL

The history of Israel may be seen first as oscillating between enmity and
friendship between God and humankind; and second as the unraveling
and restoration of creation, and the emergence of humanity into times of
redemption and restoration; and third work becoming toil and labor, yet
not without periods of creativity.

There are many narratives that set forth a vision of how the Fall will
be reversed, perhaps now, perhaps soon, or perhaps at the end of history.
These appear and reappear across the Old Testament. Hosea, writing in the
eighth century BC, prefigures a transformation of humanity and the whole
created order:

> I will make a covenant for them on that day,
> with the wild animals,
> With the birds of the air,
> And with the things that crawl on the ground.
> Bow and sword and warfare
> I will destroy from the land.
> And I will give them rest in safety.

I will betroth you to me forever:
I will betroth you to me with
justice and with judgment,
with loyalty and with compassion. (Hos 2:20–21)

A similar theme is found in the writings of Joel:

On that day
the mountains will drip new wine,
and the hills flow with milk,
All the streams of Judah
will flow with water.
A spring will rise from the house of the Lord,
watering the valley of Shittim. (Joel 4:18)

The prophet Micah writes similarly:

He shall judge between many peoples
and set terms for strong and distant nations;
They shall beat their swords into plowshares,
and their spears into pruning hooks;
One nation shall not raise the sword against another,
nor shall they train for war again.
They shall all sit under their own vines,
Under their own fig trees, undisturbed.
for the Lord of hosts has spoken.
Though all the peoples walk,
each in the name of its god,
We will walk in the name of the Lord,
our God, forever and ever. (Mic 4:3–5)

The most expressive statements of the biblical vision of the future
are found in Isaiah. There a number of themes intertwine: peace between
animals and humanity; wilderness becoming straight highways; rivers being opened up; and dry ground gushing forth springs of water. The earth
will rejoice and give glory to God, and God will restore barren places and
parched lands, and transform the desert into a verdant place:

The wilderness and the parched land will exult;
the Arabah will rejoice and bloom;
Like the crocus it shall bloom abundantly,
and rejoice with joyful song.
The glory of Lebanon will be given to it,
the splendor of Carmel and Sharon;
They will see the glory of the Lord,
the splendor of our God. (Isa 35:1–2)

Isaiah 35 takes up the same theme:

> For waters will burst forth in the wilderness,
> and streams in the Arabah.
> The burning sands will become pools,
> and the thirsty ground, springs of water;
> The abode where jackals crouch
> will be a marsh for the reed and papyrus. (6–7)

Again the theme of taming the desert and the rugged places being made plain appears in Isaiah:

> A voice proclaims:
> In the wilderness prepare the way of the Lord!
> Make straight in the wasteland a highway for our God!
> Every valley shall be lifted up,
> every mountain and hill made low;
> The rugged land shall be a plain,
> the rough country, a broad valley. (40:3–4)

Isaiah continues:

> The afflicted and the needy seek water in vain,
> their tongues are parched with thirst.
> I, the Lord, will answer them;
> I, the God of Israel, will not forsake them.
> I will open up rivers on the bare heights,
> and fountains in the broad valleys. (Isa 41:17–18)

One of the strongest statements in Isaiah has to do with divine healing, part of the process by which creation is restored:

> Strengthen hands that are feeble,
> make firm knees that are weak,
> Say to the fearful of heart:
> Be strong, do not fear!
> Here is your God,
> he comes with vindication;
> With divine recompense
> he comes to save you.
> Then the eyes of the blind shall see,
> and the ears of the deaf be opened;
> Then the lame shall leap like a stag,
> and the mute tongue sing for joy. (Isa 35:3–6)

Clearly these visions materialized in neither the Old Testament nor the New Testament periods (though they were inaugurated in the ministry of Jesus), which raises the question of how they are to be interpreted today. The fact that many of these passages are read in the Advent lectionaries of the Catholic and some other liturgical Churches clearly indicates that the ultimate reference is to the future.

THE NEW TESTAMENT AND DEEP INCARNATION

While Old Testament hopes for a new creation are ample, we find a different description of the holiness of creation in the public life of Jesus. Jesus, we are told, was baptized in water. In his first public miracle, he turns water into wine, signifying the wine of the Kingdom to come. Jesus draws an abundance of bread and meat from a few loaves and fishes, prefiguring again what is to come in the Kingdom. His agony took place in the garden of Gethsemane; he was entombed in a garden; and Mary Magdalene, when she saw him, thought he was a gardener, a man concerned only about the earth.

The strongest New Testament statement regarding the eschatological character of creation are found in Romans 8. Paul writes:

> I consider that the sufferings of this present time are as nothing compared with the glory to be revealed for us. For creation awaits with eager expectation the revelation of the children of God; for creation was made subject to futility, not of its own accord but because of the one who subjected it, in hope that creation itself would be set free from slavery to corruption and share in the glorious freedom of the children of God. We know that all creation is groaning in labor pains even until now; and not only that, but we ourselves, who have the first fruits of the Spirit, we also groan within ourselves as we wait for adoption, the redemption of our bodies. (Rom 8:18–23)

As creation is groaning in labor pains—an image from childbirth—so also is humanity groaning for restoration. The Spirit impels humankind and creation beyond themselves. Everything remains incomplete until the Kingdom is finally and completely established.

Christ relates to creation by the fact that he became incarnate in human flesh, as a consequence of which he took on the dust of the earth from which Adam and Eve were made—dust representing the basis of the natural world. Some recent theologians refer to this as "deep incarnation," a term introduced in the 1990s by the Danish Lutheran theologian Niels Henrik Gregersen.[5] For Gregersen, the incarnation of God in Christ can be understood as a "radical" or "deep" incarnation that goes beyond the human to the material, an incarnation by which Christ assumes physical matter into himself.[6] Incarnation makes the Incarnate One integrally part not only of the human race, but also of earthly reality—not only animals (with whom Jesus in his humanity shared genetic identity) but also plants and inanimate nature.

While the notion of "deep incarnation" has its critics—mostly of its pantheistic tendencies (that God is collapsed into creation), a statement of Pope John Paul II verifies the fundamental truth of this notion in his encyclical On the Holy Spirit in the Life of the Church and the World (*Dominum et Vivificantem*) of May 1986. The Pope writes:

> The Incarnation of God the Son signifies the taking up into unity with God not only of human nature, but in *this human nature, in a sense, of everything that is "flesh"*: the whole of humanity, the entire visible and material world. The Incarnation, then, also has a cosmic significance, a cosmic dimension. The "first-born of all creation," becoming incarnate in the individual humanity of Christ, unites himself in some way with the entire reality of man, which is also "flesh"—and in this reality with all "flesh," with the whole of creation.[7]

The New Testament Letter to the Colossians speaks of the way in which creation is formed in and through Christ and finds its identify in him:

> He is the image of the invisible God,
> the firstborn of all creation.
> For in him were created all things in heaven and on earth,
> the visible and the invisible,
> whether thrones or dominions or principalities or powers;
> all things were created through him and for him.
> He is before all things,
> and in him all things hold together.
> He is the head of the body, the church.
> He is the beginning, the firstborn from the dead,
> that in all things he himself might be preeminent.

5. Gregersen, "The Cross," 192–207.

6. Gregersen, *Incarnation*.

7. John Paul II, On the Holy Spirit in the Life of the Church and the World, no. 50, 96.

For in him all the fullness was pleased to dwell,
and through him to reconcile all things for him,
making peace by the blood of his cross
[through him], whether those on earth
or those in heaven. (Col 1:15–20)

Australian theologian Denis Edwards puts this matter expressively when he writes that redemption through incarnation is a theory of redemption cast in the most universal terms:[8] "God is with every sparrow, every beetle, every Great White shark, every creature hunting another for food and every creature that is the prey of another."[9] Animals, he writes, will reach their redemptive fulfillment in being taken up into the life of the Trinity. "This kind of incarnational theology provides the basis for seeing kangaroos and chimpanzees, kookaburras and dolphins as participating in redemption in Christ."[10]

ANIMALS IN HEAVEN

A question often asked is whether or not there will be animals in heaven. Isaiah intimates that there will be. The presence of animals in heaven finds its basis in Isaiah 11.

Then the wolf shall be a guest of the lamb,
and the leopard shall lie down with the young goat;
The calf and the young lion shall browse together,
with a little child to guide them.
The cow and the bear shall graze,
together their young shall lie down;
the lion shall eat hay like the ox.
The baby shall play by the viper's den,
and the child lay his hand on the adder's lair.
They shall not harm or destroy on all my holy mountain;
for the earth shall be filled with knowledge of the Lord,
as water covers the sea. (Isa 11:6–9)

It may be reasonably deduced that the presence of animals in the process of salvation will continue into the life of eternity, and that God will not destroy anything that he has made. The Catholic *Book of Blessings* contains

8. Edwards, "Redemption of Animals," 91.
9. Edwards, "Redemption of Animals," 95.
10. Edwards, "Redemption of Animals," 82.

an Order for the Blessing of Animals which implies the presence of animals in the process of salvation:

> The animals of God's creation inhabit the skies, the earth, and the sea. They share in the fortunes of human existence and have a part in human life. God, who confers his gifts on all living things, has often used the service of animals or made them symbolic remind-ers of the gifts of salvation. Animals were saved from the flood and afterwards made a part of the covenant with Noah (Genesis 9:9–10). The paschal lamb brings to mind the Passover sacrifice and the deliverance from the bondage of Egypt (Exod 12:3–14); a giant fish saved Jonah (Jon 2: 1–11); ravens brought bread to Elijah (1Kgs 17:6); animals were included in the repentance enjoined on humans (Jon 3:7). And animals share in Christ's redemption of all of God's creation. We therefore invoke the divine blessing on these animals (through the intercession of Saint N.). As we do so, let us praise the Creator and thank him for setting us over other creatures of the earth. Let us also ask him that, remembering our human dignity, we may walk always in his law.[11]

It is clear, then, that the whole creation, including animals, has an eternal value. Typically, we take for granted the resurrection of human be-ings, but what is neglected is the redemption of animals, along with the material world of water, forests, and mountains. There is a parallel between the eschatological future of humankind and the future of creation. What occurred to Christ in his resurrection will occur in all creation at the end of time. Creation will have its final Easter day.

THE BOOK OF REVELATION

The paradisal symbolism of the Book of Revelation brings the New Testa-ment to a close. At the center of the symbolism are the four living creatures expressed in natural terms: a lion, a calf, a human face, and an eagle.

The Old Testament groaning for health and the healing of nature is expressed in Revelation: The promise is that hunger and thirst will be no more:

---

11. *Book of Blessings*, 248–49. On the matter of animals in heaven, see Lewis, *Problem of Pain*, 166–67; Kreeft, *Everything You Ever Wanted to Know*, 45–46. More generally, see Deane-Drummond and Clough, *Creaturely Theology*.

They will not hunger or thirst anymore,
nor will the sun or any heat strike them.
For the Lamb who is in the center of the throne will shepherd them
and lead them to springs of life-giving water,
and God will wipe away every
tear from their eyes. (Rev 7:16–17)

The theme of the garden-city is implicit in Revelation 22:

Then the angel showed me the river of life-giving water, sparkling
like crystal, flowing from the throne of God and of the Lamb down
the middle of its street. On either side of the river grew the tree
of life that produces fruit twelve times a year, once each month;
the leaves of the trees serve as medicine for the nations. Nothing
accursed will be found there anymore. (Rev 22:1–3)

Two significant natural symbols in the Book of Revelation are the River
of Life and the Tree of Life. Water is a basic element of human sustenance.
The source of the powerful stream is the throne of God, upon which sits the
Lamb. The great river reflects the Lamb's "thirst-quenching, need-satisfying
nature."[12] Randy Alcorn says of the river that flows down the city's main
street: "Likely it has countless tributaries flowing throughout the rest of the
city."[13] Water is important because the city is a center of human life, and
water is an essential element of life. The people who lived with drought and
thirst in an arid climate readily grasped the wonder of constantly available
fresh water, pure and uncontaminated, able to satisfy the deepest thirst. The
great river reflects the overcoming of human thirst. The fact that the water
is flowing down from the King's throne suggests the throne's high elevation.
One need only follow the street—or the river—up to its source to arrive at
the city's centerpiece: the Lamb's throne.[14]

Then there is the Tree of Life. Commentator William Hendriksen suggests that the term "Tree of Life" is a collective, just like "avenue" and "river."
The idea is not that there is a single tree. There is, he says, an entire park,
whole rows of trees alongside the river. And this is also true with respect to
all the avenues of the Holy City. The city is full of rivers of life and is also
full of parks containing trees of life. These trees, moreover, are full of fruit.[15]

12. Alcorn, *Heaven*, 256.

13. Alcorn, *Heaven*, 256.

14. Alcorn, *Heaven*, 256.

15. Hendricksen, *More Than Conquerors*, 249.

This broader view of the Tree of Life, according to Hendriksen, would account for the fact that trees grow on both banks of a great river at once and yields twelve different kinds of fruit, including healing leaves. Since humankind will not experience pain or disease in heaven, the point of the healing leaves is not clear. Hendricksen says that perhaps they will have life-sustaining or life-enhancing properties that will enable unending health and energy. Physical life, health and healing derive from partaking of God's gracious provision of the fruit and leaves of the Tree of Life. Hence, our well-being is not granted once for all, but will be forever sustained and renewed as we depend on God and draw from his provision.[16]

One of the quandaries for readers of the Book of Revelation is the narration of the destruction of creation at the end of time. It is often assumed that creation has little place and is even destroyed in the accounts in Revelation. Micah D. Kiehl states that contrary to the majority opinion, the Book of Revelation is not detrimental to environmental concerns. On the contrary it offers a rich environmental point of view, if properly understood.[17] Certainly, there seems to be much destruction of the natural in Revelation. Kiehl states, "In a text like the book of Revelation, the ecosphere seems to be left smoldering, degraded, or completely destroyed."[18] But if Revelation is read not as history in the modern sense, the narratives of destruction have to be placed against the statements of God's creative power. John does not envision a destruction of the "old" world, but the destruction of all that is evil. There will be "renewal" and "transformation."[19] God does not intend to destroy the natural world, but to preserve it. Continuity between the present and the future is guaranteed.

Kiehl states that the apocalyptic destruction signifies the destruction not of the sea itself, but of the imperial power of Rome over the sea, since the sea was the key to Roman political might. If Rome lost the seas, it lost power. Since the ocean has a major part of Rome's conquering of the lands around the Mediterranean, its imperial power collapsed when the sea was "destroyed."

16. Hendricksen, *More Than Conquerors*, 258.
17. Kiehl, *Apocalyptic Ecology*, xxi.
18. Kiehl, *Apocalyptic Ecology*, 1.
19. Kiehl, *Apocalyptic Ecology*, 203.

PRAISE AND CREATION

In Chapter 8, "Feasting in the Kingdom," I will deal with creation from a different perspective. For now, I will point to some important expressions of the worshipful relationship between God and creation. In the Old Testament, the principal source of praise literature is the psalms. Psalm 148 is a good example:

I

Praise the Lord from the heavens;
praise him in the heights.
Praise him, all you his angels;
give praise, all you his hosts.
Praise him, sun and moon;
praise him, all shining stars.
Praise him, highest heavens,
you waters above the heavens.
Let them all praise the Lord's name;
for he commanded and they were created,
Assigned them their station forever,
set an order that will never change.

II

Praise the Lord from the earth,
you sea monsters and all the deeps of the sea;
Lightning and hail, snow and thick clouds,
storm wind that fulfills his command;
Mountains and all hills,
fruit trees and all cedars;
Animals wild and tame,
creatures that crawl and birds that fly;
Kings of the earth and all peoples,
princes and all who govern on earth;
Young men and women too,
old and young alike.
Let them all praise the Lord's name,
For his name alone is exalted,
His majesty above earth and heaven.
He has lifted high the horn of his people;

to the praise of all his faithful,
the Israelites, the people near to him.
Hallelujah!

Psalm 104 states the manner in which God uses creation in his work of salvation:

I

Bless the Lord, my soul!
Lord, my God, you are great indeed!
You are clothed with majesty and splendor,
robed in light as with a cloak.
You spread out the heavens like a tent;
setting the beams of your chambers upon the waters.
You make the clouds your chariot;
traveling on the wings of the wind.
You make the winds your messengers;
flaming fire, your ministers.

II

You fixed the earth on its foundation,
so it can never be shaken.
The deeps covered it like a garment;
above the mountains stood the waters.
At your rebuke they took flight;
at the sound of your thunder they fled.
They rushed up the mountains, down the valleys
to the place you had fixed for them.
You set a limit they cannot pass;
never again will they cover the earth.

Perhaps the best-celebrated expression of the manner in which creation praises God is found centuries later in Francis of Assisi's "Canticle of the Sun."

Most High, all powerful, all good, Lord!
All praise is yours, all glory, all honor
And all blessing.
To you alone, Most High, do they belong.
No mortal lips are worthy

To pronounce your name.
All praise be yours, my Lord, through all that you have made,
And first my lord Brother Sun
Who brings the day; and the light you give to us through him.
How beautiful is he, how radiant in all his splendor!
Of you, Most High, he bears the likeness.
All praise be yours, my Lord, through Sister Moon and Stars.
In the heavens you have made them,
Bright and precious and fair.
All praise be yours, my Lord, through Brothers Wind and Air,
And fair and stormy, all the weather's moods,
By which you cherish all that you have made.
All praise be yours, my Lord, through Sister Water,
So useful, lowly, precious and pure.
All praise be yours, my Lord, through Brother Fire,
Through whom you brighten up the night.
How beautiful is he, how gay! Full of power and strength.
All praise be yours, my Lord, through Sister Earth, our mother,
Who feeds us in her sovereignty and produces
Various fruits with colored flowers and herbs.[20]

ESCHATOLOGICAL ECOLOGY

What follows here may not seem to be immediately relevant to eschatology, but I propose that it is. The redemption of the earth and the salvation of the created order require what I would call an "ecological eschatology."

One cannot deal adequately with the place of nature in the story of creation—right up to the present—without adverting to the situation today in which nature is in crisis. This is the area of ecology. Without a critical ecological perspective the treatment of creation will be overly romantic. Ecological theology provides an agenda for humankind advancing toward heaven; it sets out a statement of how humankind works in the making of the New Creation.

Concern for the environment is a relatively recent phenomenon; it had its remote origin in the industrial revolution that began in England in the seventeenth century. William Blake implicitly adverted to the growing problem when in his poem "Jerusalem" he decried the advent of the "dark Satanic mills" which spewed smoke into the atmosphere and served

20. Francis of Assisi, "Canticle of Brother Sun," 81.

to turn farmers into factory workers daily confronted with slavish, un-
healthy working conditions and long hours. The Romantic poets and writers—those who saw nature in almost religious terms—were, one might say,
the first environmentalists. Prominent are William Wordsworth and such
followers as John Muir.

The concern over the degradation of the environment became more
intense in the middle of the twentieth century with the Green movement
and the multiple other movements that have since then expanded into a
plethora of political, cultural, and educational activities.

The environmental movement began with the conviction that religion
(in the West more than in the East) had provided the protocol for the despoiling of nature. The Christian socialist Lynn White's much-quoted essay
published in 1967 titled "The Historic Roots of Our Ecological Crisis" is
an example.[21] White squarely blames the opening chapters of Genesis for
the fact that God gave Adam the commission to "subdue" the earth and to
have "dominion" over it. White's view continues to be promoted in many
quarters today, but is challenged by other commentators, not least on the
grounds that non-Christian areas of the world have their own disastrous
problems in this area. (One thinks of China, for instance, which has the
worse industrial pollution in the world).

One of the more reasonable assertions about the relationship between
religion and nature is that when Western theology developed spiritually at
the beginning of the second millennium, it focused more on the spiritual
at the expense of the corporeal. It incorporated the language of despising
the world and escaping from it. This trend was found in the Modern Devo-
tion (*devotio moderna*) of the fourteenth century and was compounded by
the Protestant Reformation, particularly by John Calvin, who advocated
getting away from the world by seeking the otherworldly. The "world" was
thought to be evil, and the human person was called to focus on the spiritual rather than the material.

In our own time, however, religion has begun to take a lead in environmental matters. Numerous Christian (Catholic, Orthodox, Protestant)
and non-Christian (Judaism, Islam, Buddhism) leaders and organizations
have been working for some time to offer analyses and solutions to the
ecological problems.[22]

---

21. White, "Historical Roots," 1203–7.

22. The most comprehensive treatment of this topic is provided in *The Oxford Handbook of Religion and Ecology*, ed., Gottlieb. The *Handbook* deals with ecological concerns

Within Catholicism there have been numerous initiatives taken at the regional, national, and international levels. Catholic theologians have been writing on the matter for decades.[23] Catholic concern for the environment has its remote origins in Pope Leo XIII's landmark encyclical published in 1891 On the Condition of Labor (*Rerum Novarum*), considered the first social encyclical. While ecology is not dealt with directly, the encyclical laid the ground by its concern for labor, the health conditions of workers, and a just wage. Vatican Council II did not discuss environmental issues directly, but reflected the concerns of Leo XIII's encyclical. The Council did touch on the matter briefly in its document The Church in the Modern World (*Gaudium et Spes*).

Starting with John Paul II, the environment began to receive greater prominence in official Catholic thought. The Pope dealt with the matter when he wrote, "Christians, in particular, realize that their responsibility with creation and their duty toward nature and the creator are an essential part of their faith."[24] The areas of concern for the Pope were the following: the greenhouse effect and climate change; alternative and nuclear energies; deforestation, desertification, and reforestation; oceans, marine life, and sea creatures; scarcity of clean, fresh water; poverty, which is the "worst pollution"; oppression and exclusion of women and others; population growth, limited resources; and responsible parenthood; farming and conservation; indigenous peoples; environmental racism; loss of biodiversity; endangered species and their interdependence; chemical and industrial pollution; war and peace.[25]

In June, 2002, Pope John Paul II and Ecumenical Patriarch Bartholomew (spiritual head of Orthodoxy worldwide) issued a common

---

in Catholic, Orthodox, Protestant, and non-Christian religions. See also Bouma-Prediger, *For the Beauty of the Earth*; Wirzba, *From Nature to Creation*; D. Moo and J. Moo., *Creation Care*; Fergusson, *Creation*; Granberg-Michaelson, ed., *Tending the Earth*; Deane-Drummond, *A Primer in Ecotheology*; Huntzinger, *The Trees will Clap Their Hands*.

23. For a broad survey, see Hart, *What Are They Saying About Environmental Theology?*; Winright, ed., *Green Discipleship*; Cloutier, *Walking God's Earth*; Fragomeni and Pawlikowski, eds., *The Ecological Challenge*; Cummings, *Eco-Spirituality*; Bergant, *The Earth is the Lord's*.

24. John Paul II, *Ecological Crisis*, no. 30. The list of John Paul II's writings and speeches on ecology are quite extensive; see 351–55 of the book just mentioned.

25. This list is adapted from Lorbiecki, written and compiled, *Following St. Francis*, 10–11.

declaration on the environment.[26] The result is that this subject has emerged as a major topic in ecumenical relations.

Pope Benedict XVI also addressed the issue extensively starting with his homily at his inaugural Mass on April 24, 2005. Benedict emphasized moral (i.e., human) ecology as a complement to natural ecology, and he saw the former as an intrinsic factor in looking at the ecology question in general. For him the moral sense of society must be brought into any discussion of ecology. Benedict wrote and spoke often on the subject, thus was christened the "Green Pope" by the media.[27]

Pope Francis's Encyclical On Care for Our Common Home (*Laudato Sí'*) is probably the most celebrated contribution on ecological matters by a Church leader—and it has the status of an "encyclical," the most authoritative kind of papal document.

Pope Francis himself took his name from St. Francis of Assisi in order to emphasize the simple lifestyle he intended to assume, but more centrally to seek inspiration for dealing with the environmental crisis that he thought a major threat to humankind. For this, he, too, was christened the "Green Pope."

Francis, following the Saint of Assisi, calls the earth our "common home," similar to our own sister and mother. He states that we are damaging this familial relationship when we harm the environment, as we are damaging our relationship with fellow men and women, especially the poor as well as future generations. We are neglecting our connectedness with the earth and with those who depend on our good stewardship of the gift of creation.

In *Laudato Sí'* Pope Francis presents six principles regarding the environment, all of which can be read eschatologically and in relation to the future of the earth and its heavenly end.

- "What is Happening to our Common Home?" elaborates the various symptoms of environmental destruction, especially climate change, considered alongside the depletion of fresh water and loss of biodiversity. While there is no substantial discussion of the science of global warming, Francis points to the overwhelming consensus among scientists concerning the negative impact of carbon-intensive economies on the natural world and on human life. Caring for ecosystems

26. Lorbiecki, *Following St. Francis*, 100–101; 364–66.
27. Pope Benedict XVI, *Garden of God*

demands farsightedness, since no one looking for quick and easy financial profit is truly interested in ecological preservation.

- In the treatment of "The Gospel of Creation," he considers the world the way God intended it to be. It surveys the rich scriptural traditions to show that there is no biblical justification for a lack of concern for other creatures.

- "The Human Roots of the Ecological Crisis" examines the more "technocratic" viewpoint and an exclusive focus on the human that sees nature as devoid of any spiritual or transcendent values.

- In "Integral Ecology," the encyclical seeks to recapture awareness of the interconnectedness of all aspects of creation. To do so, it is essential to appreciate the impact of environmental degradation on "cultural ecology," meaning those ways of life bound up with the environment.[28]

- "Lines of Approach and Action" sets out the various international collective actions needed. It highlights the critical necessity of switching away from fossil fuels to renewable energy sources and identifies the need for international agreements and legislation not only in relation to climate change but also to animals and natural life in the oceans.

- "Ecological Education and Spirituality" draws attention to the individual believer, as well as families and communities. Consumer choices, the cultivation of ecological virtues such as reducing wastefulness, and the environmental education of the young are part of the practical steps leading to a deeper, spiritual ecological conversion through which the follower of Christ recognizes the true worth of all created entities. The statement "God created the world means . . . that human beings have no right to ignore."

I already mentioned Orthodox Patriarch Bartholomew, who is today probably more involved in environmental issues than any other Church leader East or West—and is also often referred to as the "green" Patriarch. Bartholomew's attention to the environment makes him not only an important figure within Christianity, but also a world leader in the area of ecology.[29]

---

28. Pope Francis, *Laudato Si'*, no. 17.

29. For a general introduction to Orthodox ecology, see Chryssavgis and Foltz, eds., *Toward an Ecology of Transfiguration*. See also Theokritoff, *Living in God's Creation*.

This section of the chapter on the environment and ecology may seem extraneous to a theology of the New Creation. I argue that we cannot treat the New Creation without looking at ecological and environmental matters. A theology of creation must inevitably be an eschatological theology. The present creation will be part of the New Creation, and human stewardship of creation now is a preparation for the world to come. Heaven will include the physical order of creation redeemed; and human work now toward the preservation of the earth is an essential part of eschatological vision.

CONCLUSION

The divine mandate to our first parents to tend the earth and to share in God's dominion over it is as valid today as it ever was, and will continue into the Kingdom of heaven. In heaven, the saints (and all men and women of goodwill) will tend, till, and protect animals, waters, plants, food, fields, and all the elements of creation. Grass, flowers and trees will grow; animals will play (and not serve consumer needs). Fruit and vegetables of all kind will flourish. There will be no abusing, controlling, or "dominating" in the secular sense. In the New Creation all human despoiling of nature, and nature's own antagonism toward humankind will have passed away. God will once again look at his creation and find it "very good."

Chapter Seven

MODEL SEVEN:
DWELLING IN THE HOLY CITY

A city is not gauged by its length and width, but by the broadness of its vision and the height of its dreams
—Herb Caen and Dong Kingman.[1]

IN CHAPTER SIX, I began by referring to heaven as a garden-city. I proposed that, for the sake of analysis, heaven may be examined separately as a garden and as a city, though in the end both coalesce. Chapter 6 examined natural creation symbolized by the garden. Chapter 7 will examine the city as another symbolic model of heaven. I will proceed by looking at four themes: two patristic cities; the city in the scriptures; three cities that represent humanity reaching for the heavenly city; and the liturgical shape of the traditional Christian city. The aim of this chapter is to propose that those who have died will dwell in the holy city.

TWO CITIES

The theme of the two cities has long been a favorite of Christian authors. Caesarius of Arles wrote as follows:

> There are two cities, dearest brethren. The first is the city of this world, the second, the city of paradise. The good Christian is always journeying in the city of the world, but he is recognized as a citizen of the city of paradise. The first city is full of labor, the second, is restful; the first is full of misery, the second, blessed; in

1. Caen and Kingman, *San Francisco*, 1.

the first there is labor, in the second repose; if a man lives sinfully in the first he cannot arrive in the second. We must be pilgrims in this world in order to merit to be citizens of heaven. If one wants to love this world and remain a citizen of it, he has no place in heaven, for we prove our pilgrim status by our longing for our true country. Let no one deceive himself, beloved brethren; the true country of Christians is in heaven, not here. The city of Christians, their blessed state, their true, eternal happiness is not here. The one who searches for happiness in this world will not find it in heaven. Our true fatherland is paradise, our city of Jerusalem is the heavenly one.[2]

St. Augustine, writing in the fifth century AD, contrasted the two cities: the heavenly and the earthly. At the end of his famed book *City of God,* he writes of how the earthly city and the heavenly City are intermingled from the beginning to the end of history.

One of them, the earthly city, has created for herself such false gods as she wanted, from any source she chose—even creating them out of men—in order to worship them with sacrifices. The other city, the Heavenly City on pilgrimage in this world, does not create false gods. She herself is the creation of the true God and she herself is to be his true sacrifice. Nevertheless, both cities alike enjoy the good things, or are afflicted with the adversities of this temporal state, but with a different faith, a different expectation, a different love, until they are separated by the final judgement, and each receives her own end, of which there is no end.[3]

In recent times, the more notable contrasting views of the city are presented in Harvey Cox, *The Secular City,* and Jacques Ellul, *The Meaning of the City.* Ellul casts the human city in the worst possible light by saying that the city symbolizes the supreme work of man—and, as such, represents the ultimate rejection of God. He declares, "All the inhabitants of the city are sooner or later to become prostitutes and members of the proletariat."[4] On the other end of the spectrum, Harvey Cox, Harvard University Divinity School professor emeritus, views the secularized modern city as the fullest

2. Quoted in Halton, *Church,* 185.

3. Augustine, *City of God,* 842. An overview of the Christian views of the city over the centuries is found in Martindale, ed., *Journey to the Celestial City.* For modern interpretations of the theme of the two cities from differing perspectives, see Boice, *Two Cities, Two Loves,* esp. 111–36; Braaten and Jenson, *Two Cities of God*; Linthicum. *City of God, City of Satan.*

4. Ellul, *Meaning of the City,* 55.

expression of Christian faith. For Cox, secularization "is the loosing of the world from religious and quasi-religious understandings of itself, the dispelling of all closed world-views, the breaking of all supernatural myths and sacred symbols."[5] The second is "the liberation of man from religious and metaphysical tutelage, the turning of his attention away from other worlds and towards this one."[6] Cox is not anti-religious, of course; he is a Christian theologian; but he credits the secularity of the modern city with a breakthrough into a new way of being religious. For Cox, the secular city is a radically new development.[7] Unlike Caesarius and Augustine, Cox has a very positive view of the earthly city.

THE BIBLICAL CITY

I turn now to biblical treatments of the city. In the Book of Micah, there is set forth a strong vision of the eschatological place to which all peoples will journey:

> In the days to come
> the mount of the Lord's house
> Shall be established as the highest mountain;
> it shall be raised above the hills,
> And peoples shall stream to it:
> Many nations shall come, and say,
> "Come, let us climb the Lord's mountain,
> to the house of the God of Jacob,
> That he may instruct us in his ways,
> that we may walk in his paths." (Mic 4:1–2)

In the Book of Isaiah, there is set forth a noble view of the city. God's glory, we are told, will envelop the holy mountain and the city of heaven, and all evil will be overcome:

> Arise! Shine, for your light has come,
> the glory of the Lord has dawned upon you.
> Though darkness covers the earth,

5. Cox, *Secular City*, 2.

6. Cox, *Secular City*, 21.

7. Commentators on the physical configuration of the modern city note that, while the centrally-located medieval cathedral was symbolically the highest building in the city, it has been replaced by the skyscraper—a transition from the religious to the secular. The skyscraper is the secular cathedral. See generally, Leeuwen, *Skyward Trend of Thought*; Kingwell, *Nearest Thing to Heaven*.

and thick clouds, the peoples,
Upon you the Lord will dawn,
and over you his glory will be seen. (Isa 60:1–2)

On the holy mountain there shall be a radiant dawn, and the nations will be gathered in glory. Sons, daughters, and their children will stream to the holy city:

Nations shall walk by your light,
kings by the radiance of your dawning.
Raise your eyes and look about;
they all gather and come to you—
Your sons from afar,
your daughters in the arms of their nurses. (Isa 60:3–4)

The riches shipped from the sea shall be great, including animals—camels and dromedaries; gold and frankincense will be brought to the holy mountain:

Then you shall see and be radiant,
your heart shall throb and overflow.
For the riches of the sea shall be poured out before you,
the wealth of nations shall come to you.
Caravans of camels shall cover you,
dromedaries of Midian and Ephah;
All from Sheba shall come
bearing gold and frankincense,
and heralding the praises of the Lord.
All the flocks of Kedar shall be gathered for you,
the rams of Nebaioth shall serve your needs;
They will be acceptable offerings on my altar,
and I will glorify my glorious house. (Isa 60:5–7)

In the New Jerusalem, there will be a great gathering of God's children, rich in silver and gold, who will come from afar:

Who are these that fly along like a cloud,
like doves to their cotes?
The vessels of the coastlands are gathering,
with the ships of Tarshish in the lead,
To bring your children from afar,
their silver and gold with them—
For the name of the Lord, your God,
for the Holy One of Israel
who has glorified you. (Isa 60:8–9)

Isaiah proclaims that a timely rebuilding of the walls of the holy city will occur. And, most notably, the gates of the city will be open to all—a departure from other ancient cities, which kept the gates closed against the stranger and the enemy. All the glories of nature will bring beauty to the holy sanctuary.

> The glory of Lebanon shall come to you—
> the juniper, the fir, and the cypress all together—
> To bring beauty to my sanctuary,
> and glory to the place where I stand. (Isa 60:13)

In the new age, the oppressors and the oppressed will be reconciled and will convert their enmity into prayer. To God, Zion will become the joy of nations, a city of rejoicing:

> The children of your oppressors shall come,
> bowing before you;
> All those who despised you,
> shall bow low at your feet.
> They shall call you "City of the Lord,"
> "Zion of the Holy One of Israel."
> No longer forsaken and hated,
> with no one passing through,
> Now I will make you the pride of the ages,
> a joy from generation to generation.
> You shall suck the milk of nations,
> and be nursed at royal breasts;
> And you shall know that I, the LORD, am your savior,
> your redeemer, the Mighty One of Jacob. (Isa 60:14–16)

The gifts of nations will edify the holy city. Peace will be the governor and justice the ruler:

> Instead of bronze, I will bring gold,
> instead of iron I will bring silver;
> Instead of wood, bronze;
> instead of stones, iron.
> I will appoint peace your governor,
> and justice your ruler. (Isa 60:17)

The city envisioned by Isaiah has a magnetism about it; it draws people in. They are gathered from many places. Isaiah foresees a city into which technology, political rulers, and people from many nations are brought together. God will redeem and transform that which is corroded, distorted, and perverted.[8]

Turning to Psalm 48, which expresses a similar praise of the heavenly city, we find a powerful affirmation of the stronghold of the great King and praise on the holy mountain.

> Great is the Lord and highly praised
> in the city of our God:
> His holy mountain,
> fairest of heights,
> the joy of all the earth,
> Mount Zion, the heights of Zaphon,
> the city of the great king. (Ps 48:2–3)

While the city is faced with destruction, the enemies are routed:

> God is in its citadel,
> renowned as a stronghold.
> See! The kings assembled,
> together they advanced.
> When they looked they were astounded;
> terrified, they were put to flight!
> Trembling seized them there,
> anguished, like a woman's labor,
> As when the east wind wrecks
> the ships of Tarshish! (Ps 48:4–8)

In the verses that follow, there is praise of Zion on the holy mountain:

> What we had heard we have now seen
> in the city of the Lord of hosts,
> In the city of God,
> which God establishes forever.
> We ponder, O God, your mercy
> within your temple.
> Like your name, O God,
> so is your praise to the ends of the earth.
> Your right hand is fully victorious.
> Mount Zion is glad!
> The daughters of Judah rejoice,
> because of your judgments! (Ps 48:9–12)

Psalm 48 ends with a great blaze of praise for Zion:

---

8. See Mouw, *When Kings*, 9–12.

Go about Zion, walk all around it,
note the number of its towers.
Consider her ramparts, examine its citadels,
that you may tell future generations:
That this is God,
our God forever and ever;
He will lead us until death. (Ps 48:13–15)

THE NEW TESTAMENT CITY

The New Testament is also directed toward a holy city, a place in which God's redemptive purposes for creation and humanity will be realized. Human creativity and work are preparations for future life in the heavenly city. Thus, as Richard J. Mouw points out, "there are grounds for looking for patterns of continuity between our present lives as people immersed in cultural contexts and the life to come."[9] The old city will not be destroyed but transformed and drawn into the holy city.

The most notable descriptions of the holy city in the New Testament are found in the Letter to the Hebrews and the Book of Revelation. The author of Hebrews envisages a powerful city on Mount Zion:

> No, you have approached Mount Zion and the city of the living God, the heavenly Jerusalem, and countless angels in festal gathering, and the assembling of the firstborn enrolled in heaven, and God the judge of all, and the spirits of the just made perfect, and Jesus, the mediator of a new covenant, and the sprinkled blood that speaks more eloquently than that of Abel. (Heb 12:18–24)

Here there is an element of liturgical praise in the vision of the city of God, with a great assembling of humanity and angels in festal gathering.

The most marvelous image that Christians have of eternity is that of the holy city on Mount Zion in the Book of Revelation expressed in chapter 21:

> Then I saw a new heaven and a new earth. The former heaven and the former earth had passed away, and the sea was no more. I also saw the holy city, a new Jerusalem, coming down out of heaven from God, prepared as a bride adorned for her husband. I heard a loud voice from the throne saying, "Behold, God's dwelling is with the human race. He will dwell with them and they will be his

9. Mouw, *When Kings*, 1–12.

people and God himself will always be with them [as their God].
He will wipe every tear from their eyes, and there shall be no more
death or mourning, wailing or pain, for the old order has passed
away. (Rev 21:1–4)[10]

Into the heavenly city of God will gather at the end of time humanity,
creation, and history. Divine redemption will assume the human city into
the heavenly city. Eternity will not be an eternity of disembodied spirits; it
will be an eternity of all that is most noble, graceful, and beautiful in the human city. If our human existence is inextricable from the life of the human
city, then humanity and the human city will be raised up, freed from all that
is enslaving and dehumanizing.

THE CULTURE OF THE CITY

It is on the city as cultural artifact that I want to focus now. The more that
the culture of a city is based on a rich, expressive symbol system, the more
significant it is. Cities are often founded, for instance, on a claim to religious
origins: Rome on the myth of Romulus and Remus; Jerusalem on the spot
where Adam is said to be buried; Salt Lake City on a dream of creating the
New Jerusalem. The human city at its best builds and generates its initiatives from dreams of a great and unlimited future, not from short-term or
purely pragmatic ideas. The city is the place of hopes and dreams, as we find
in the utopian thought of Plato, Augustine, and Thomas More. The city is
the repository of common memories (which is why we love old cities). The
city symbolizes deeds and achievements not yet possible (which is why we
love bustling cities and dislike dull cities). The city at its most humane is not
a faceless or shapeless amalgam, but a patterned and harmonious ordering of household, neighborhood, public institutions, and civic activity. In
the good city, industry and commerce, education and intellectual pursuit,
religion and spiritual expression, art and festival, coexist dynamically and
interconnectedly. This calls for well-planned cities.[11]

---

10. Commentaries relevant to this passage include Malina, *The New Jerusalem in the Revelation of John*; Dow, *Images of Zion*.

11. Two landmark books on the problems of the badly-planned city, its inhumane characteristics, and the possibilities of renewal are Mumford, *The Culture of Cities*; Ja-cobs, *The Death and Life of Great American Cities*. On broad expositions of this theme, see Sheldrake, *The Spiritual City*; Jacobsen, *The Space Between*.

The ancient art of civility is the art of living together in the city grace-fully and cooperatively. Civility exists to make good citizens. The lack of civility occasions the worst evils of the city. Civic virtue is practiced in great part by the advancement of established personal and communal rituals that are beautiful, dignified, and graceful.[12] The opposite of civility is fighting in the streets!

The more a city has a well-defined ritual and symbol system, the more humane, noble, and beautiful it is. The public rituals of a city are particularly important. Washington is never more Washington than when it inaugurates or buries a president. London is never more London than when its citizenry gathers for a great royal occasion. Salt Lake City is never more Salt Lake City than on July 24, when its foundation on that date in 1847 is remembered and celebrated. In its civic rituals, manners, symbols, monuments, and historic spaces, the life of a city is condensed, unified, and displayed.

If it is in its civic rituals and symbols that the earthly city in all of its features is most fully manifested and displayed, it is in the liturgy of the Church that the holy and eternal city is given its central and fullest expres-sion. The task of the earthly liturgy of the Church is to invoke, embody, symbolize, and sacramentalize the liturgy of the heavenly city in the midst of the earthly city. Through its liturgical life the liturgical Church becomes a living icon of heaven, a place in which the drama of the holy city is enacted, an anticipation of the redeemed life of the New Jerusalem. The Christian liturgy is a prefigurement of the holy city. This understanding of the liturgy has been set forth classically in modern times in article 8 of the Constitu-tion on the Sacred Liturgy of the Second Vatican Council (*Sacrosanctum Concilium*) in which we read:

> In the earthly liturgy we take part in a foretaste of that heavenly liturgy which is celebrated in the Holy City of Jerusalem toward which we journey as pilgrims, where Christ is sitting at the right hand of God, Minister of the holies and of the true tabernacle. With all the warriors of the heavenly army we sing a hymn of glory to the Lord; venerating the memory of the saints, we hope for some part and fellowship with them; we eagerly await the Savior, our Lord Jesus Christ, until he our life shall appear and we too will appear with him in glory.[13]

12. On the crucial necessity of a renewal of civility, see Allman and Beatty, eds., *Cultivating Citizens*; Sistare, ed., *Civility and its Discontents*; Carter, *Civility.*

13. Vatican Council II, no.8, 5.

In the Western city for nearly two millennia, the liturgical Church has played a crucial role in unifying the heavenly city and the earthly city. If in the liturgical Church the holy city descends to earth, then in the liturgical church the earthly city is raised up, its sight lifted to heaven. The liturgy of the human city is the embodiment on earth of the life and language of the heavenly city. Maximus the Confessor writes: "It is a most admirable thing that a small church can be like the vast universe . . . Its raised dome is like the heavens . . . and rests solidly on its lower part. Its arches represent the four corners of the earth."[14]

The earthly Church, great not only in magnificence but even in beautiful smallness, is a sign of the New Jerusalem taking shape in the earthly city. The liturgy of the liturgical Church gathers up the liturgy of the human city, what Pierre Teilhard de Chardin called the "Mass on the World" and the "Hymn of the Universe," and what Karl Rahner spoke of as the "Liturgy of the World." The liturgy in this regard gives expression to the worshipful impulses of the human city. This is what Louis Bouyer meant when he said that in the vision of the fathers of the Church, "the whole world is essentially liturgical."[15]

THE LITURGICAL CITY

The Church's liturgy is the sacrament of the heavenly city conducted in the midst of the earthly city for the redemption of the latter. The liturgy, wrote Aidan Kavanagh, is the Church doing the business of the city. Kavanagh calls the Church the central "workshop of the human City."[16] He is emphatic that the Church's concerns "must be with nothing less than the real, both socially and universally perceived."[17] Christ, he says, "recreates the World not by making new things but by making all things new."[18]

Because the work of the Church is city and cosmos, Kavanagh says, this truth acts as an effective control upon the Church's lapsing "into self-aggrandizing solipsism."[19] The danger of internal focus begins to occur when "the Church allows itself by pious fits to float free of World and City,

---

14. Quoted in Evdokimov, *Art of Icon*, 145.

15. Bouyer, *Cosmos*, 200.

16. Kavanagh, *Liturgical Theology*, 42.

17. Kavanagh, *Liturgical Theology*, 44.

18. Kavanagh, *Liturgical Theology*, 50.

19. Kavanagh, *Liturgical Theology*, 44.

becoming thereby unworldly, spiritualized, abstracted, idealized, sectarian, and gnostic."[20] For Kavanagh, there is nothing more deadly for the Church and its liturgy than introversion, privatization, and the evasion of the public world.

The Church, says Kavanagh, is—or should be—never more intensely aware of the city than when at worship. In worship, the Church is opened out to the world, and the world in all its dimensions is drawn into the act of worship. Kavanagh writes: "*What* the liturgical assembly of Christian orthodoxy does is the world. *Where* the liturgical assembly does this is the public forum of the world's radical business, [the place] of a restored and redeemed creation. *When* the liturgical assembly does this is the moment of the world's rebirth—the eighth day of creation, the first day of the last and newest age."[21] Nothing less, Kavanagh says, "rides upon the act of the assembly, determines its style, lays bare its service and mission for the life of the world."[22]

The Jesuit liturgical theologian John Baldovin has shown how early Christian worship was a highly civic affair, just as the Church building itself was from the beginning a public, urban institution. Baldovin writes:

> In medieval Jerusalem, Rome, Constantinople, and many other cities besides, a world in which Christianity formed the symbolic basis for social life, worship was not confined to the neighborhood church. It was public; it acclaimed the society's connectedness with the sacred; it made the streets and plazas sacred places in addition to the churches and shrines. To put it simply, the city became a church.[23]

During the Middle Ages, cities were often built in a manner inspired by images of heaven.[24] John Chrysostom was especially fond of speaking about the city itself as a Church reflecting heaven. In Antioch, he preached on processions in times of great civic turmoil, declaring: "The whole city has become a church for us."[25] Even more significantly, Baldovin says, the

---

20. Kavanagh, *Liturgical Theology*, 44–45.

21. Kavanagh, *Liturgical Theology*, 176.

22. Kavanagh, *Liturgical Theology*, 176.

23. Baldovin, "City as Church," 8. See also Hanawalt and Reyerson, eds., *City and Spectacle in Medieval Europe*.

24. See Frugoni, *A Distant City*; Simson, *The Gothic Cathedral*, esp. 8–13; Le Goff, *Medieval Civilization 400–1500*; Thompson, *Cities of God*.

25. Quoted in Baldovin, *Worship*, 8.

early Churches were not only part of the city, they represented it. They were a miniature representation of public life. Civic and religious rituals were often intertwined. The early Christian Church buildings did not separate Christians from the city, like a kind of sacred oasis, but rather brought the city and its concerns into the Church. Augustine could say: "The house of God is itself a city."[26]

The reader may now be asking how the liturgical Church represents all this? The answer, of course, is that it cannot. This brings us to a most crucial point. The liturgy is not contained or restricted within the time and space of Sunday morning. The authentic celebration of the liturgy is only the beginning of the Church's sacramental work for the redemption of the human city. The Constitution on the Sacred Liturgy (*Sacrosanctum Concilium*) of Vatican II pointed out that the liturgy is the "fount" and "summit"—the beginning and the end—of the Church's life; but it is not all there is or all that needs to be. It stated: "The sacred liturgy does not exhaust the entire activity of the Church."[27] Liturgy flows out into catechesis, charity, education, pastoral care, evangelization, and an entire plethora of other ministries and apostolates.

There are numerous ways in which I could proceed here. I propose to do so by reference to three biblical places which symbolize human needs at their most severe. They are Babel, Raamses, and Philistia. Two are cities; the third a quasi-city. These three places represent, in different ways, human deprivation in civic configuration: Babel, the city of confusion; Raamses, the city of injustice and oppression; and Philistia, the quasi-city of ugliness.

Over these three reigns the city that is their radical opposites: the holy city, the New Jerusalem, the heavenly city of goodness, truth, and beauty. The Church, in its liturgy and the ministries consequent to the liturgy, is called to do nothing less than embody the holy city in the midst of the modern city in which the ghosts of Babel, Raamses, and Philistia are sighted often.

FROM BABEL TO THE CITY OF TRUTH

First is the city of Babel. In Genesis chapter 11 we have an account of the origins of Babel:

26. Quoted in Baldovin, *Worship*, 9.
27. *Vatican Council II*, no. 9, 6.

The whole world had the same language and the same words . . .
Then they said, "Come let us build ourselves a city and a tower
with its top in the sky, and so make a name for ourselves; otherwise we shall be scattered all over the earth."

The Lord came down to see the city and the tower that the
people had built. Then the Lord said: If now, while they are one
people, and all have the same language, they have started to do
this, nothing they presume to do will be out of their reach. Come,
let us then go down there and confuse their language, so that no
one will understand the speech of another." So the Lord scattered
them from there over all the earth, and they stopped building the
city. That is why it was called Babel, because there the Lord confused the speech of all the world. From there the Lord scattered
them all over the earth. (Gen 11:1–9)

Without going into the exegetical details of this story, I want to highlight Babel as the biblical model of the confused, disoriented, fragmented,
city, a condition not of divine making but of human pride.

The confusion of Babel is significant because it has been replicated in
every city in history. In the poem "The Rock," T. S. Eliot described modern
London as a city full of the "knowledge of words, and ignorance of the
Word."[28] The Notre Dame University scholar James Dougherty described
the modern city as follows: "The city is never silent; it speaks with a voice of
its own, the voice of false prophets in Jerusalem, of sophists in Athens and
Carthage, of gramophones and television in London and Wichita. Like the
prophet's cry, the city's own voice summons the citizens to believe—but to
believe in their common self-sufficiency and in the durability and satisfaction of the city's goods. Its call to worship is ultimately to self-worship."[29]

The mission of the Church in every age is to reverse Babel, to give new
voice and understanding to society struggling to achieve meaning. Such a
reversal began in the Pentecost event:

When the time for Pentecost was fulfilled, they [the disciples] were
in one place together. And suddenly there came from the sky a
noise like a strong, driving wind, and it filled the entire house in
which they were. Then there appeared to them tongues as of fire,
which parted and came to rest on each one of them. And they were
filled with the holy Spirit, and began to speak in different tongues
as the spirit enabled them to proclaim.

28. Eliot, *Waste Land*, 8.

29. Dougherty, *Fivesquare City*, 118.

> Now there were devout Jews from every nation under heaven staying in Jerusalem. At this sound, they gathered in a large crowd, but they were confused because each one heard them speaking in his own language. They were astounded, and in amazement they asked, "Are not all these people who are speaking Galileans? Then how does each of us hear them in his own native language? We are Parthians, Medes, and Elamites, inhabitants of Mesopotamia, Judea and Cappadocia, Pontus and Asia, Phrygia and Pamphylia, Egypt and the districts of Libya near Cyrene, as well as travelers from Rome, both Jews and converts to Judaism, Cretans and Arabs, too, yet we hear them speaking in our own tongues of the mighty acts of God." (Acts 2:1–11)

In modern America we have lost faith in words, in coherent meanings, in the possibility of common language, in the very idea of truth. We live increasingly in a culture in which language is suspect, a culture of confusion and disorientation regarding meaning, a world of illusions and hyperreality. W. B. Yeats' words in his poem "The Second Coming" are true in numerous respects in North America today: "Things fall apart; the center cannot hold; Mere anarchy is loosed upon the world."[30]

The mission of the Church is to speak the voice of Pentecost, to introduce it into the city of Babel, and to find in Babel, and dialogue with, those voices which seek out and give expression to truth. This is the task of prophecy which James Dougherty described as follows: "The task of the prophet is to bear into the historical city the image of another city, the eschatological Jerusalem over the mountains. But if he is to bring a redemption in time as well as at the end of time, the prophet must also bring to the city the summoning word of God."[31] Christians individually and the Church corporately are called to a ministry of the word which will redeem the language of the city, provide a meaningful account of life, and enable the citizenry to speak a language that is unitive, cooperative, and dialogical.

The liturgical Church can only be a sacrament of the redeemed city when it begins to believe the word. When it believes the word, there will be a renewal of preaching of a worthy kind, a renaissance of the Christian intellectual tradition and Christian humanism, a pastoral catechesis capable of making true disciples, a powerful and compelling moral tradition and a wise fearlessness about challenging conventional cultural mores, a

---

30. Yeats, "The Second Coming," 187.
31. Dougherty, *Fivesquare City*, 118.

reanimation of the practices of contemplation, of *lectio divina,* and of silence—all practices which are crucial to *hearing* the word.

But talk alone will not do. The urban Church is not yet a sacrament until it practices the word. The Church as symbolized by these institutions must be a city of the word embodied; a place in which what Pope John Paul II calls "the splendor of truth" must shine forth in concrete forms of expression. Only by being its authentic self can the Church credibly speak to the human city.

Assuming that it has its own house in proper order, the liturgical Church can only then become a credible place of public education, conversation, dialogue. It can go out to, and invite in, the city and its institutions—including the university, the government, business, theaters, and professions—so that the wisdom of God and the voices of the city may meet for the salvation of the world. Around the ambos and pulpits in our churches on Sunday morning gather the citizens of the human city to hear and celebrate a redeeming word that, were it fully effected, would mean the triumph of the New Jerusalem over Babel. The journey from Babel to the heavenly city is the awesome responsibility of the Church and its institutions. Standing as a permanent sacrament of Pentecost, the Church draws the world forward out of the old city and into the new and eternal holy city.

FROM RAAMSES TO THE CITY OF FREEDOM

The second symbolic city I want to examine is Raamses, the human city in desperate need of justice and dignity. Raamses in Egypt was one of the dreadful places where the enslaved Hebrew people were forced to construct a "supply city" for Pharaoh. In Exodus 1 we read:

> Then a new king, who knew nothing of Joseph, rose to power in Egypt. He said to his people, "See! The Israelite people have multiplied and become more numerous than we are. Come, let us deal shrewdly with them to stop their increase; otherwise, in time of war they too may join our enemies to fight against us, and so leave the land."
>
> Accordingly, they set supervisors over the Israelites to oppress them with forced labor. Thus they had to build for Pharaoh the garrison cities of Pithom and Raamses. Yet the more they were oppressed, the more they multiplied and spread, so that the Egyptians began to loathe the Israelites. So the Egyptians reduced the Israelites to cruel slavery, making life bitter for them with hard

labor at mortar and brick and all kinds of field work—cruelly oppressed in all their labor. (Exod 1:8–14)

Chapter 5 of Exodus describes the harshness and misery of life in Raamses. Hebrew male babies were constantly in danger of death because the Pharaoh feared the excessive growth of the Hebrew population. One of the boys who survived the Egyptian policy of slaughter or abandonment of male Hebrew infants was Moses—whose name is derived from the name of the city of Raamses. It was from Raamses that Moses led the Exodus out of Egypt toward the Promised Land after the whole area was infested with plagues.

The Bible is replete with dreadful cities like Raamses, as is human history, ancient and modern. In the human city has been gathered together and intensified all the personal and communal vices of which human beings are capable: injustice, opportunism, inequality, racism, competitiveness, and general destructiveness. These vices are by no means unique to the city, but the city seems to put them under pressure, to advertize them and give them notable profile. Because of this, not a few commentators have taken a distinctly negative view of the human city. Yet, while no city past or present lacks the typical evils of the human city, few cities in history have totally lacked virtuous citizens and noble institutions.

The history of the human city may be read in biblical terms as a movement from Raamses to the New Jerusalem. Jesus prefigured the advent of the eternal city of holiness, goodness, and liberation in a key moment in Nazareth at the beginning of his public ministry. We read in Luke 4:

> Jesus returned to Galilee in the power of the Spirit, and news of him spread throughout the whole region. He taught in their synagogues and was praised by all.
>
> He came to Nazareth, where he had grown up, and went according to his custom into the synagogue on the sabbath day. He stood up to read and was handed a scroll of the prophet Isaiah. He unrolled the scroll and found the passage where it was written:

> The spirit of the Lord is upon me;
> because he has anointed me
> to bring glad tiding to the poor.
> He has sent me to proclaim liberty to captives
> and recovery of sight to the blind
> and to let captives free
> and to proclaim a year acceptable to the Lord.

Rolling up the scroll, he handed it back to the attendant and
sat down, and the eyes of all the synagogue looked intently at him.
He said to them: "Today this Scripture passage is fulfilled in your
hearing." (Luke 4:16–21)

In this crucial event, Jesus gathered up all the hopes of Israel, all the
dreams of Isaiah and the prophets, and he announced the inauguration of
the long-expected era of divine salvation, redemption, healing, and joy. In
that moment in Nazareth, everything that Jesus was to do in his public
ministry thereafter was prefigured: healing the sick, lifting up the down-
trodden, giving sight to the blind, forgiving the sinner.

Jesus' ministry of inaugurating the holy city within the conditions of
the human city continues in the life of the Church today, even if imperfectly. The Nazareth event is irrevocably imprinted in the Church's identity.
This ministry is, like all others, condensed in the liturgy. The worshiping
assembly of the Christian community embodies and sacramentalizes a
whole ethical philosophy and way of life founded on the holiness, justice,
and righteousness of God. When we step into the world of the liturgy, we
are already in the world of an ethical and moral goodness transcending
anything available in the human city; we are already living out the ethics of
the holy city. In the liturgy is set forth a whole system of redeemed interrelationships. Liturgy offers a communal model of existence rather than an
individualistic one. At the Lord's table people of all classes and races are
welcome—surely a model of community that is by no means in place in the
human city.

Where but in the liturgical assembly are governors and bag ladies, rich
and poor, white, black, and brown brought together in solidarity? That all
share the one bread and one cup is a most unique act, unique because we do
not behave in the same manner in the human city. In the Eucharist we share
our resources by offering gifts—surely a challenge to capitalist and *laissez
faire* economics. In the Mass we offer a sacrifice that, to mean anything, as
the scriptures constantly declare, must be translated into daily acts of mercy
and justice. In the Eucharist we seek forgiveness publicly and offer each
other the sign of peace—gestures that have much to say in a world of self-
assertiveness, division, hostility, and violence. We take the Eucharist out to
the home-bound and the institution-bound, thereby taking a stance against
the abandonment and marginalizing of the poor, sick, and old. In Baptism
men and women are declared children of God and are endowed with a
value beyond anything they could ever earn for themselves. In sacramental
Confession we say that no one is beyond the pale of God's mercy. What a

vision this holds up in a world so prone to vengeance, condemnation, and rejection of the sinner, the prisoner, and the criminal! We anoint the sick and minister to them as Christ himself, fighting every social tendency to see illness and old age as meaningless. In all our liturgies we pray for the Church, the world, the local community, and those in need—then to be dismissed to enact that for which we have prayed.

Theologian Peter Leithart published a most original essay in *First Things* in 1996 titled "The Politics of Baptism." The author, citing Max Weber, points to the difference between the pre-Christian cities of the ancient world and the medieval cities in which Christianity was operative. The ancient cities, he says, were "socially structured by a separation between those who made a claim of descent from the founding clans (patricians) and those who could make no such claim (plebeians), a separation often spatially represented by the isolation of plebeians either at the foot of the sacred hill of the city (*polis*) or in ghettos clustered at the walls."[32] The Hebrews in Raamses were an example of people who did not belong in the Egyptian cities, but were set apart in outcast cities.

In medieval times, under the impulse of Christianity, religious exclusions began to come apart. Leithart observes that the medieval city, for all its inequities and flaws, was "a partial realization of a social order ritually imagined in Christian baptism."[33]

> The waters of baptism became the universal solvent not only of traditional religious distinctions within Judaism but also of the foundation stones on which the ancient city rested; for the church, it was the sole initiation and was not confined to a single family, clan, race, or social class. Everyone within the watery walls of this city participates in the rites and shares in the saints; holy things are for holy people, but all the baptized are saints.[34]

Why Christian liturgies today do not seem to have the ethical and socially transforming power I am describing is a complex matter.[35] We can be sure, however, that if the liturgy is not a public event, is not a liturgy of the city, then its interests will not be in social transformation. If liturgy is a small group gathering for quasi-therapeutic purposes, then its gaze will be inward and, both conceptually and practically, it will abandon the city.

32. Leithart, "Politics of Baptism," 5; see also Leithart, *The Priesthood of the Plebs.*

33. Leithart, "Politics of Baptism," 5.

34. Leithart, "Politics of Baptism," 5.

35. Mannion, "Crisis of Culture," 98–132; Mannion, "Worship and the Public Church," 11–14; Mannion, *The Cathedral as Sacrament of the Redeemed City*, 5–24.

What is required today of the Church and of Christians is a new awareness of what Christians are actually doing ethically in the liturgy and of taking seriously one of the most neglected rites of all: the dismissal rite—which sends worshippers into the human city on a sanctifying mission. If believers do not take the dismissal seriously, then the liturgy becomes, as the Old Testament prophets never tired of saying, false worship.

The Church building as sacrament of the redeemed city is called—like the Church at large—to be a model of goodness, justice, peace, righteousness, holiness, and charity—to be a zone of holy and redeemed life. Such a vocation is monumental, frightening, and frustrating, but unavoidable. Only when its own house is in order can the Church go out to, and call in, the citizens of Raamses and lift up the human city from its poverty and oppression.

The work for justice and charity is not extrinsic, but intrinsic, to the Church's life. The Church's social teaching is not a matter of ecclesiastical dabbling in politics. We cannot forget that the word "politics" comes from the Greek word *polis,* the city. The Church should never "dabble" in politics; it must competently, systematically, and confidently immerse itself in the life of the *polis.* As Urban Holmes pointed out, "The goal of all ministry is political."[36] The Church must avoid, of course, intrusion into governmental politics, steer clear of secular platforms, and shun party allegiances, but it must involve itself in what Robert Webber and Rodney Clapp call "depth politics,"[37] or what Robert Jenson calls "eschatological politics"—politics in its deepest connection to the coming of God's Kingdom.[38]

Catholic, Anglican, and Orthodox Church buildings generally exist within parishes. A parish is a unit of territory. The mentality called "parochialism" is often put down. I suggest the need for a renewed parochialism in the sense of a renewed responsibility on the part of every local Church for each and every person, every event, every decision made within the boundaries of the parish. Every Church should have in one way or another a social ministry to the city that constitutes the territory of the parish. The liturgical building is called to prefigure the redeemed city in which there will be no more death or mourning, crying out or pain, no more evil or sin. As such it should be a place of notable, energetic, and systematic charity and service, hospitality and welcome, advocacy, and truth-telling—a place

36. Holmes *Ministry and Imagination,* 21.

37. Webber and Clapp, *People of Truth,* 34–83.

38. Jenson, *Theology and Culture,* 16–27.

of sanctuary for the poor, homeless, lonely, alien, depressed, a place of forgiveness, wisdom, and dialogue.

The journey from Raamses to the New Jerusalem is the awesome responsibility of the urban Church. Standing as a permanent sacrament of the Nazareth event, it draws the world forward out of the old city and into the holy city. The eschatological city becomes the inspiration and model for the human city.

FROM PHILISTIA TO THE CITY OF GLORY

I turn finally to the quasi-city of Philistia. More a confederation of cities than a single city, Philistia is synonymous with ugliness and anti-aestheticism. In the dictionary, a "Philistine" is not only a native or inhabitant of ancient Philistia, but a crass, prosaic, often priggish individual guided by material rather than intellectual or artistic values.[39] (If the Philistines have been unfairly caricatured in this regard, as recent scholars have suggested, then the lesson is that every city is Philistia; every city embodies ugliness, crassness, and materialism.)

I want to look again at the theme of glory as a key to understanding the movement of glory from Philistia to the holy city. The theme of glory pervades the Old Testament. God's glory was said to dwell in a unique way among the people during the Exodus, in the Ark of the Covenant, and in the Temple of Jerusalem. The glory of God is thought of as a brilliant and marvelous light. This conception is probably at the base of passages which proclaim that the earth is full of the glory of God, or that the earth is bright with God's glory, or that the glory of God dwells in the heavens.

The New Testament reflects the Old Testament conceptions of glory. The glory of God which illuminated the shepherds at Bethlehem had the form of a brilliant light. In his person, Jesus shared the glory, the luminous brilliance of the Father. Through his passion, death and resurrection, Christ revealed the Father's glory. Christians already reflect the glory of the Father by being changed into the likeness of Christ. In the Book of Revelation, the glory of God is a brilliant light which illuminates the New Jerusalem.

If Pentecost stands between Babel and the New Jerusalem; if Jesus' proclamation in the Nazareth synagogue stands between Raamses and the holy city; then the Transfiguration of Jesus stands between Philistia and the glorious city of heaven. We read in the Gospel of Luke, chapter 9:

39. "Philistine," *Webster's Seventh,* 634.

About eight days after he said this, he [Jesus] took Peter, John, and James and went up the mountain to pray. While he was praying his face changed in appearance and his clothing became dazzlingly white. And behold, two men were conversing with him, Moses and Elijah, who appeared in glory and spoke of his exodus that he was going to accomplish in Jerusalem. Peter and his companions had been overcome by sleep, but becoming fully awake, they saw his glory and the two men standing with him. As they were about to part from him, Peter said to Jesus, "Master, how good that we are here. Let us make three tents, one for you, one for Moses, and one for Elijah." But he did not know what he was saying. While he was still speaking, a cloud came and cast a shadow over them, and they became frightened when they entered the cloud. Then from the cloud came a voice that said, "This is my chosen Son: listen to him." After the voice had spoken, Jesus was found alone. They fell silent and did not at that time tell anyone what they had seen. (Luke 9:28–36)

If the liturgy is the principal manifestation of God's worldly presence, then it is, by that fact, the primordial place of God's glory; it is an ongoing process of Transfiguration. The liturgy of the Church is at its best an invocation, an embodiment, an anticipation of the glorious city, the New Jerusalem. The *Catechism* aptly describes the sacraments and the liturgy in artistic terms as "God's masterpieces" and "the masterworks of God." [40]

It surely could not be said that the liturgy of the West lacks beauty or is unconcerned about glory—although philistinism in liturgical guise is far too readily identifiable today, and modern American liturgical practice is not generally known for an ethos of beauty, glory, and solemnity. Western liturgy has had and continues to have its glorious expressions. Think of Chartres Cathedral, Michelangelo's Sistine Chapel, the Abbey of Melk, Palestrina, Mozart, Britten, Vaughan Williams, Cranmer's English, the homilies of Augustine, St. John Henry Newman, and Bishop Robert Barron, Evensong at King's College Cambridge, the liturgy of monasteries. Yet beauty in Western liturgy is all too often regarded as accidental to the liturgy. The basic problem is that the Churches of the West—unlike those of the East—lack an adequate theology of glory—something recently being compensated for by the magisterial work of Hans Urs von Balthasar and Anglican theologians like John Riches and Richard Harries, former Bishop of Oxford.

---

40. *Catechism*, nos. 1091, 1116.

But because glory is regarded in Western liturgy as an accidental, a luxury, a decoration, it should not be surprising that Western culture has made glory accidental also.[41] Witness everything that has happened since the industrial revolution. Consider that the modern movement in architecture and urban planning which, in its rationalism and functionalism, has left our cities and our public spaces very inglorious indeed.[42] In the West, we imprison glory in museums and concert halls; we have taken beauty off the streets and out of our public places. In the process, popular culture has become severely ugly, superficial, and stultifying. In the modern West, we have lost the ability to celebrate, to hold festivals, to be playful in the most profound sense. Our social rituals are increasingly rough and primitive. America today is not a polite society, meaning that the public rituals of the *polis* have disintegrated.

In an increasingly materialistic culture, the ordinary, the mundane, and the worldly are not, ironically, taken more seriously than in religious cultures; they are taken less seriously. What, for example, do water, wine, wheat, work, creativity, and leisure mean in popular cultural terms? The answer is that they are merely functional, utilitarian. But place these in a sacramental context, as occurs habitually in the East, and they become elements of God's glory. Orthodox theologian Paul Evdokimov says about created reality that "everything is destined for a liturgical fulfillment."[43] Olive oil and water "attain their fulness as conductor elements for grace on regenerated man. Wheat and wine achieve their ultimate *raison d'être* in the eucharistic chalice."[44] The Church's worship "integrates the most elementary actions of life: drinking, eating, washing speaking, acting, communing . . . . It restores to them their meaning and true destiny, that is, to be blocks in the cosmic temple of God's glory."[45]

The journey from Philstia to the holy city is the awesome responsibility of the Church, its institutions, its cathedrals, basilicas, monasteries, and universities. Standing as a permanent sacrament of the transfiguration, it draws forward the world out of the old city into the new city of glory, a city in which truth, justice, and beauty embrace in the heart of God, a city in

---

41. Wilder, *Theopoetic*, 8–11.

42. See Bess, *Till We Have Built Jerusalem*; Bakke, *A Theology as Big as the City*; Bell. *City of the Good*; Pasquariello, Shriver, and Geyer, *Redeeming the City*.

43. Evdokimov, *Art of Icon,* 117.

44. Evdokimov, *Art of Icon,* 117.

45 Evdokimov, *Art of Icon,* 117.

which all men and women (whether they know it or not), have already set their hearts.

CONCLUSION

Into the holy city of God, the New Jerusalem, will be gathered at the end of time humanity, creation, cosmos, and history. Divine redemption will assume the earthly city into the heavenly city. Eternity will not be an eternity of disembodied spirits; it will be the eternity of all that is most noble, graceful, and beautiful in the human city. If our human existence is inextricable from the life of the city, then the human city will be raised up, freed from all this is enslaving, dehumanizing and tragic. The task of Christians in the meantime is to renovate the earthly city so that the earthly and heavenly will in God's time become one, the eternal dwelling place for redeemed humankind.

Chapter Eight

MODEL EIGHT:
FEASTING IN THE KINGDOM

All their days are days of feasting
—Alfred de Musset[1]

IN THIS FINAL CHAPTER, I turn to one of the central models of heaven: the sacred meal. I propose that this is more than an incidental feature of both the Old and New Testaments—and of Christian life in general. I shall first examine food in its social roles. Then I will look at meals in the Old and New Testaments and at the Wedding Feast of the Lamb in the Book of Revelation. Finally, I shall review the eschatological features of the Christian eucharistic meal today.

THE CULTURE OF FOOD

In recent decades much attention has been paid to a short story titled "Babette's Feast," written by Isak Dinesen (Karen Blixen) and published along with four other stories.[2] The storyline is simple yet compelling. A French woman named Babette now living in Denmark is welcomed by two sisters who belong to an austere Christian sect. Babette moves into the home of the sisters and participates in the life of the household. Babette wins the French lottery and with the money prepares a lavish feast for the sisters. The dinner is a great success.

1. Musset, *Confession*, 103.

2. Dinesen, *Babette's Feast*, 23–68. The story was produced as a movie in 1987 by Danish film director Gabriel Axel.

Some commentators interpret this story in transcendent terms. Liturgical theologians Christopher Carstens and Douglas Martis write as follows: "On the natural level, *Babette's Feast* has a great deal in common with the Wedding Feast of the Lamb and its sacramental presentation in the Mass."[3] The eschatological theme is especially expressed at the end of the story, when Philippa, one of the sisters, says to Babette: "Yet, this is not the end! I feel, Babette, that this is not the end! In paradise you would be the great artist God meant you to be!"[4]

While food in modern societies tends to be functional and to lack symbolism, the use of food in traditional societies was replete with symbolic meanings. I will set forth in this chapter the various meanings of food as a way of providing a basis for understanding the quintessential biblical meals, those of the Old and New Testaments, especially the Last Supper—and on the Wedding Feast of the Lamb in the Book of Revelation.

It is evident that food and eating are cultural, religious, and symbolic matters.[5] In one way or another, people need to eat for their survival and growth. But they also eat for non-functional purposes. In the words of Ángel F. Méndez-Montoya: "Eating is a primal mark and act of life that evokes the cosmos as a great cosmic banquet."[6] Food, then, is a central cultural and social reality with diverse meanings and functions. The French sacramental theologian Philippe Rouillard wrote an essay in the late 1970s which has since become a classic, entitled "From Human Meal to Christian Eucharist."[7] Rouillard's thesis is that we best understand the Christian Eucharist if we can trace its historical development to its roots in the human meal from pre-Christian times to the present.[8]

3. Carstens and Martis, *Mystical Body*, 63.

4. Dinesen, *Babette's Feast*, 68.

5. Works which provide a theory of food and its various cultural meanings include Veit, *Modern Food, Moral Food*; Zeller et al., *Religion, Food, and Eating in North America*; Vester, *A Taste of Power*; Ritzer, *The McDonaldization of Society*; Schlosser, *Fast Food Nation*; Finn, *Discriminating Taste*; Julier, *Eating Together*; Berry, *Bringing it to the Table*; Harvey, *Food, Sex and Strangers*. Broad surveys of this topic include Murcott, *Introducing the Sociology of Food and Eating*; and Douglas, "Deciphering a Meal," 61–81.

6. Méndez-Montoya, *Theology of Foods*, 1.

7. Rouillard, "From Human Meal to Christian Eucharist," 125–56.

8. Works on eucharistic meanings from a specifically theological perspective include Feely-Harnik, *The Lord's Table*; Vanderslice, *We Will Feast*; McGann, *The Meal that Reconnects*; McCormick, *A Banqueter's Guide to the All-Night Soup Kitchen of the Kingdom of God*; Wirzba. *Food and Faith*; Hellwig, *The Eucharist and the Hungers of the World*.

The human meal fundamentally meets the physical needs of people and the experience of hunger and thirst. Food is the assurance of energy and life. Every piece of bread is the result of a history from planting, tilling, growing, and harvesting. Wine, too, results from the planting, pruning, harvesting, crushing under a press, fermenting, and aging. "Hunger" and "thirst" are often employed to symbolize the desires of the human person not just for physical satisfaction, but for spiritual fulfillment. Bread and wine and all the elements of human nourishment are brought together in the meal, particularly in events such as the celebration of important occasions like birth, initiation, marriage, funerals, and anniversaries.

The meal is usually taken in common. It seals communities great and small. It recognizes the communion and kinship that individuals hunger for. Most religions feature a sacred meal in which the gods are present in some way, either as a means of obtaining their favor or to receive sacrificial offerings.

OLD TESTAMENT MEALS

In the Old and New Testaments, meals often accompanied important occasions. Numerous Old Testament passages mention the banquet to describe the coming age of salvation. The most explicit description of a meal anticipating the age to come is found in Isaiah 25. Here the author portrays the coming of the age of the Lord in terms of a banquet:

> On this mountain the Lord of hosts
> will provide for all peoples
> A feast of rich food and choice wines,
> juicy, rich food and pure, choice wines.
> On this mountain he will destroy
> the veil that veils all peoples,
> the veil that is woven over all nations.
> He will destroy death forever.
> The Lord God will wipe away
> the tears from all faces;
> The reproach of his people he will remove
> from the whole earth; for the Lord has spoken.
> On that day it will be said:
> "Indeed, this is our God; we looked to him, and he saved us!
> This is the Lord to whom we looked;
> let us rejoice and be glad that he has saved us!" (Isa 25: 6–9)

Human sadness and tears will be resolved in a joyful feast on God's holy mountain, where there will be no more loss, sadness, or death.

Several other occurrences of the image of the banquet in the Old Testament point to a salvific feast for the poor and the hungry:

> All you who are thirsty,
> come to the water!
> You who have no money,
> come, buy grain and eat;
> Come, buy grain without paying the cost!
> Why spend your money for what is not bread;
> your wages for what does not satisfy?
> Only listen to me, and you shall eat well,
> you shall delight in rich fare.
> Pay attention and come to me;
> listen, that you may have life.
> I will make with you an everlasting covenant,
> the steadfast loyalty promised to David. (Isa 55:1–3)

The age to come is announced in terms of plenteous water, grain, wine, and milk. No more will there be hunger and famine among the descendants of David. Wheat and wine will no more be given to the enemies of Israel. Those who harvest the grain and those who gather the grapes will be the beneficiaries of their own work. Thus, we read:

> The Lord has sworn by his right hand
> and by his mighty arm:
> No more will I give your grain
> as food to our enemies;
> Nor shall foreigners drink the wine,
> for which you toiled.
> But those who harvest the grain shall eat,
> and praise the Lord. (Isa 62: 8–9)

The prophet continues the theme of liberation and freedom of God's servants in terms of plenteous food:

> Therefore, thus says the Lord God:
> My servants shall eat,
> but you shall go hungry:
> My servants shall drink,
> but you shall be thirsty;
> My servants shall rejoice,
> but you shall be put to shame. (Isa 65:13)

In a different key, the Book of Proverbs invokes the same theme in which a house is built in which to hold a banquet with Wisdom as host:

> Wisdom has built her house,
> she has set up her seven columns;
> She has dressed her meat, mixed her wine,
> yes, she has spread her table. (Prov 8:9)

Proverbs elaborates this theme simply:

> Come, eat of my food,
> and drink of the wine I have mixed!
> Forsake foolishness that you may live. (Prov 9:5–6)

Scripture scholar Brant Pitre identifies several aspects of the biblical feast. I will select four. First, the feast is no ordinary occasion; it has an extraordinary character. The eschatological aspect is evident from the fact that the banquet finds fulfillment in the overthrow of suffering and oppression. God will destroy death forever and wipe away all tears. Second, the banquet signifies redemption and the forgiveness of sins. God will take away the guilt of his people and bring them salvation. Third, the coming feast will have a sacrificial dimension: there will always be sanctification by human self-offering. Fourth, the eschatological banquet will accompany the return from exile of the tribes of Israel, as well as of the gentile nations. The feast will be for all peoples and will result in the lifting of the veil that is cast over all peoples.[9]

It is clear that the Old Testament passages cited above have an eschatological orientation, though one must be careful not to interpret them in a defined Christian eschatological sense. Yet one might say that the Old Testament feasts are foretastes of the sacred meals revealed in the New Testament, especially in Revelation.

The most notable Old Testament festive meal was the yearly Passover. Whether the Last Supper of Jesus and his apostles was a Passover meal or not remains an open question among scholars. But it seems clear that elements of the Passover found their place in the Last Supper. We read in Exodus the original account of Passover:

> The Lord said to Moses and Aaron in the land of Egypt: This
> month will stand at the head of your calendar: you will reckon
> it the first month of the year. Tell the whole community of Israel:
> on the tenth of this month every family must procure for itself a

---

9. Pitre, *Last Supper*, 449–50; also Pitre, *Jesus and the Jewish Roots of the Eucharist*.

lamb, one apiece for each household. If a household is too small for a lamb, it along with its nearest neighbor will procure one and apportion the lamb's cost in proportion to the number of persons according to what each household consumes. Your lamb must be a year-old male and without blemish. You may take it from either the sheep or the goats. You will keep it until the fourteenth day of this month, and then, with the whole community of Israel assembled, it will be slaughtered during the evening twilight. They will take some of its blood and apply it to the two doorposts and the lintel of the houses in which they eat it. They will consume its meat that same night, eating it roasted with unleavened bread and bitter herbs. (Exod 12:1–8)

The German theologian Joachim Jeremias writes about both the retrospective and prospective aspects of the Passover:

> The Jewish Passover celebration at the time of Jesus is both retrospect and prospect. At this festival the people of God remember the merciful immunity granted to the houses marked with the blood of the paschal lamb and the deliverance from the Egyptian servitude. *At the same time the Passover is looking forward to the coming deliverance of which the deliverance from Egypt is the prototype.*[10]

This is essentially an eschatological statement.

JESUS' MEAL MINISTRY

The meal ministry of Jesus also had an eschatological character. The significance of the sharing of meals during Jesus' itinerant ministry has traditionally been understood in miraculous terms: they demonstrate Jesus' divinity. Recent scholars, as I noted, have come to see these meals more in eschatological terms, prefiguring the banquet of the Kingdom of heaven. N. T. Wright, the English theologian and former Bishop of Durham states that table fellowship is a "symbolic evocation of the coming messianic banquet."[11]

---

10. Jeremias, *Eucharistic Words*, 206; emphasis in the original.

11. Wright, *Jesus and Victory*. Arthur Juste states that Jesus' table fellowship was an expression of the coming of the eschatological Kingdom. See Juste, *Ongoing Feast*, xiii.

In what follows I will look at the meals of Jesus not as isolated events or merely practical accounts of the need to satiate hunger, but as part of Jesus' ministry of inaugurating the Kingdom.

The wedding feast at Cana was the first of Jesus' meal miracles. The turning of water into wine was a fundamentally eschatological event. The "human" water was turned into "heavenly" wine. This transformation signified Jesus' eschatological ministry. On the third day, we are told, there was a wedding in Cana of Galilee, and the mother of Jesus was there. Jesus and his disciples were also invited. When the wine ran short, the mother of Jesus said to her son, "They have no wine."

> [And] Jesus said to her, "Woman, how does your concern affect me? My hour has not yet come." His mother said to the servers, "Do whatever he tells you." Now there were six stone water jars there for Jewish ceremonial washings, each holding twenty to thirty gallons. Jesus told them, "Fill the jars with water." So they filled them to the brim. Then he told them, "Draw some out now and take it to the headwaiter." So they took it. And when the head-waiter tasted the water that had become wine, without knowing where it came from (although the servers who had drawn the water knew), the headwaiter called the bridegroom and said to him, "Everyone serves good wine first, and then when people have drunk freely, an inferior one, but you have kept the good wine until now." (John 2:4–11)

Commentators see this event not only as miraculous, but as signifying the beginning of the new age in Jesus. The wine showed the power of Jesus over nature, which will find fulfilment in the age to come, when all creation is transformed.

The next eschatological miracle to which we pay attention is the dinner with Levi. This happened in Capernaum, located on the north shores of the sea of Galilee.

> Once again [Jesus] went out again along the sea. All the crowd came to him and he taught them. As he passed by, he saw Levi the son of Alphaeus, sitting at the customs post. He said to him, "Follow me." And he got up and followed him. While he was at table in his house, many tax collectors and sinners sat with Jesus and his disciples; for there were many who followed him. Some scribes who were Pharisees saw that he was eating with sinners and tax collectors and said to his disciples, "Why does he eat and drink with tax collectors and sinners?" Jesus heard this said to them,

"Those who are well do not need a physician, but the sick [do]. I have not come to call the righteous but sinners." (Mark 2:13-17)

Levi was a tax collector for the Roman authorities, therefore a despised man. By calling Levi to follow him, Jesus was inviting the marginal and the rejected into his circle of disciples, and this is celebrated with a meal prepared by Levi. By Jesus invitation, the tax collector was brought into the realm of the Kingdom of God.

Next there was the feeding of the five thousand, which signified the coming of the bread of salvation from heaven. This was an eschatological "sign," which for the apostle John signified a miracle.

> After this, Jesus went across the Sea of Galilee [of Tiberias]. A large crowd followed him, because they saw the signs he was performing on the sick. Jesus went up on the mountain, and there he sat down with his disciples. The Jewish feast of Passover was near. When Jesus raised his eyes and saw that a large crowd was coming to him, he said to Philip, "Where can we buy enough food for them to eat?" He said this to test him, because he himself knew what he was going to do. Philip answered him, "Two hundred days wages worth of food would not be enough for each of them to have a little [bit]." One of his disciples, Andrew, the brother of Simon Peter, said to him, "There is a boy here who has five barley loaves and two fish; but what good are these for so many?" Jesus said, "Have the people recline." Now there was a great deal of grass in that place. So the men reclined, about five thousand in number. Then Jesus took the loaves, gave thanks, and distributed them to those who were reclining, and also as much of the fish as they wanted. When they had their fill, he said to his disciples, "Gather the fragments left over, so that nothing will be wasted." So they collected them, and filled twelve wicker baskets with fragments from the five barley loaves that had been more than they could eat. When the people saw the sign he had done, they said, "This is truly the Prophet, the one who is to come into the world." (John 6:1-14)

Another important occasion was of Jesus curing a man with dropsy at a meal provided by the scribes and Pharisees. By breaking the law to perform the miracle on the Sabbath, Jesus' healing ministry had an implicit eschatological reference. We read:

> On a sabbath he [Jesus] went to dine at the home of one of the leading Pharisees, and the people there were observing him carefully. In front of him there was a man suffering from dropsy. Jesus spoke to the scholars of the law and Pharisees in reply, asking, "Is

it lawful to cure on the sabbath or not?" But they kept silent; so he took the man and, after he had healed him, dismissed him. Then he said to them, who among you, if your son or ox falls into a cistern, would not immediately pull him out on the sabbath day?" But they were unable to answer his question. (Luke 14: 1–6)

The next healing event was the conversion of a sinful woman in the context of a meal. In this event the life of the Kingdom is already made present. We read:

A Pharisee invited him [Jesus] to dine with him, and he entered the Pharisee's house and reclined at table. Now there was a sinful woman in the city who learned that he was at table in the house of the Pharisee. Bringing an alabaster flask of ointment, she stood behind him at his feet weeping and began to bathe his feet with her tears. Then she wiped them with her hair, kissed them, and anointed them with the ointment. When the Pharisee who had invited him saw this he said to himself, "If this man were a prophet, he would know who and what sort of woman this is who is touching him, that she is a sinner" (Luke 7:36–39).

The principal and most significant of Jesus' meals with his disciples was the Last Supper:

When the day of the feast of Unleavened Bread arrived, the day for sacrificing the Passover lamb, he sent out Peter and John, instructing them, "Go and make preparations for us to eat the Passover." They asked him, "Where do you want us to make the preparations?" And he answered them, "When you go into the city, a man will meet you carrying a jar of water. Follow him into the house that he enters and say to the master of the house, the teacher says to you, Where is the guest room where I may eat the Passover with my disciples? He will show you a large upper room which is furnished. Make the preparations there." Then they went off and found everything exactly as he had told them, and there they prepared the Passover. (Luke 22:7–13)

The core of the Last Supper with its eschatological orientation is recounted as follows:

When the hour came, he took his place at table with the apostles. He said to them, "I have eagerly desired to eat this Passover with you before I suffer, for, I tell you, I shall not eat it [again] until there is fulfillment in the kingdom of God." Then he took a cup, gave thanks, and said, "Take this and share it among yourselves; for I tell you [that] from this time on I shall not drink of the fruit of the vine until the kingdom of God comes." Then he took the bread, said the blessing, broke it, and gave it to them, saying, "This is my body, which will be given for you; do this in memory of me." And likewise, the cup after they had eaten, saying, "This cup is the new covenant in my blood, which will be shed for you. (Luke 22:14–20)

The eschatological heart of this event is Jesus' words about the coming of the Kingdom:

For I tell you [that] from this time I shall not drink of the fruit of the vine until the kingdom of God comes. (Luke 22:18)[12]

The fact that Jesus did not drink of the fourth cup signifies the eschatological character of the Last Supper. The different events narrated in the passages already narrated underline the eschatological ministry of Jesus expressed in common meals.

POST-RESURRECTION MEALS

The relationship between Jesus and his disciples was radically changed by the event of the resurrection. The principal post-resurrection meal was eaten at Emmaus, a few miles from Jerusalem. After interpreting for the disciples the events of his betrayal and death, Jesus and the disciples draw near to the town of Emmaus:

As they approached the village to which they were going, he gave the impression that he was going on farther. But they urged him, "Stay with us, for it is nearly evening and the day is almost over." So he went in to stay with them. And it happened that, while he was with them at table, he took bread, said the blessing, broke it, and gave it to them. With that their eyes were opened and they recognized him, but he vanished from their sight. Then they said to each other, "Were not our hearts burning [within us] while he spoke to us on the way and opened the scriptures to us? So they set out at once and returned to Jerusalem where they found gathered together the eleven and those with them who were saying, "The Lord has truly been raised and has appeared to Simon!" Then the two recounted what had taken place on the way and how he was made known to them in the breaking of the bread. (Luke 24:28–35)

---

12. The most articulate position in favor of the Last Supper as a Passover event is that of Brant Pitre, *Jesus and the Last Supper*.

In chapter 24 of Luke we read that in Jerusalem, while the disciples were explaining what had occurred in Emmaus, Jesus appeared to them and was made known in the breaking of bread.

> While they were still speaking about this, he stood in their midst and said to them, "Peace be with you." But they were startled and terrified and thought that they were seeing a ghost. Then he said to them, "Why are you troubled? And why do questions arise in your hearts? Look at my hands and my feet, that it is I myself. Touch me and see, because a ghost does not have flesh and bones as you can see I have." And as he said this, he showed them his hands and his feet. While they were still incredulous for joy and were amazed, he asked them, "Have you anything here to eat?" They gave him a piece of baked fish; he took it and ate it in front of them. (Luke 24: 36–43)

The Old and New Testaments narrated above together constitute the fact that Jesus' eschatological ministry took place typically in the context of meals.

THE WEDDING FEAST OF THE LAMB

I turn next to the theme of the wedding of Christ the Lamb victorious and the Church as bride. Jesus is here an eschatological figure in that his appearance brings the world to come into the present. This topic is found most prominently in the Book of Revelation. In chapter 19 we read:

> Then I heard something like the sound of a great multitude or the sound of rushing water or mighty peals of thunder, as they said:
>
> "Alleluia!
> The Lord has established his reign,
> [our] God, the almighty.
> Let us rejoice and be glad
> and give him glory.
> For the wedding day of the Lamb has come,
> his bride has made herself ready.
> She was allowed to wear
> A bright, clean linen garment." (Rev 19:6–8)

The Lamb represents Christ, while the bride represents the Church. This theme is elaborated as follows:

> Then the angel said to me, "Write this: Blessed are those who have been called to the wedding feast of the Lamb." And he said to me, "These words are true, they come from God." I fell at his feet to worship him. But he said to me, "Don't! I am a fellow servant of yours and of your brothers who bear witness to Jesus. Worship God. Witness to Jesus is the spirit of prophecy." (Rev 19:9–10)

The great wedding banquet in Revelation expressed the future hope of Israel. Jesus' whole public ministry was seen as looking forward to the eschatological wedding banquet. In this, Jesus combines the tradition of the eschatological banquet with the symbolism of marriage in order to present the end of all things as a wedding banquet.[13] We read:

> One of the seven angels who held the seven bowls filled with the seven last plagues came and said to me, "Come here. I will show you the bride, the wife of the Lamb." (Rev 21:9)

The image of Christ the bridegroom is found already in St. Paul with the Church as a bride and St. Paul as the best man who guards the bride's virginity, and Christ, the bridegroom as his pure body. The same image is found in Ephesians, where the love of Christ for his people is presented in nuptial terms (Eph 5:22–33).

Pursuing this theme, we are given one of the most beautiful passages in Revelation:

> Then I saw a new heaven and a new earth. The former heaven and the former earth had passed away, and the sea was no more. Jerusalem, coming down out of heaven from God, prepared as a bride adorned for her husband. I heard a loud voice from the throne saying, "Behold, God's dwelling is with the human race. He will dwell with them and they will be his people" and God himself will always be with them [as their God]. (Rev 21:1–3)

Horton Davies states of the marriage festival that it is "one of utmost joy, for it proclaims the indissoluble union of Christ and his faithful disciples of every century, the complete establishment of the communion of saints."[14]

---

13. On Jesus as bridegroom, see Long, *Jesus the Bridegroom*; McWhirter, *The Bridegroom Messiah and the People of God*; Pitre. *Jesus the Bridegroom*.

14. Davies, *Bread of Life*, 89–90.

Then there is the matter of fasting. Jesus answers the question of why the disciples of the Pharisees and John the Baptist fast while Jesus' disciples do not by saying, "Can the wedding guests mourn as long as the bridegroom is with them? The days will come when the bridegroom is taken from them and they will fast (Matt 9:15). Now, Jesus says, is the time for celebration and banqueting, rather than fasting. Banquets evoke the blessings of God's presence, belonging, and friendship in God's family, the joyful celebration of victory over evil, and the hopeful expectation of the final coming of the Kingdom. Indeed, the wedding banquet is an image for the messianic Kingdom and its joys.

THE JOYFUL FEAST

Feasts in the Bible are blessed events. They are not simply parties in the modern sense, but celebrations of God's goodness towards his people. They provide occasions of communal solidarity. If the people of Israel had good harvests over many years, the feasts were accompanied with joyful music and dancing, giving thanks for abundance. At the same time, the communities shared their sorrows at feasts. The nearest similarities to the ancient feast today might be celebrations of birthdays, wedding anniversaries, funerals, and public recognitions of achievements of distinction.

Feasts without blessings, as the modern conceptions allow, make a striking contrast with those in the Old and New Testaments. The differences may well be attributed to Western civilization's outlook in which the soul and body are split, with food assigned to the realm of the body. The feasts in the Bible express physical, psychological, and spiritual joy. The pleasure of a festive meal is depicted in Tobit (Tob 2:1) and as a drink of good wine in Judges (Jgs 9:13). Music and dancing were expressions of communal joy (Job 21:12). Occasions to express joy included the birth of children, especially sons (Jer 20:15), long life (Eccl 30:23), love of spouse (Prov 5:18), and, of course, prosperity and abundance at the harvest of grain and vintage (1 Chr 12:4). Deliverance from enemies or victories also were occasions of joyful feasting (1 Sam 18:6). Joy was seen as a gift of God and was associated with religious feasts and liturgical worship.[15]

In light of the milieu in which he lived, Jesus inaugurated salvation by feasts of many kinds. He directed his followers' attention to the wedding banquet, which he expressed prominently in parables such as those of the

15. I adapt this summary from Davies, *Bread of Life*, 93–94.

parable of the monarch celebrating the wedding of his son (Matt 22.4) and the wealthy landowner preparing a great supper (Luke 14:16ff).

As I said already, the blessing of the Passover feast prefigured in Christian perspective the sanctified feast in the Kingdom of heaven, an eternal feast of which earthly feasts are an anticipation. The feast in the Kingdom of heaven will respond to the aspirations of people by means of a blessing: the meeting of friends long lost, the reconciliation of those who were enemies, the end of all alienations, the rejoicing of families reunited. The celebrations will be blessed with the heavenly joy at the eschatological table and with a superabundance of food and wine of the highest quality.

The blessing of food sets the proper tone of all communal celebrations, and the Christian liturgy establishes the foundation of that joy. But we never forget that Christian joy is always forged in the deathly passing over of Christ. Scripture scholar Walter Brueggemann speaks of "pain as the matrix of praise."[16] The feast is eschatological, even in sadness, a foretaste of the feast of heaven in which all sadness is overcome. The Christian feast is essentially a joyous remembrance of the Lord's death and resurrection, and a participation in the superabundance of life and love that has been ever present and available to us since the first Easter morning.

The Church on earth participates in the worship of heaven, and its true citizenship is renewed and deepened because the Church in its eucharistic worship looks forward to the second coming of Christ when the Lord will return in joy and heaven and earth are united.

ESCHATOLOGY AND EUCHARIST TODAY

I will now focus on the eschatological aspect of the Church's eucharistic liturgy today, which is the place in which we encounter most fully the heavenly liturgy on earth. The core of this eschatological aspect is implicitly the Eucharist which stands at the center of the Church's liturgy. The Constitution on the Sacred Liturgy of Vatican II sets forth the eschatological nature of the liturgy. We read:

> In the earthly liturgy we take part in a foretaste of that heavenly liturgy which is celebrated in the holy city of Jerusalem toward which we journey as pilgrims, where Christ is sitting at the right

---

16. Brueggemann, *Israel's Praise*, 136. German theologian Karl Rahner describes the liturgical feast of the ascension as a "festival of holy pain," of fear and blessing combined; in Rahner, "Festival of the Future of the World," 182–85.

hand of God, minister of the holy of holies and of the true tabernacle. With all the warriors of the heavenly army we sing a hymn of glory to the Lord; venerating the memory of the saints, we hope for some part and fellowship with them; we eagerly await the Savior, our Lord Jesus Christ, until he our life shall appear and we too will appear with him in glory (no.8).[17]

The Dogmatic Constitution on the Church of Vatican II states similarly of the eschatological nature of the Church and the eucharistic sacrifice that stands at its core:

It is especially in the sacred liturgy that our union with the heavenly church is best realized; in the liturgy, through the sacramental signs, the power of the Holy Spirit acts on us, and with community rejoicing we celebrate together the praise of the divine majesty, when all those of every tribe and tongue and people and nation (cf. Apoc. 5.9) who have been redeemed by the blood of Christ and gathered together into one church glorify, in one common song of praise, the one and triune God. When, then, we celebrate the eucharistic sacrifice we are most closely united to the worship of the heavenly church; when in the fellowship of communion we honor and remember the glorious Mary ever virgin, St. Joseph, the holy apostles and martyrs and all the saints (no. 50.)[18]

The *Catechism* deals with the heavenly community at worship in a cosmic liturgy:

Recapitulated in Christ," these are the ones who take part in the service of the praise of God and the fulfillment of his plan: the heavenly powers, all creation (the four living beings), the servants of the Old and New Covenants (the twenty-four elders), the new People of God (the one hundred and forty-four thousand) especially the martyrs "slain for the word of God," and the all-holy Mother of God (the Woman), the Bride of the Lamb, and finally "a great multitude which no one could number, from every nation, from all tribes, and peoples and tongues.[19]

The liturgically-minded Christian touched by such descriptions may well ask: Where does this biblical conception of the liturgy find practical expression today? Is this the kind of vision that one actually experiences in the average Sunday celebration of the Eucharist, not to speak of the other

---

17. *Vatican Council II*, vol. 1, 5.

18. *Vatican Council II*, 77.

19. *Catechism*, no. 1138.

liturgies of the Churches? Few will be inclined to answer these questions in a positive manner. So the question arises: Why has the eschatological vision of the scriptures, of the modern liturgical movement, and of Vatican II, not been realized?

The problem here is not, of course, new, and some history will be useful. There appears to be general consensus that the eschatological features of Roman Catholicism were at something of a low ebb as the Church moved out of its neo-scholastic mold in the nineteenth century. Eschatology in that framework was regarded largely as the discrete study of the last things: death, particular judgment, heaven, hell, and purgatory. In the standard sacramental theology of the pre-Vatican II era, the focus was primarily on what was *present* in the liturgy, but not adequately on what was *yet to come*. The English Dominican scholar Aidan Nichols is, for instance, critical of this aspect of *Mediator Dei* published by Pope Pius XII in 1947. Reflecting its time, Nichols says, *Mediator Dei* focused on the rendering present of "the most holy being of Jesus . . . to the effective exclusion of any concern for the liturgy as the realized anticipation of the future Parousia of the Lord."[20] But, Nichols writes, the Eucharist is not merely the "rendering actual in present time of a *past* reality" but is also "an anticipation of a future to come."[21] He does not hesitate to say that, in most respects, *Mediator Dei* is theologically superior to *Sacrosanctum Concilium*. But in its strong eschatological emphasis, Nichols finds the Vatican II document far superior.

The focus in the liturgy before Vatican II, we might say, was on the incarnational rather than the eschatological. This emphasis found expression in the attention given in the standard manuals of Catholic sacramental theology to Christ's eucharistic presence. That Christ is really and truly present in the Eucharist is an affirmation that remains firmly implanted in Roman Catholic teaching. But the laudable desire to insist on the reality of that presence, especially after the Council of Trent, was often worked out at the expense of the recognition that the Eucharist has an intrinsically and systemically crucial eschatological element. Theologian Owen Cummings points out that "in the polemics of eucharistic theology during the Reformation and Catholic Reformation periods, the almost exclusive concerns of theologians were with the two eucharistic doctrines of sacrifice and

---

20. Nichols, "Tale," 24–25.

21. Nichols, "Tale," 29. Nichols praises the strength of the eschatological emphasis in the *Catechism*, especially in the earlier section of part two, which deals with liturgical theology generally.

presence" to the effect that "the eschatological dimension of the Eucharist faded into the background,"[22] even if it never quite disappeared.

The issue has played itself out symbolically in the question of which image of the Eucharist is more fundamental: the Last Supper, the Sacrifice of Calvary, the Emmaus meal, or the Banquet of the Lamb Victorious. There is, or course, no theological competition between these images, yet there is much to be said for choosing the latter—the Banquet of the Lamb Victorious—as the one that is both more fundamental theologically and more inclusive of the others.

If eucharistic eschatology has had a poor presence in Roman Catholicism in recent centuries, this oversight was awakened with the modern liturgical movement's encounter with Eastern Christianity and with the renewal of New Testament and patristic scholarship. The major leaders of the Roman Catholic liturgical renewal, such as Lambert Beauduin of Belgium, and Odo Casel and Joseph Jungmann of Germany, found strong inspiration for a revival of the eschatological in the life of the Eastern churches where it has always had a stronger and more explicit presence.

In the eschatological consciousness of early twentieth-century Western thought, then, there developed a growing awareness that the Christ who is present in the Eucharist is also the Christ who stands above and beyond the liturgy, drawing the Church forward into the amplitude of eternity. In this vision, the worship of the Church is not self-enclosed, complete in itself, but always has a dimension of reaching forward—of being pulled ahead of itself into the Kingdom to come. The dimension of future glory is the dimension of the *eschaton,* of what is yet to come, even as it is already present in sacrament.[23] To suggest that the eschatological was simply absent in Western Christianity after the patristic period would not, of course, be accurate.[24] The famous Corpus Christi hymn written by St. Thomas Aquinas praises the sacred banquet "in which Christ is received as food, the memory of his Passion is renewed, the soul is filled with grace, and a pledge

22. Cummings, *Coming to Christ*, 243, 241ff.

23. For treatments of the liturgy and eschatology, see Shepherd, *Paschal Liturgy and the Apocalypse*; Cothenet, "Earthly Liturgy and Heavenly Liturgy," 115–36; Wainwright, "Church as Worshiping Community," 19–33; Schaffer, "Heavenly and Earthly Liturgies," 482–505; Jean-Pierre Ruiz, "Apocalypse of John and Contemporary Roman Catholic Liturgy," 482–504.

24. For a fuller analysis of the themes dealt with here, see Mannion, "Rejoice, Heavenly Powers!" 37–60.

of future glory is given to us."[25] The same theme found strong representation in some parts of the Anglican and Methodist traditions.[26]

THE CULTURAL PROBLEM

If reviving the eschatological vision focused on the Eucharist appears to have waned since the Second Vatican Council, the problem seems to be related largely to the cultural climate of the 1960s and after. In those decades, the eschatological quickly became translated into secular concern, that is, concern for the concrete *now* of the human world. Indeed, it seems as though the strong cultural openness of the Vatican II Constitution on the Church in the Modern World (*Gaudium et spes*) began to provide the new hermeneutic for practical liturgical renewal after Vatican II.[27] The advent of political and liberation theologies (which did contribute something immeasurably important in postconciliar Catholicism) had a downside: a preoccupation with the present that easily led to the political and social instrumentalization of eschatological themes. The relevance of the liturgy to social concerns had always been a strong conviction of the liturgical movement, but the controlling themes therein were of comprehensive cultural transformation in the light of the gospel. The liturgy, it was fervently hoped, would transform the culture. However, in the 1970s, the conception of the Church and its liturgy as *of service* to culture and society took the upper hand, so that the liturgy began to be instrumentally harnessed to secular, socially-conscious ends.[28] Rather than liturgy transforming culture, the culture set the agenda for liturgical conceptions and practice.

By no means am I playing down the importance of the eucharistic liturgy engaging its social context; nor am I suggesting that the eschatological

25. See *Catechism* no. 1042, 354.

26. See Wainwright. *Eucharist and Eschatology*, 1–17, 123–54. One of the more prominent Anglican representatives, Jeremy Taylor, speaks of the Eucharist as "the antepast of heaven," quoted in Taylor, *Selected Works*, 194; see also McAdoo and Stevenson, *The Mystery of the Eucharist in the Anglican Tradition*. As I will show later, John and Charles Wesley's Hymns are notable for their high eucharistic eschatology (examples will be presented at the end of this chapter).

27. For an advocacy of this development, see the chapters entitled, "Two Models of Christian Worship" and "Liturgical Spirituality," in Madigan, *Spirituality Rooted in Liturgy*, 89–115; 117–37.

28. On the strengths and weaknesses of the "servant" model of the Church, see the chapter entitled, "The Church as Servant," in Dulles, *Models of the Church*, 89–102; also, Dulles, "Imaging the Church for the 1980s," 1–18.

and the political are opposed. On the contrary, eschatology is inescapably political; but it may not be collapsed into the narrowly political and pragmatic as defined by secular culture.[29] The task of the church is not to remake the human city according to the more progressive insights of the age, but to remake it in the light of the New Jerusalem, the glorious city of God, which the eschatological liturgy expresses.[30]

Another factor in the reversal of the emerging eschatological eucharistic consciousness has been the reductionist christologies generally subsumed under the "third quest for the historical Jesus." These are decidedly biased against eschatological conceptions of Christ risen and glorified. "Historical quest" christologies, precisely because of their "low" theological character and their preoccupation with historical data generally, do not adequately consider Jesus' eschatological character. Rather, the emphasis is on Jesus' table fellowship as a subversion of societal norms of association, authority, and hierarchy. The eschatology of these conceptions is a radically realized one. Conceptions of Christ in majesty and glory are set in the shadows.

In tandem with this factor, post-Vatican II theology of the more radical type assumed a decidedly negative approach to traditional eschatology, regarding it as oppressive and escapist. Eschatological themes were thought to be imperialist male politics of domination in liturgical guise. Radical theology set out to deconstruct Christian eschatological conceptions.[31]

In summary, eschatological consciousness, so central to New Testament and early Christianity, began to decline—more in the West than the East—soon after the patristic era. It was never, of course, completely absent in the West, but it did lie fallow for quite long periods. With the liturgical, biblical, and patristic movements of the late nineteenth and early twentieth centuries, the theme was recovered and renewed. This development found official approbation at the Second Vatican Council. However, a decline set in thereafter so that what Cardinal Christoph Schönborn has

---

29. See Webber and Clapp, *People of the Truth*, 17–83; also, "Eschatological Politics and Political Eschatology," in Jenson, *Essays in Theology of Culture*, 16–27; Berger and Neuhaus, eds., *Against the World, For the World*.

30. Mannion, "Church and City," 31–36; also, Urban Holmes, *Ministry and Imagination*, 13–34.

31. For a summary of radically realized eschatologies, see Cummings, *Coming to Christ*, 203–6.

called "eschatological amnesia" came to prevail in late modern Christiani-ty.[32] Following Vatican II liturgy began to be increasingly secularized and instrumentalized.

How can the eschatological be more generally restored and renewed in liturgy? I suggest that the Christian imagination should be grasped anew by the Book of Revelation. This interest can serve to bring back into Christian focus the heavenly liturgy as the model for the earthly. Scholars disagree on the extent to which the dramatic portrayals of the New Jerusa-lem in the Book of Revelation reflect the worship life of early Christianity; the model of Revelation does seem, however, to be deeply liturgical. In this understanding, the liturgy of heaven and earth are united as the former gathers up the latter.[33] In my view, the importance of this theme cannot be overestimated.

CONCLUSION

I began the eighth model of this book by looking at the meal from both human and religious perspectives. The eschatological meal was highlighted in particular in the New and Old Testaments, and reached its high point in the Book of Revelation. The culmination of biblical feasts at the wedding of the Lamb unites eschatology to the liturgy.

The eucharistic hymns of the founders of Methodism, John and Charles Wesley, are a good place to end this chapter. These hymns represent perhaps the strongest and most expressive statements of the eschatological character of the Eucharist, the Supper of the Lamb, in Western liturgy and are a model of liturgical hymnody and prayer in a renewed eschatological liturgy.

> Admitted to the heavenly feast,
> We shall his choicest blessings taste,
> And banquet on His richest love.
> We soon the midnight cry shall hear,
> Arise, and meet the Bridegroom near,
> The marriage of the Lamb is come;

32. Schönborn, *Death to Life*, 14.

33. A convergence of thought on this matter is a marked feature of ecumenical eucharistic theologies. See Stookey, *Eucharist*; Saliers, *Worship as Theology*; Juste, *The Ongoing Feast*; Wainwright, *Eucharist and Eschatology*. This is also evidenced in the joint common statements of Protestant and Catholic ecumenists.

Attended by His heavenly friends,
The glorious King of Saints descends
To take His bride in triumph home.

. . . . .

By faith and hope already there,
Even now the marriage-feast we share,
Even now we by the Lamb are fed;
Our Lord's celestial joy we prove,
Led by the Spirit of His love,
To springs of living comfort led. (Hymn 93)

. . . . .

He hallow'd the cup Which now we receive,
The pledge of our hope With Jesus to live,
(Where sorry and sadness Shall never be found,)
With glory and gladness Eternally crown'd.
The fruit of the vine (The joy it implies)
Again we shall join To drink in the skies,
Exult in His favour, Our triumph renew;
And I, saith the Saviour, Will drink it with you. (Hymn 95)

. . . . .

In heaven the mystic banquet leads;
Let us to heaven ascend,
And bear this joy upon our heads
Till it in glory end.
Till all who truly join in this,
The marriage supper share,
Enter into their Master's bliss,
And feast for ever there. (Hymn 99)

. . . . .

For all that Joy which now we taste,
Our happy hallow'd souls prepare;
O let us hold the earnest fast,
This pledge that we Thy heaven shall share,
Shall drink it new with Thee above,
The wine of Thy eternal love. (Hymn 108)[34]

---

34. These hymn texts and their numbering are quoted from Wainwright, *Eucharist and Eschatology*, 56–57. They are also found in numerous hymnals. Fuller presentations of this hymnody are found in Rattenbury, *The Eucharistic Hymns of John and Charles Wesley*.

EPILOGUE

I choose to live toward eternal life.
—John S. Dunne[1]

IF THERE IS ONE thing I would like readers to take away from this book, it is a sense of the dynamic, overwhelming, and magnificent reality of heaven. The theoretical and popular views of heaven have, for reasons I need not repeat here, suffered from weak and vague conceptions. That heaven is more real than anything we experience in earthly life is a lesson that is hard to get across due to people's ingrained and meager understandings of life after death. In reality, heaven is most majestic and glorious and is the foundation and end of all existence. The following points, which serve partly as a summary of this book, seek to underline a more affective and spiritually rich vision of heaven.

- Earthly life is often tedious and beset by restlessness. It is characterized by anxiety and a sense of a never-ending lack of ease. When, at funerals we wish the deceased "eternal rest," we are not condemning him or her to an eternity of boredom. Rather, heavenly rest is dynamic and vibrant. It opens up the possibility of creativity and imaginative achievement. It is the very opposite of boredom and anxiety of soul.

- There is much in life that is beautiful: people, nature, and art that lifts the mind beyond the present moment. One can discipline one's mind to interpret earthly beauties as signs of the ultimate beauty that is God and that permeates the heavenly Kingdom. By the same token, human beings are inspired to beautify the world in which they live, so that the beauty of the world becomes a kind of sacrament of heaven's glory.

---

1. Dunne. *Dark Light*, 73.

- The concept of living in the Trinity is remote from people's ordinary understanding. But there is much in nature and in life in general that shows traces of the Trinity. Reflection on life can develop a trinitarian mindset—seeing signs of the threeness of God imprinted in all things—community, human cooperation, even politics. The dance, an ancient metaphor, can help us imagine the artful relationships between Father, Son, and Spirit, as well as the relationships between God and humanity.

- In an age of individualism, the experience of community is not as strong as it was in traditional societies, when people depended on each other for most things. People do not generally regard human existence today as a foretaste of the eschatological community. Yet heaven is a great and universal community in which all humankind will live in graceful interrelationships. Human efforts to live communally—not least in the community of the family—are prefigurements of the communion of saints. Therefore, earthly relationships have an eschatological character, and earthly friendships will grow into heavenly bonds.

- The singing voice of earthly humanity reflects the singing of the angels. Every beautiful song, symphony, chant reflect the harmony of heaven, even as they express the many moods and experiences of ordinary life. When we make music or listen to music, we are drawn already into the cosmic choir, and our souls are lifted beyond the noise of the human world. Great music opens the soul to the heavenly universe. The harmony of music on earth gives voice to the harmony of heaven.

- Since the industrial revolution, life in cities is a combination of glory and squalor. Yet, human work, both public and private, often seeks a harmony that brings order to society. Human beings can see something heavenly in the well-built house or the well-planned city. People are habitually attracted to the architecture of Paris, Rome, London (or, at least, the better parts of them). The work of making the human environment beautiful is implicitly an attempt to bring heaven to earth and to prepare the earthly city to be lifted into heaven.

- The state of the environment stands as, perhaps, the greatest area of crisis that grips the world today. The pollution of water, the chemical poisoning of large areas of the world, deforestation, poor air quality, all seem to be on the rise as the climate changes. There are heroic efforts at work to relieve these problems, but many worry that it may

166

be too late. As Genesis makes clear, the earth we have inherited is Paradise despoiled. The challenge facing humankind is the reversal of this trend. This is not just a "secular" task, but also an eschatological one. We are called to remake the earth as a preparation for heaven, to prefigure the heavenly world in earthly work.

- The human feast prefigures the feast of heaven. This notion goes against the modern conception of meals as merely functional. The earthly feasts, such as we experience at birthdays, weddings, and funerals, have a transcendent ethos that carries us for a moment into heaven. The traditional practice of invoking God's blessing before meals sanctifies human eating and blesses meals as prefigurements of the heavenly feast.

In summary, earthly life is, in all its positive and noble aspects, eschatological. We are called to live now with heaven in view, to have a spirituality that is eschatological, always looking forward to the life to come, to seeing death as the door to heaven, to seeing present life as pale by comparison with the fulness of life in heaven. I give the last word to Victor Hugo:

> For half a century I have been translating my thoughts into prose and verse: history, drama, philosophy, romance, tradition, satire, ode, and song; all of these I have tried. I feel I haven't given utterance to the thousandth part of what lies within me. When I go to the grave I can say, as others have said, "My day's work is done." But I cannot say, "My life is done." My work will recommence the next morning. The tomb is not a blind alley; it is a thoroughfare. It closes upon the twilight, but opens upon the dawn.[2]

---

2. Quoted in Alcorn, *Eternal Perspectives*, 603–4.

BIBLIOGRAPHY

Adler, Mortimer. *The Angels and Us.* New York: Collier, 1982.

Alcorn, Randy. *Heaven.* Carol Stream, IL: Tyndale House, 2000.

———. *Eternal Perspectives: A Collection of Quotations on Heaven, the New Earth, and Life After Death.* Carol Stream, IL: Tyndale, 2012.

Alexandra, Mother. *The Holy Angels.* Minneapolis, MN: Light and Life, 1987.

Alkon, Alison Hope and Julian Agyeman, eds. *Cultivating Food Justice: Race, Class, and Sustainability.* Cambridge, MA: MIT Press, 2011.

Allman, Dwight D. and Michael D. Beatty, eds. *Cultivating Citizens: Soulcraft and Citizenship in Contemporary American.* Lanham, MD: Lexington, 2002.

Aquilina, Mike. *Angels of God: The Bible, the Church, and the Heavenly Hosts.* Cincinnati, OH: Servant, 2009.

Auden, W. H. *Selected Poems.* Edited by Edward Mendelson. New York: Vintage International, 1979.

Augustine. *City of God.* Translated by Henry Bettensnor. London: Penguin, 1972.

———. *Confessions.* Translation by Henry Chadwick. Oxford: Oxford University, 1991.

———. *On the Trinity.* Quoted in Douglas F. Kelly, *Systematic Theology II—The Beauty of Christ: A Trinitarian Vision.* Ross-shire, Scotland: Christian Focus, 2014.

———. "The Beauty of Creation." *The Liturgy of Hours,* vol. 3. New York: Book Publishing, 1975.

Bakke, Ray. *A Theology as Big as the City: Effective Ministry in Today's Urban World.* Downers Grove, IL: Intervarsity, 1997.

Baldovin, John F. *Worship: City, Church and Renewal.* Washington, DC: Pastoral, 1991.

Balthasar, Hans Urs von. *The Christian and Anxiety,* Foreword by Yves Tourenne, OFM, translated by Dennis D. Martin and Michael J. Miller. San Francisco: Ignatius, 2000.

———. *The Glory of the Lord. A Theological Aesthetic 1: Seeing the Form.* San Francisco: Ignatius, 2009.

Barth, Karl. *Wolfgang Amadeus Mozart.* Translated by Clarence K. Pott. Foreword by John Updike. Grand Rapids: Eerdmans, 1986.

Barron, Robert. *And Now I See . . . A Theology of Transformation.* New York: Crossroad, 1998.

Bauerschmidt, Frederick Christian. "Trinity, Politics, and Modernity." In *The Oxford Handbook of the Trinity,* edited by Gilles Emery, OP, and Matthew Levering, 531–43. Oxford: Oxford University Press, 2011.

Beatty, Michael D. and Dwight D. Allman, eds. *Cultivating Citizens: Soulcraft and Citizenship in Contemporary America.* Lanham, MD: Lexington, 2002.

Bede the Venerable. "Sermon on All Saints' Day," around A.D. 710. In William Jennings Bryan, ed., *The World's Famous Orations*. New York: Funk and Wagnalls, 1906.

Bell, Michael M. *City of the Good: Nature, Religion and the Ancient Search for What is Right*. Princeton University Press, 2018.

Benedict XVI. *The Environment*. Collected and edited by Jacquelyn Lindsay. Huntington, IN: Our Sunday Visitor, 2012.

———. *The Garden of God: Toward a Human Ecology*. Foreword by Archbishop Jean-Louis Brugùes. Washington, DC: Catholic University of America Press, 2014.

———. The Sacrament of Charity (*Sacramentum Caritatis*). Washington, DC: United States Conference of Catholic Bishops, 2007.

Benko, Stephen. *The Meaning of Sanctorum Communio*. London: SCM, 1964.

Bergant, Diane, CSA. *"The Earth is the Lord's:" The Bible, Ecology and Worship*. Collegeville, MN: Liturgical Press, 1998.

Berger, John. *Ways of Seeing*. Based on the BBC television series. London: British Broadcasting Corporation and Penguin, 1972.

Berry, Wendell. *Bringing It to the Table: On Farming and Food*. Berkeley: Counterpoint, 2009.

Bess, Philip. *Till We Have Built Jerusalem: Architecture, Urbanism, and the Sacred*. Wilmington, DE: ISI, 2006.

Bloesch, Donald G. *The Last Things: Resurrection, Judgment, Glory*. Downers Grove, IL : LUP Academic, 2004.

Bloy, Léon. *La Femme pauvre*, 1897. Paris: FB Editions, 1939.

Boff, Leonardo. *Trinity and Society*. Translated by Philip Berryman. Maryknoll, NY: Orbis, 2000.

———. *Holy Trinity, Perfect Society*. Translated by Paul Burns. Maryknoll, NY: Orbis, 2000.

Boice, James Montgomery. *Two Cities, Two Loves: Christian Responsibility in a Crumbling Culture*. Translated by Peter D. Hertz. New York: Harper and Row, 1971.

Bonhoeffer, Dietrich. *The Communion of Saints: A Dogmatic Inquiry into the Sociology of the Church*. London: Forgotten, 2015.

Book of Common Prayer. New York: Church Hymnal Society/Seabury, 1977.

Book of Blessings. Collegeville, MN: Liturgical, 1989.

Boudreau, J., SJ. *The Happiness of Heaven*. Rockford, IL: Tan Books, 1984.

Bouma-Prediger, Steven. *For the Beauty of the Earth: A Christian Vision of Creation Care*. 2nd edition. Grand Rapids, MI: Baker Academic, 2010.

Bouyer, Louis. *Cosmos: The World and the Glory of God*. Translated by Pierre de Fontnouvelle. Petersham, MA: St. Bede's, 1988.

Braaten, Carl E. and Robert W. Jenson, eds. *The Last Things: Biblical and Theological Perspectives on Eschatology*. Grand Rapids: Eerdmans, 2002.

———. *The Two Cities of God: The Church's Responsibility for the Earthly City*. Grand Rapids, MI: Eerdmans, 1997.

Brontë, Emily. *The Complete Poems of Emily Jane Brontë*. Edited by C. W. Hatfield. New York: Columbia University Press, 1941.

Brueggemann, Walter. *Israel's Praise: Doxology Against Idolatry and Ideology*. Philadelphia, PA: Fortress, 1988.

———. *Sabbath as Resistance: Saying No to the Culture of Now*. Louisville, KY: Westminster John Knox, 2014.

Buckley, James J. and David S. Yeago, eds. *Knowing the Triune God: The Work of the Spirit in the Practices of the Church*. Grand Rapids: Eerdmans, 2001.

Bulgakov, Sergius. *Jacob's Ladder: On Angels*. Translated with an introduction by Thomas Allan Smith. Grand Rapids: Eerdmans, 2010.

Byerly, T. Ryan and Eric V. Silverman, eds. *Paradise Understood: New Philosophical Essays about Heaven*. Oxford: Oxford University Press, 2006.

Caen, Herb and Dong Kingman. *San Francisco: City on Golden Hills*. Garden City, New York: Doubleday and Company, 1967.

Carlyle, Thomas. *Critical and Miscellaneous Essays*. New York: Peter Fenelon Collier, 1897.

Carroll, Thomas K., ed. *Jeremy Taylor: Selected Works*. Mahway, NJ: Paulist, 1990.

Carstens, Christopher and Douglas Martis, *Mystical Body, Mystical Voice: Encountering Christ in the Words of the Mass*. Chicago: Liturgy, 2011.

Carter, Stephen L. *Civility: Manners, Morals, and Etiquette of Democracy*. New York: Basic, 1998.

Catechism of the Catholic Church 2nd ed. Washington, DC: United States Conference of Catholic Bishops/*Libreria editrice Vaticana,* 2000.

Catherine of Genoa. *Fire of Love! Understanding Purgatory*. Manchester, NH: Sophia Institute, 1996.

Chervin, Ronda et al., *What the Saints Said About Heaven: 101 Holy Insights about Everlasting Life*. Charlotte, NC: Tan, 2011.

Christensen, Michael J. and Jeffery A. Witting, eds. *Partakers of the Divine Nature: The History and Development of Deification in the Christian Traditions*. Grand Rapids: Baker, 2007.

Christianson, Drew and Michael Grazer, eds. *And God Saw That It Was Good: Catholic Theology and the Environment*. Washington, DC: United States Conference of Catholic Bishops, 1996.

Chryssavgis, John, ed. *On Earth as in Heaven: Ecological Vision and Initiatives of Ecumenical Patriarch Bartholomew*. New York: Fordham University Press, 2012.

Chryssavgis, John and Bruce V. Foltz, eds. *Toward an Ecology of Transfiguration: Orthodox Christian Perspectives on Environment, Nature, and Creation*. New York: Fordham Press, 2013.

Cloutier, David. *Walking God's Earth: The Environment and Catholic Faith*. Collegeville, MN: Liturgical, 2014.

Colde, Mary L., ed. *Creation is Groaning: Biblical and Theological Perspectives*. Collegeville, MN: Liturgical, 2013.

Collins, Paul M. *Partaking in Divine Nature: Deification and Communion*. London/New York: T. & T. Clark, 2010.

Corbon, Jean. *The Wellspring of Worship*. Translated by Matthew J. O'Connell. San Francisco: Ignatius, 2005.

Cothenet, Edouard. "Earthly Liturgy and Heavenly Liturgy according to the Book of Revelation." In *Roles in the Liturgical Assembly: The Twenty-Third Liturgical Conference Saint Serge,* edited by Matthew J. O'Connell, 118–35. New York: Pueblo, 1961.

Cox, Harvey. *The Secular City: Secularization and Urbanization in Theological Perspective*. New York: Macmillan, 2013.

Csikszentmihalyi, Mihalyi. *Flow: The Psychology of Optimal Experience*. New York: Harper Perennial Modern Classics, 2008.

————. *Beyond Boredom and Anxiety: Experiencing Flow in Work and Play.* San Francisco: Jossey-Bass, 2000.

Csikszentmihalyi, Mihalyi and Rick E. Robinson. *The Art of Seeing: An Interpretation of the Aesthetic Encounter.* Malibu, CA: J. Paul Getty, 1990.

Cummings, Charles. *Eco-Spirituality: Toward a Reverent Life.* Mahwah, NJ: Paulist, 1991.

Cummings, Owen. *Coming to Christ: A Study in Christian Eschatology.* Lanham, MD: University Press of America, 1998.

Cunningham, Lawrence. *A Brief History of Saints.* Malden, MA: Blackwell, 2005.

————. *The Meaning of Saints.* San Francisco, CA: Harper and Row, 1980.

Daley, Brian E. *The Hope of the Early Church: A Handbook of Patristic Eschatology.* Cambridge: Cambridge University Press, 1991.

Daniélou, Jean, SJ. *The Angels and their Mission According to the Fathers of the Church.* Translated by David Heimen. Westminster, MD: Christian Classics, 1987.

Daniels, Marilyn. *The Dance in Christianity: A History of Religious Dance through the Middle Ages.* Ramsay, NJ: Paulist, 1981.

Davidson, Gustav. *All Things are Holy.* Introduction by Cornel Lengyel. Georgetown, CA: Dragon's Teeth, 1970.

————. *A Dictionary of Angels, Including Fallen Angels.* New York: Free, 1967.

Davies, Horton. *Bread of Life and Cup of Joy: Newer Ecumenical Perspectives on the Eucharist.* Eugene, OR: Wipf and Stock, 1999.

Davison, Peter. "The Singer and the Song." In the convention handbook of the Royal Canadian College of Organists, Ontario, 1981.

Deane-Drummond, Celia and David Clough, eds. *Creaturely Theology: On God, Human and Other Animals.* London: SCM, 2009.

Deane-Drummond, Celia. *A Primer in Ecotheology: Theology for a Fragile Earth.* Eugene, OR: Cascade Books, 2017.

DeLorenzo, Leonard J. *Work of Love: A Theological Reconstruction of the Communion of Saints.* Notre Dame, IN: University of Notre Dame Press, 2017.

Delumeau, Jean. *History of Paradise: The Garden of Eden in Myth and Tradition.* Translated by Matthew O'Connell. New York: Continuum, 1995.

Dick, Larry. *A Taste of Heaven.* Victoria, BC: Trafford, 2003.

Dinesen, Isak (Karen Blixen). *Babette's Feast and Other Short Stories.* London: Penguin Classics, 2013.

Dominite, Meriçor and Stelian Onica. "The Concept of Beauty in the Orthodox Esthetic and Iconography" in *European Journal of Science and Theology* 2 (June 2006) 1–32.

Dostoevsky, Fyodor. *The Idiot.* Translated by Henry and Olga Carlisle. New York: New American Library, 1969.

Dougherty, James. *The Fivesquare City: The City in the Religious Imagination.* Notre Dame, IN: University of Notre Dame Press, 1980.

Douglas, Mary. "Deciphering a Meal." *Daedalus: Journal of the American Academy of Arts and Sciences* (Winter 1992) 61–81.

Dow, Louis K. Fuller. *Images of Zion: Biblical Antecedents for the New Jerusalem.* Sheffield, UK: Sheffield Phoenix, 2010.

Downey, Michael. *Altogether Gift: A Trinitarian Spirituality.* Maryknoll, NY: Orbis, 2000.

Dulles, Avery, SJ. *A Church to Believe In: Discipleship and the Dynamics of Freedom.* New York: Crossroad, 1982.

————. *Models of the Church: Expanded edition.* New York: Image, 1987.

————. *Models of Revelation.* Maryknoll, NY: Orbis, 1992.

Dunne, John S. *Dark Light of Heaven*. Notre Dame, IN: University of Notre Dame Press, 2014.

Dupuis, Jacques, ed. *The Christian Faith in the Doctrinal Documents of the Catholic Church*. New York: Alba, 2001.

Durand, Emmanuel, OP. "A Theology of God the Father." In *The Oxford Handbook of the Trinity*. Editors Gilles Emery, OP, and Matthew Levering, 371–86. Oxford: Oxford University Press, 2011.

Edwards, Denis. "The Redemption of Animals in an Incarnational Theology." In *Creaturely Theology: On God, Human and Other Animals*, edited by Celia Deane-Drummond and David Clough. London: SCM, 2009.

Edwards, Jonathan. *Heaven: A World of Love*. Amityville, TX: Calvary Press, 1999.

Eliot, T. S. *The Waste Land and Other Poems*. Orlando, FL: Harcourt, 1934.

Ellsberg, Robert. *The Saints' Guide to Happiness*. New York: North Point, 2003.

Ellul, Jacques. *The Meaning of the City*. Translated by Dennis Pardee, introduction by John Wilkinson. Grand Rapids: Eerdmans, 1970.

Emery, Gilles, OP, and Matthew Levering, eds. *The Oxford Handbook of the Trinity*. Oxford: Oxford University Press, 2011.

Emery, Pierre-Yves. *The Communion of Saints*. Translated by D. J. and M. Watson. London: Faith Press, 1966.

Enright, D. J., ed. *The Oxford Book of Death*. Oxford: Oxford University Press, 1983.

Evdokimov, Paul. *The Art of the Icon: A Theology of Beauty*. Translated by Fr. Steven Bingham. Redondo Beach, CA: Oakwood, 1990.

Feely-Harnik, Gillian. *The Lord's Table: The Meaning of Food in Early Judaism and Christianity*. Washington, DC: Smithsonian Books, 1991.

Fergusson, David. *Creation*. Grand Rapids, MI: Eerdmans, 2014.

Finn, S. Margot. *Discriminating Taste: How Class Anxiety Created the American Food Revolution*. New Brunswick: Rutgers University Press, 2017.

Forte, Bruno. *The Portal of Beauty: Toward a Theology of Aesthetics*. Translated by David Glenday and Paul McPartlan. Grand Rapids: Eerdmans, 2008.

Fortman, Edmund J., SJ. *The Triune God: A Historical Study of the Doctrine of the Trinity*. Eugene, OR: Wipf and Stock, 1999.

———. *Everlasting Life After Death*. New York: Alba House, 1977.

Foster, Roger. *Trinity: Song and Dance*. London: Ichthus, 2004.

Fragomeni, Richard N. and John T. Pawlikowski, eds. *The Ecological Challenge: Ethical, Liturgical, and Spiritual Responses*. Collegeville, MN: Liturgical, 1994.

Francis, Pope. On Care for Our Common Home (*Laudato Si'*) Washington, DC: United States Conference of Catholic Bishops, 2015.

Francis of Assisi. "Canticle of Brother Sun." Translated by Paul M. Allen and John DeRis Allen, in *Canticle of the Creatures: A Modern Spiritual Path*. New York: Continuum, 1996.

Franz, Ignaz. "Holy God, We Praise Thy Name." No. 366. In *The Hymnal 1982 according to the use of The Episcopal Church*. New York: The Church Hymnal Corporation, 1982.

Frugoni, Chiara. *A Distant City: Images of Urban Experience in the Medieval World*. Translated by William McCuaeg. Princeton: Princeton University Press, 1991.

Garijo-Guembe, Miguel M. *Communion of the Saints: Foundation, Nature and Structure of the Church*. Translated by Patrick Madigan, S J. Collegeville, MN: Liturgical, 1994.

Geyer, Alan, Ronald D. Pasquariello and Donald W. Shriver, Jr. *Redeeming the City: Theology, Politics and Urban Policy*. New York: Pilgrim, 1982.

Gifford, James D., Jr. *Perichōrētic Salvation: The Believer's Union with Christ as a Third Type of Perichōrēsis.* Eugene, OR: Wipf and Stock, 2011.

Godwin, Joscelyn, ed. *The Harmony of the Spheres: A Sourcebook of the Pythagorean Tradition in Music.* Rochester, VT: Inner Traditions, 1993.

Godwin, Malcolm. *Angels: An Endangered Species.* New York: Simon and Schuster, 1990.

Gottlieb, Roger S., ed. *The Oxford Handbook of Religion and Ecology.* Oxford: Oxford University Press, 2006.

Granberg-Michaelson, Wesley, ed. *Tending the Earth: Essays on the Gospel and the Earth.* Grand Rapids: Eerdmans, 1987.

Grant, Robert. "O Worship the King." In *The Hymnal 1982 according to the use of The Episcopal Church.* New York: The Church Hymnal Corporation, 1982.

Gregersen, Niels Henrik. "The Cross of Christ in an Evolutionary World." *Dialog* 40 (2001) 192–207.

———. Editor. *Incarnation: On the Scope and Depth of Christology.* Minneapolis: Fortress, 2015.

Gregory of Nyssa. *Homilies on the Psalms*, 6. Translation in Hugo Rahner, *Man at Play.* Providence, RI: Cluny Media, 2019.

Grogan, Brian. *Where to from Here? The Christian Vision of Life After Death.* Dublin: Veritas, 2011.

Guiley, Rosemary Ellen. *Encyclopedia of Angels.* New York: Facts on File, 1996.

Habib, John. *Orthodox Afterlife.* Sandie, TX: Mt. Mary and St. Moses Abbey Press, 2016.

Hahn, Scott. *The Fourth Cup: Unveiling the Mystery of the Last Supper and the Cross.* New York: Image, 2018.

———. *The Lamb's Supper: The Mass as Heaven and Earth.* New York: Doubleday, 1999.

Hahnenberg, Edward J. *Purgatory: An Historic and Contemporary Analysis.* Livermore, MA: Wing Span, 2008.

Halton, Thomas. *The Church.* Eugene, OR: Wipf and Stock, 2002.

Hanawalt, Barbara A. and Kathryn L. Reyerson, eds. *City and Spectacle in Medieval Europe.* Minneapolis: University of Minnesota Press, 1994.

Harries, Richard. *Art and the Beauty of God: A Christian Understanding.* London: Mowbray, 1993.

Harrison, Carol. *Beauty and Revelation in the Thought of Saint Augustine.* Oxford: Clarendon, 1992.

Hart, John. *What Are They Saying About Environmental Theology?* New York: Paulist, 2004.

Harvey, Graham. *Food, Sex and Strangers: Understanding Religion as Everyday Life.* Durham, UK: Acumen, 2014.

Haydon, Geoffrey. *John Tavener: Glimpses of Paradise.* London: Indigo, 1995.

Hayes, Zachary. *Visions of a Future: A Study of Christian Eschatology.* Collegeville, MN: Liturgical, 1989.

Heinberg, Richard. *Memories and Visions of Paradise: Exploring the Universal Myth of a Lost Golden Age.* Wheaton, IL: Guest, 1995.

Hellwig, Monika K. *The Eucharist and the Hungers of the World,* 2nd edition, Lanham, MD: Sheed and Ward, 1992.

Hendriksen, William. *More Than Conquerors: An Interpretation of the Book of Revelation.* Grand Rapids: Baker, 1961.

Heschel, Abraham. *The Sabbath: Its Meaning for Modern Man.* Introduction by Susannah Heschel. New York: Farrar, Strauss and Giroux, 2005.

Heupp, Roderick T. *The Renewal of Trinitarian Theology: Themes, Patterns, and Explorations.* Downers Grove, IL: Intervarsity, 2008.

Hildegard of Bingen. *Symphonia: A Critical Edition of the Symphonia armonie celestium revelationum.* Translated by Barbara Newman. Ithaca, NY: Cornell University Press, 1998.

Hill, William J., OP. *The Three-Personed God: The Trinity as a Mystery of Salvation.* Washington, DC: The Catholic University of America Press, 1982.

Hippolytus, *Homilies on the Pasch/Easter 6.* Translation in Rahner, *Man at Play,* 108.

Hofer, Andrew, OP, ed. *Divinization: Becoming Icons of Christ through the Liturgy.* Chicago/Mundelein, IL: Hillenbrand, 2015.

Hölderlin, Friedrich. "Schicksalsied," from *Hyperion: Handbook of Vocal Works of Brahms.* London: W. M. Reeves, 1912.

Holmes, Urban T., III. *Ministry and Imagination.* New York: Seabury, 1976.

Hopkins, Gerard Manley. "God's Grandeur." In *Poems and Prose of Gerard Manley Hopkins,* edited by W. H. Gardner. Harmondsworth, UK: Penguin, 1953.

Howard, Ebenezer. *To-morrow: A Peaceful Path to Real Reform.* London: Swan and Sonnenschein, 1898.

Huntzinger, Jon. *The Trees Will Clap Their Hands: A Garden Theology.* Bloomington, IN: West Bow, 2012.

Jacobs, James M., ed. *A Piercing Light: Beauty, Faith and Transcendence.* Washington, DC: American Maritain Association/The Catholic University of America Press, 2015.

Jacobs, Jane. *The Death and Life of Great American Cities.* New York: Vintage, 1961.

Jacobsen, Eric O. *The Space Between: A Christian Engagement with the Built Environment.* Grand Rapids: Baker, 2012.

James, William. *The Varieties of Religious Experience: A Study in Human Nature.* Edited and with introduction by Martin Marty. New York: Penguin Books, 1985.

Jeanrond, Werner G. *A Theology of Love.* London: T. & T. Clark, 2010.

Jenson, Robert W. *Essays in Theology and Culture.* Grand Rapids: Eerdmans, 1995.

Jeremias, Joachim. *The Eucharistic Words of Jesus.* Eugene, OR: Wipf and Stock, 2001.

John Paul II. Apostolic Letter *Dies Domini.* Guide to Keeping Sunday Holy. Chicago: Liturgy Training, 1998.

———. *The Ecological Crisis: A Common Responsibility.* Washington, DC: United States Catholic Conference, 1990.

———. On the Holy Spirit in the Life of the Church and of the World (*Dominum et Vivificantem*). Boston: Daughters of St. Paul, 1986.

Jones, David Albert. *Angels: A Very Short Introduction.* Oxford: Oxford University Press, 2011.

Jones, Jamie. *The Music of the Spheres: Music, Science, and the Natural Order of the Universe.* New York: Grove, 1993.

Jullien, Claudia. *Paul Claudel interroge Le Cantique des cantiques.* Paris: Annales Littéraires, 1994. English translation in Henri de Lubac, *The Splendor of the Church.* San Francisco: Ignatius, 1999.

Julier, Alice P. *Eating Together: Food, Friendship and Inequality.* Urbana, IL: University of Illinois Press, 2013.

Juste, Arthur A., Jr. *The Ongoing Feast: Fellowship and Eschatology at Emmaus.* Collegeville, MN: Liturgical, 1993.

Kaam, Adrian Van. *The Music of Eternity.* Notre Dame, IN: Ave Maria, 1990.

Kant, Immanuel. *Religion and Rational Theology*. Translated by A. W. Wood and G. di Giovanni. from *The Cambridge Edition of the Works of Immanuel Kant*. Cambridge: Cambridge University Press, 1996.

Kasper, Walter. *The God of Jesus Christ*. New York: Crossroad, 1984.

Kavanagh, Aidan. *On Liturgical Theology*. New York: Pueblo Publishing, 1984.

Keeble, Brian, editor. *The Music of Silence: A Composer's Testament*. London: Faber and Faber, 1999.

Kelly, Anthony. *Eschatology and Hope*. Maryknoll, NY: Orbis, 2006. 172.

Kelly, Douglas R. *Systematic Theology*, vol II. Fearn, Ross-shire: Christian Focus Publications, 2014.

Kiehl, Micah D. *Apocalyptic Ecology: The Book of Revelation, the Earth, and the Future*. Foreword by Barbara R. Rossing. Collegeville, MN: Liturgical, 2017.

Kingwell, Mark. *Nearest Thing to Heaven: The Empire State Building and American Dreams*. New Haven, CN: Yale University Press, 2006.

Kirsch, J. P. *The Doctrine of the Communion of Saints in the Ancient Church: A Study in the History of Doctrine*.

Kloppenburg, Bonaventure. *The People's Church*. Chicago, IL: Franciscan Herald, 1978.

Kreeft, Peter. *Angels (and Demons): What Do We Really Know about Them?* San Francisco: Ignatius, 1995.

———. *Everything You Ever Wanted to Know about Heaven . . . But Never Dreamed of Asking!* San Francisco, CA: Ignatius, 1990.

Kruger, C. Baxter. *The Great Dance: The Christian Vision Revisited*. Vancouver, BC: Regent College Publishing, 2005.

Küng, Hans. *Mozart: Traces of Transcendence*. Translated by John Bowen, foreword by Yehudi Menuhun. Grand Rapids: Eerdmans, 1993.

LaCugna, Catherine Mowry. *God for Us: The Trinity and Christian Life*. San Francisco: Harper, 1991.

———. "The Practical Trinity." *The Christian Century* 109 (22) 681.

La Due, William J. *The Trinity Guide to Eschatology*. New York: Continuum, 2000.

Leeuw, Gerardus van der. *Sacred and Profane Beauty: The Holy in Art*. Translated by David E. Green. New York: Holt, Rinehart and Winston, 1963.

Lane, Dermot A. *Keeping Hope Alive: Stirrings in Christian Theology*. Dublin: Gill and Macmillan, 1996.

Lang, Bernhard. *Meeting in Heaven: Modernizing the Christian Afterlife 1600—2000*. New York: Peter Lang, 2011.

LaVerdiere, Eugene. "Musician: Model for Church Ministry." *Pastoral Music* 10 (October–November 1985).

Lawrence, D. H. *Collected Works*. Edited with introduction and notes by Vivian DeSola Pinto and F. Warren Roberts. Harmondsworth, UK: Penguin, 1980.

Leeuwen, Thomas P. van. *The Skyward Trend of Thought: The Metaphysics of the American Skyscraper*. Cambridge, MA: MIT Press, 1988.

Le Goff, Jacques. *Medieval Civilization 400–1300*. Translated by Julia Barrow. New York: Barnes and Noble, 1964.

Leithart, Peter J. "The Politics of Baptism." *First Things* 68 (December, 1996).

———. *The Priesthood of the Plebs: A Theology of Baptism*. Eugene, OR: Wipf and Stock, 2003.

Lewis, C. S. *The Four Loves: An Exploration of the Nature of Love*. Boston: Mariner, 2012.

———. *The Problem of Pain*. New York: MacMillan, 1948.

———. "The Weight of Glory." *The Weight of Glory and Other Addresses.* San Francisco: Harper, 2001.

Linthicum, Robert C. *City of God, City of Satan: A Biblical Theology of the Urban Church.* Grand Rapids: Zondervan, 1991.

Liturgy of the Hours, vol. 1 (Christmas Season). New York: Catholic Book Publishing, 1975.

Long, Philip J. *Jesus the Bridegroom: The Origins of the Eschatological Feast as a Wedding Banquet in the Synoptic Gospels.* Eugene, OR: Pickwick, 2013.

Longbottom, Henri, ed. "An Overview of *Laudato Si'.*" *The Jesuit Post* (18 June, 2015).

Lorbiecki, Marybeth. *Following St. Francis: John Paul II's Call for Ecological Action.* New York: Rizzoli, 2014.

Lorensen, Lynne Faber. *The College Students' Introduction to the Trinity.* Collegeville, MN: Liturgical, 1999.

Lutheran Book of Worship. Minneapolis: Augsburg, 1978.

Macmurray, John. *Persons in Relation.* New York: Harper and Brothers, 1961.

———. *The Self as Agent.* New York: Harper and Brothers, 1957.

Macquarrie, John. *Principles of Christian Theology* 2nd edition. New York: Charles Scribner's Sons, 1977.

Madigan, Shawn. *Spirituality Rooted in Liturgy.* Washington, DC: Pastoral, 1988.

Madrid, Patrick. *Any Friend of God Is a Friend of Mine: A Biblical and Historical Explanation of the Catholic Doctrine of the Communion of Saints.* San Diego, CA: Basilica, 1996.

Malina, Bruce J. *The New Jerusalem in the Revelation of John: The City as Symbol of Life with God.* Collegeville, MN: Liturgical, 2000.

Maloney, George A., SJ. *Communion of Saints.* Hauppauge, NY: Living Flame, 1978.

Mannion, M. Francis. "The Cathedral as Sacrament of the Redeemed City." The Second Annual Anne Brand Stolborg Lecture, delivered at the Cathedral Basilica at Covington, KY, on February 4, 1997.

———. "The Church and the City." *First Things* 100 (February 2000) 31–36.

———. "Liturgy and the Present Crisis of Culture," *Worship* 62:2 (March 1988) 98–123.

———. "Rejoice, Heavenly Powers! The Renewal of Liturgical Doxology." *Pro Ecclesia* 12 (no. 1) 37–60.

———. "Worship and the Public Church." *Liturgy* 80 (1990) 11–14.

Marechal, Elias. *Tears of an Innocent God: Conversations on Silence, Kindness and Prayer.* New York: Paulist, 2015.

Maritain, Jacques. *Art and Scholasticism with Other Essays.* Translated by Reverend John O'Connor. Miami, FL: HardPress, 2019.

Martin, James, SJ. *My Life with the Saints.* Chicago: Loyola University Press, 2006.

Martin, Thomas F., OSA. *Our Restless Heart: The Augustinian Tradition.* Maryknoll, NY: Orbis, 2003.

Martindale, Wayne, ed. *Journey to the Celestial City: Glimpses of Heaven from Great Literary Classics.* Chicago: Moody, 1995.

Martis, Douglas and Christopher Carstens. *Mystical Body, Mystical Voice: Encountering Christ in the Words of the Mass.* Chicago: Liturgy Training, 2011.

Maurer, Armand Augustine. *About Beauty: A Thomistic Interpretation.* Dockey: Archive Press, 2000.

May, Rollo. *The Meaning of Anxiety.* New York: W. W. Norton, 1977.

McAdoo, Henry R. and Kenneth Stevenson. *The Mystery of the Eucharist in the Anglican Tradition.* Norwich: Canterbury, 1995.

McCarthy, David Matko. *Sharing God's Company: A Theology of the Communion of Saints.* Grand Rapids: Eerdmans, 2012.

McCormick, Patrick T. *A Banqueter's Guide to the All-Night Soup Kitchen of the Kingdom of God.* Collegeville, MN: Liturgical Press, 2004.

McDannell, Colleen and Bernhard Lang. *Heaven: A History*, 2nd ed. New Haven: Yale University,2001.

McGann, Mary E. *The Meal that Reconnects: Eucharistic Eating and the Global Food Crisis.* Collegeville, MN: Liturgical, 2020.

McGinnis, Charles F. *The Communion of Saints.* Introduction by Most Referend John Ireland. n.d.

McGrath, Alister E. *A Brief History of Heaven.* Oxford: Blackwell, 2003.

McGuire, Matthew, editor. *Irish Poems.* New York: Knopf, 2011.

McKinnon, James. *Music in Early Christian Literature.* Cambridge: Cambridge University Press, 1987.

McWhirter, Jocelyn. *The Bridegroom Messiah and the People of God: Marriage in the Fourth Gospel.* Cambridge: Cambridge University Press, 2006.

Meconi, David, SJ. and Carl E. Olson. *Called to be the Children of God: The Catholic Theology of Human Deification.* San Francisco: Ignatius, 2016.

Mechtild of Magdeburg, vii.1. English translation in Hugo Rahner, *Man at Play*, 79.

Medley, Mark S. *Imago Trinitatis: Toward a Relational Understanding of Becoming Human.* Lanham, MD: University Press of America, 2002.

Mellers, Wildrid. *Celestial Music? Some Masterpieces of European Religious Music.* Woodbridge, UK: Boydell, 2002.

Méndez-Montoya, Ángel. *The Theology of Food: Eating and the Eucharist.* Chichester, UK: Blackwell, 2012.

Miller, Joel J. *Lifted by Angels: The Presence and Power of our Heavenly Guides and Guardians.* Nashville: Thomas Nelson, 2012.

Mitchell, Nathan. "Toward a Liturgical Aesthetics." *Liturgy Digest* (1996) 71–85.

Molinar, Paul, SJ. *Saints: Their Place in the Church.* Translated by Dominic Maruca, SJ, preface by Cardinal Larroana. New York: Sheed and Ward, 1965.

Moltmann, Jürgen. *The Trinity and the Kingdom: The Kingdom of God.* Translated by Margaret Kohl. London: SCM, 1981.

Moo, Douglas J. and Jonathan A. Moo. *Creation Care: A Biblical Theology of the Natural World.* Grand Rapids: Zondervan, 2018. Electronic book.

Morrell, Mike and Richard Rohr. *The Divine Dance: The Trinity and Your Transformation.* New Kensington, PA: Whitaker House, 2016.

Mouw, Richard J. *When Kings Come Marching In: Isaiah and the New Jerusalem.* Grand Rapids: Eerdmans, 2002.

Mumford, Lewis. *The Culture of Cities.* San Diego, CA: Harvest, 1970.

Murcott, Anne. *Introducing the Sociology of Food and Eating.* London: Bloomsbury, 2019.

Murphy, Francesca Aran. *Christ the Form of Beauty: A Study in Theology and Literature.* Edinburgh: T&T Clark, 1995.

Murphy-O'Connor, Jerome, OP. *Becoming Human Together: The Pastoral Anthropology of St. Paul*, 3rd. ed. Atlanta: Society of Biblical Literature, 2009.

Musset, Alfred de. *The Confession of a Child of the Century.* Translated and with an introduction and notes by David Coward. London: Penguin, 2013.

Navone, John. *Enjoying God's Beauty.* Collegeville, MN: Liturgical, 1997.

———. *Self-Giving and Sharing: The Trinity and Human Fulfillment.* Collegeville, MN: Liturgical, 1989.

———. *Toward a Theology of Beauty.* Collegeville, MN: Liturgical, 1996.

Newman, John Henry. *The Dream of Gerontius.* Introduction by Rev. Gregory Winterton. Oxford: Family Publications, 2001.

Nichols, Aidan, O.P. *The Art of God Incarnate: Theology and Image in the Christian Tradition.* New York: Paulist, 1980.

———. *A Key to Balthasar: Hans Urs von Balthasar on Beauty, Goodness and Truth.* Grand Rapids, MI: Baker, 2011.

———. *Redeeming Beauty: Soundings in Sacred Aesthetics.* Burlington, VT: Ashgate, 2007.

———. "A Tale of Two Documents: *Sacrosanctum Consilium* and *Mediator Dei.*" *Antiphon* 5:1 (2000) 24–25.

Nichols, Terence. *Death and Afterlife: A Theological Introduction.* Grand Rapids, MI: Brazos, 2010.

Nietzsche, Friedrich Wilhelm. *Thus Spake Zarathustra.* Translated by Thomas Common. Edinburgh and London: T. N. Foulis, 1990.

Nygren, Anders. *Agape and Eros.* Translated by Philip S. Watson. New York: Harper Touchbooks, 1932/1937.

Oakes, Edward T. *Patterns of Redemption: The Theology of Hans Urs von Balthasar.* New York: Continuum, 1994.

O'Callaghan, Paul. *Christ Our Hope: An Introduction to Eschatology.* Washington, DC: The Catholic University of America Press, 2011.

O'Collins, Gerald, S. J. *The Tripersonal God: Understanding and Interpreting the Trinity.* New York/Mahwah, NJ: Paulist, 1999.

O'Donohue, John. *Beauty: The Invisible Embrace.* New York: Perennial, 2005.

Olsen, Glenn W. *The Turn to Transcendence: The Role of Religion in the Twenty-First Century.* Washington, DC: The Catholic University of America Press, 2010.

Ombres, Robert, OP. *The Theology of Purgatory.* Butler, WI: Clergy Book Service, 1978.

Order for the Blessing of Animals. Book of Blessings. Collegeville, MN: Liturgical, 1998.

Order of Christian Funerals. New York: International Committee on English in the Liturgy, 1989.

Order of the Christian Initiation of Adults. Washington, D.C.: International Committee of English in the Liturgy, 1985.

Outka, Gene. *Agape: An Ethical Analysis.* New Haven: Yale University Press, 1976.

Parente, Pascal P. *The Angels in Catholic Teaching and Tradition.* Charlotte, NC: Tan, 2013.

Park, Seong Hyun, Aéda Besançon Spencer, and William David Spencer. *Reaching for the New Jerusalem: A Biblical and Theological Framework for the City.* Eugene, OR: Wipf and Stock, 2013.

Pasquariello, Ronald D., Donald W. Shriver, Jr., and Alan Geyer. *Redeeming the City: Theology, Politics, and Urban Policy.* New York: Pilgrim, 1982.

Patella, Michael. *Angels and Demons: A Christian Primer of the Spiritual World.* Collegeville, MN: Liturgical, 2012.

Paterson-Smyth, J. *The Gospel of the Hereafter.* London: Hodder and Stoughton, n.d.

Perham, Michael. *The Communion of Saints: An Examination of the Place of the Christian Dead in the Belief, Worship, and Calendars of the Church.* London: Alcuin/SPCK, 1980.

Peterson, Eric. *The Angels and the Liturgy.* Translated by Ronald Wall. New York: Herder and Herder, 1964.

Pew Research Center. "Religious Beliefs and Practices." https//www.pewresearch.org.

Phan, Peter C., editor. *The Cambridge Companion to the Trinity*. Cambridge: Cambridge University Press, 2011.

———. *Living into Death, Dying to Life: A Christian Theology of Death and Life Eternal*. Hobe Sound, FL: Lection Publishing, 2014.

———. *Responses to 101 Questions on Death and Eternal Life*. New York/Mahwah, NJ: Paulist, 1997.

Pieper, Joseph. *Leisure, the Basis of Culture*. Translated by Alexander Dru. San Francisco: Ignatius, 2009.

Pitre, Brant. *Jesus the Bridegroom: The Greatest Love Story Ever Told*. New York: Image, 2014.

———. *Jesus and the Jewish Roots of the Eucharist: Unlocking the Secrets of the Last Supper* Foreword by Scott Hahn. New York: Doubleday, 2011.

———. *Jesus and the Last Supper*. Grand Rapids, MI: Eerdmans, 2015.

Pivarnik, R. Gabriel. *Toward a Trinitarian Theology of Liturgical Participation*. Collegeville, MN: Liturgical Press, 2012.

Pseudo-Dionysius. "The Celestial Hierarchy." In *Pseudo-Dionysius: The Complete Works*. Translated by Luibheid, Colm. The Classics of Western Spirituality. New York: Paulist, 1987.

Purtill, Richard J. *Thinking about Religion: A Philosophical Introduction to Religion*. Englewood Cliff, NJ: Prentice Hall, 1978.

Quasten, Johannes. *Music and Worship in Pagan and Christian Antiquity*. Translated by Boniface Ramsey, OP. Washington, DC: National Association of Pastoral Musicians, 1983.

Rahner, Hugo. *Man at Play*. Preface by Walter J. Ong. Providence, RI: Cluny, 2019.

Rahner, Karl. "Angels," in *Encyclopedia of Theology, The Concise Sacramentum Mundi*. New York: Crossroad, 1975.

———. *The Church and the Sacraments*. New York: Herder and Herder, 1963.

———. *Theological Investigations* vol. 7: *Further Theology of the Spiritual Life*. London: Darton, Longman and Todd, 1972.

———. *The Trinity*. Translated by Joseph Donceel, with an introduction by Catherine Mowry LaCugna. New York: Crossroad Herder, 2010.

Rattenbury, J. Ernest. *The Eucharistic Hymns of John and Charles Wesley*. Eugene, OR: Wipf and Stock, 2014.

Ratzinger, Joseph. *Church, Ecumenism, and Politics: New Essays in Ecclesiology*. New York: Crossroad, 2011.

———. *Eschatology: Death and Eternal Life*. Washington, DC: The Catholic University of America Press, 2020.

Rausch, Thomas P. *Eschatology, Liturgy, and Christology: Toward Recovering an Eschatological Imagination*. Collegeville, MN: Liturgical Press, 2012.

Reeves, Michael. *Delighting in the Trinity: An Introduction to the Christian Faith*. Downers' Grove, IL: IUP Academics.

Riches, John, ed. *The Analogy of Beauty: The Theology of Hans Urs von Balthasar*. Edinburgh: T&T Clark, 1986.

Ritzer, George. *The McDonaldization of Society: Into the Digital Age*, 8th edition. Los Angeles: Sage, 2018.

Robb, David A. "Praise the Living God Who Sings." Chicago: Liturgy Training Publications, 1997.

Rohr, Richard and Mike Morrell. *The Divine Dance: The Trinity and Your Transformation.* New Kensington, PA: Whitaker House, 2016.

Rolheiser, Ronald. *The Restless Heart: Finding Our Spiritual Home.* New York: Doubleday, 2004

Roman Missal, 3rd ed. International Commission on English in the Liturgy. Washington, DC: United States Conference of Catholic Bishops, 2010.

Rordorf, Willy. *The History of the Day of Rest and Worship in the Earliest Centuries of the Christian Church.* Philadelphia: Westminster, 1968.

Rouillard, Philippe. "From Human Meal to Christian Eucharist." In *Living Bread, Saving Cup: Readings on the Eucharist,* edited by R. Kevin Seasoltz, 127–56. Collegeville, MN: Liturgical, 1987.

Ruiz, Jean-Pierre. "The Apocalypse of John and Contemporary Roman Catholic Liturgy" *Worship* 68:6 (November 1994), 482–504.

Rushby, Kevin. *Paradise: A History of the Idea that Rules the World.* New York: Carroll and Graf, 2007.

Russell, Jeffrey Burton. *Paradise Mislaid: How We Lost Heaven and How We Can Regain It.* Oxford: Oxford University Press, 2006.

Ryken, Philip Graham, ed. *The Communion of Saints: Living in Fellowship with the People of God.* Phillipsburg, NJ: RR Publishing, 2001.

Saliers, Don E. *Worship as Theology: Foretaste of Divine Glory.* Nashville, TN: Abington, 1994.

Sánchez-Escobar, Ángel. *Orthodox Church Music.* Winston-Salem, NC: Stephen Harding, 2014.

Saward, John. *Sweet and Blessed Country: The Christian Hope for Heaven.* Oxford: Oxford University Press, 2005.

Schaffer, Mary M. "Heavenly and Earthly Liturgies: Patristic Prototypes, Medieval Perspectives and a Contemporary Application," *Worship* 70:6 (November 1996) 19—33.

Schillebeeckx, Edward. *Christ the Sacrament of the Encounter with God.* New York: Sheed and Ward, 1963.

Schlosser, Eric. *Fast Food Nation: The Dark Side of the All-American Meal.* Boston: Marina, 2012.

Schönborn, Christoph, *From Death to Life: The Christian Journey,* Translator, Brian McNeil, CRV. San Francisco: Ignatius, 1977.

———. *God's Human Face: The Christ-Icon.* San Francisco: Ignatius, 1994.

Schwarz, Hans. *Eschatology.* Grand Rapids, MI: Eerdmans, 2000.

Scruton, Roger. *Beauty: A Very Short Introduction.* Oxford: Oxford University Press, 2011.

Seviér, Christopher Scott. *Aquinas on Beauty.* Lanham, MD: Lexington, 2015.

Shapiro, Rami. *The Angelic Way: Angels Through the Ages and Their Meaning for Us.* New York: BlueBridge, 2009.

Shaw, George Bernard. *A Treatise on Parents and Children.* No publication data.

Sheldrake, Philip. *The Spiritual City: Theology, Spirituality, and the Urban.* Chichester, West Sussex, UK: John Wiley and Sons, 2014.

Shepherd, Massey H., Jr. *The Paschal Liturgy and the Apocalypse.* Richmond, VA: John Knox, 1960.

Sherry, Patrick. *Spirit and Beauty: An Introduction to Theological Aesthetics.* London: SCM, 2002.

Shriver, Donald W., Jr. Ronald D. Pasquariello and Alan Geyer. *Redeeming the City: Theology, Politics, and Urban Policy.* New York: Pilgrim, 1982.

Silverman, Eric V. and T. Ryan Byerly, eds. *Paradise Understood: New Philosophical Essays about Heaven.* Oxford: Oxford University Press, 2006.

Simson, Otto von. *The Gothic Cathedral: Origins of Architecture and the Medieval Concept of Order.* Princeton: Princeton University Press, 1988.

Sistare, Christine T., editor. *Civility and its Discontents: Civic Virtue, Toleration, and Cultural Fragmentation.* Lawrence, KS: University Press of Kansas, 2004.

Smith, Gary Scott. *Heaven in the American Imagination.* Oxford: Oxford University Press, 2011.

Solkeld, Brett. *Can Catholics and Evangelicals Agree about Purgatory and the Last Judgment?* Mahwah, NJ: Paulist, 2011.

Spinks, Bryan D. *Sanctus in the Eucharistic Prayer.* Cambridge: Cambridge University Press, 1991.

Spitzer, Robert, SJ. *The Soul's Upward Yearning: Clues to Our Transcendent Nature, from Experience and Reason.* San Francisco: Ignatius, 2015.

Stapert, Calvert R. *A New Song for an Old World: Musical Thought in the Early Church.* Grand Rapids, MI: Eerdmans, 2007.

Stevenson, Kenneth and Henry R. McAdoo. *The Mystery of the Eucharist in the Anglican Tradition.* Norwich: Canterbury, 1995.

Stookey, Laurance Hull. *Eucharist: Christ's Feast with the Church.* Nashville, TN: Abington, 1993.

Strossel, Scott. *My Age of Anxiety: Fear, Hope, Dread, and the Search for Peace of Mind.* New York: Knopf, 2014.

Tavener, John. *The Music of Silence: A Composer's Testament.* Edited by Brian Keeble. London: Faber and Faber, 1999.

Taylor, Michael J., SJ. *Purgatory.* Huntington, IN: Our Sunday Visitor, 1988.

Theocritoff, Elizabeth. *Living in God's Creation: Orthodox Perspectives on Ecology.* Crestwood, NY: St. Vladimir's Press, 2009.

Thiel, John E. *Icons of Hope: The "Last Things" in Catholic Imagination.* Notre Dame, IN: University of Notre Dame Press, 2013.

Thiessen, Gesa Elsbeth, ed. *Theological Aesthetics: A Reader.* Grand Rapids, MI: Eerdmans, 2005.

Thompson, OP. *Cities of God: The Religion of the Italian Communes 1125—1325.* University Park, PA: Pennsylvania State University Press, 2005.

Tillich, Paul. *The Protestant Era.* Translated by James Luther Adams. Chicago: University of Chicago, 1947.

———. *The Courage to Be.* New Haven: Yale University, 1952.

———. *The Shaking of the Foundations.* New York: Charles Scribner's Sons, 1948.

———. *The Eternal Now.* New York: Charles Scriber's Sons, 1963.

Vagaggini, Cyprian, OSB. *Theological Dimensions of the Liturgy: A General Treatise on the Theology of the Liturgy.* Translated by Leonard J. Doyle and W. A. Jurgens. Collegeville, MN: Liturgical, 1976.

Vanderslice, Kendall. *We Will Feast: Rethinking Dinner, Worship, and the Community of God.* Foreword by D. L Mayfield. Grand Rapids, MI: Eerdmans, 2019.

Vatican Council II: The Conciliar and Post Conciliar Documents. Revised edition. Edited by Austin Flannery, OP. Northport, NY: Costello, 1996.

Veit, Helen Zoe. *Modern Food, Moral Food: Self-Control, Science, and the Rise of American Modern Eating in the Early Twentieth Century*. Chapel Hill: University of North Carolina Press, 2013.

Vester, Katharina H. *A Taste of Power: Food and American Identities*. California: University of California Press, 2015.

Visal, Jeana, OSB *Icons in the Western Church: Towards a More Sacramental Encounter*. Collegeville, MN: Liturgical, 2016.

Vogt, Brandon. *Saints and Social Justice: A Guide to Changing the World*. Huntington, IN: Our Sunday Visitor, Inc. 2013.

Volf, Miroslav. *After Our Likeness: The Church as the Image of the Trinity*. Grand Rapid, MI: Eerdmans, 1997.

Vonier, Dom Anscar. *The Angels*. Assumption, IL: Assumption Press, 2013.

Wainwright, Geoffrey. *Eucharist and Eschatology*. New York: Oxford University Press, 1971.

———. "The Church as Worshiping Community." In *Worship with One Accord: Where Liturgy and Ecumenism Embrace*. New York: Oxford University Press, 1997.

Walford, Stephen. *Communion of Saints: The Unity of Divine Love in the Mystical Body of Christ*. Foreword by Cardinal Gérald Cyprien Lacroix. Kettering, OH: Angelico, 2016.

Walls, Jerry L. *Heaven: The Logic of Eternal Joy*. Oxford: Oxford University Press, 2002.

———. *Purgatory: The Logic of Total Transformation*. Oxford: Oxford University Press, 2012.

———. ed. *The Oxford Handbook of Eschatology*. Oxford: Oxford University Press, 2009.

Walsh, Milton. *In Memory of Me: A Meditation on the Roman Canon*. San Francisco: Ignatius, 2011.

Ware, Kallistos. "The Human Person as an Icon of the Trinity." *Sobornost* 8 (1986) 17–18.

———Ware, [Timothy]. *The Orthodox Church*. New York: Penguin, 1976.

Webber, Robert E. and Rodney Clapp. *People of the Truth: The Power of the Worshiping Community in the Modern World*. San Francisco: Harper and Row, 1988.

White, Lynn. "The Historical Roots of Our Ecological Crisis." In *Science* 155 (10 March 1967) 1203–1207.

Wilder, Amos Niven. *Theopoetic: Theology and the Religious Imagination*. Philadelphia: Fortress, 1976.

Winright, Tobias, ed. *Green Discipleship: Catholic Theological Ethics and the Environment*. Winona, MI: Anselm, 2011.

Wirzba, Norman. *Food and Faith: A Theology of Eating*, 2nd edition. Cambridge: Cambridge University Press, 2019.

———. *From Nature to Creation: A Christian Vision for Understanding and Loving Our World*. Grand Rapids, MI: Baker Academic, 2015.

Witvliet, John D. "Toward a Liturgical Aesthetic: An Interdisciplinary Review of Aesthetic Theory." *Liturgy Digest* 3 (1996) 19–34.

Wood, Susan K. "Participatory Knowledge of God in the Liturgy," in *Knowing the Triune God: The Work of the Spirit in the Practices of the Church*. Editors James J. Buckley and David S. Yeago. Grand Rapids, MI: Eerdmans, 2001.

Woodward, Kenneth L. *Making Saints: How the Catholic Church Determines Who Becomes a Saint, Who Doesn't, and Why*. New York: Touchstone, 1996.

Wright, N. T. *Jesus and the Victory of God: Christian Origins and the Question of God*. Vol. 2. Atlanta, GA: Fortress, 1996.

————. *Surprised by Hope: Rethinking Heaven, the Resurrection, and the Mission of the Church.* New York: HarperOne, 2008.

Yeats, W. B. *The Collected Poems of W. B. Yeats.* Editor, Richard J. Finneran. New York: Collier, 1991.

Zahnd, Brian. *Beauty Will Save the World: Rediscovering the Allure and Mystery of Christianity.* Lake Mary, FL: Charisma, 2012.

Zeller, Benjamin E. et al. *Religion, Food, and Eating in North America.* New York: Columbia University Press, 2014.

Zizioulas, John D. *Being as Communion: Studies in Personhood and the Church.* Foreword by John Meyendorff. Crestwood, NY: St. Vladimir's Seminary Press, 1985.

————. *Communion and Otherness: Further Studies in Personhood and the Church.* Edited by Paul McPartlan. London: T&T Clark, 2006.